TRIALS
N'
TRIUMPH

Jim Davis

JIM DAVIS

TRIALS
—— N' ——
TRIUMPH

ISBN: 978-1-4866-0403-6

Word Alive Press
131 Cordite Road, Winnipeg, MB R3W 1S1
www.wordalivepress.ca

WORD ALIVE
—P R E S S—

Cataloguing in Publication information may be obtained through Library and Archives Canada

ACKNOWLEDGEMENTS

I give sincere and loving thanks to my dear and devoted wife, Trish, for all her help and assistance in so many areas of my life, without which this book would have never happened.

I am grateful to my dear friend and advisor, Virginia Yarjau, who has worked tirelessly for the past five or six years with me, typing and editing the manuscript and preparing it for publication (as well as handling the computer end of things of which I am totally ignorant).

CONTENTS

Introduction...ix

I
Risky Business

Roots 1

School Daze 1935–1948... 9

Poor Boys' Institute 1948–1950 43

Disaster–1950... 55

Finishing at Prairie 1950–1952.. 65

Gordon College Round One–1952... 79

Alberta Bound–1953 85

Back to Boston or Bust! Gordon College Round Two–1954 99

Last Dash to Boston–1954 109

Gordon College–1955 119

Teaching Special Needs Boys–1957..133

II
Betty

Courtship...149

Marriage 173

Long Years of Betty's Illness 179

Manitoba 189

On The Move Again 201

Books..207

On The Colony 211

A Wild Ride 217

High River and Loss..221

Seven Lonely, Frustrating Years 229

III
Pat-Trisha

Courtship and Marriage 247

Home to Alberta and a New Beginning 255

Life Enriched 263

"I Will Repay"..285

Biography 289

INTRODUCTION

"God has been using all the events and experiences of our lives to prepare us for the kind of service He's called us to now. Whether our past was happy or sad, godly or sordid, God is building on that experience to make us into effective servants for Him." This quote is from *The Calling*, a book by Brother Andrew. Furthermore, as an ancient proverb says, "The journey of a thousand miles begins with the first step." These are a few of the thoughts that crowd my mind as I begin the monumental task of writing my memoirs, mostly chronologically, in three stages—"Risky Business," "Betty," and "Pat-Trisha."

"Risky Business" covers memories related to my family history, my journey through childhood, becoming a follower of Christ Jesus, a disastrous turn of events in my life, and then my struggles to achieve an education to finally becoming a teacher of "slow learners," now referred to more appropriately as "special needs students." These students have requirements that are more involved than learning the ABCs, as they are often encumbered with problems associated with mental, physical and/or emotional wellbeing. Further, they have often endured at least two years of failure in regular classroom studies where heartless kids may have teased and bullied them by calling them "retards" or worse and/or mistreating them in one way or another. Presently in most jurisdictions, it seems that those in authority have decided that these students must be integrated into regular grades where they become "lame ducks at a dry-land chicken's convention." Their teachers are challenged with a variety of problems for which they have little time, interest, or training. The goal of the teacher then often becomes simply passing on the problems these children are encountering to the teacher in the next grade. After all, the new norm is that teachers must not delay any child's school progress for fear of endangering their self esteem—children must not be failed regardless of their incompetence. As former prime minister John Diefenbaker would say, while shaking his jowls vigorously, "Balderdash!" There are many children with serious problems that do not do well in regular classroom situations, nor do they fit into the twenty-first century school system. Many of these children often find even the ringing of bells and the stampede or lagging progress from classroom to classroom disturbing and unsettling. They are often exposed to expectations for which they have little ability or motivation. No matter how simple their needs may be, they may not necessarily be easy to provide! I have found that some of these students' biggest requirements center on *acceptance, security* and *motivation*. My teaching years also taught me why the same class was disruptive with one teacher and not with another. Today, because of the new constraints on educators, any attempt to maintain discipline in a very unruly class is almost impossible.

The second part of this narrative, entitled "Betty," revolves around my courtship of and marriage to my first wife and the trials and triumphs which we shared. Betty was a courageous companion during those years. This segment is also a recap of the perils, problems, and challenges of living with a terminally ill, disabled spouse during sixteen of our nineteen years together, which finally ended in her death. The frustrations of being single once again while raising a family and seeking a new life partner are covered along with the precarious problems, difficulties, and loneliness of a single male in married culture which I lived out for seven long years. During these years, I constantly prayed, "Lord, please send me another good wife." You have probably experienced answers to prayers in one or all of the four possibilities which I have found to be true: "*yes,*" "*no,*" "*not now,*" or "*something better.*" The last answer, "*something better,*" is the one I like best. If many of my prayers had been answered "*yes*" I would be in deep trouble today. As I prayed, I often complained to God as the dairyman, Tevye, did in *Fiddler on the Roof* while pushing his milk cart: "What are *You* doing up there today?"

Ultimately, the last section of the book deals with my rescue from the frustrating condition of singleness. I relate how I renewed my acquaintance with Trish, a good friend of Betty's, who consented to be my wife, much to my relief and amazement. Through the years, I was always in the habit of picking up pennies whenever and wherever I found them. As you may well have noticed, the back of a penny is stamped with two maple leaves on one branch, which to me is a symbol of marriage—two people connected on the same branch, that branch being Christ. When I see a penny now, I say, "Thanks, Lord. You sure did a good job." Now in my eighties, I believe even more firmly that two heads are better than one—especially if they are both Christian—even if one head happens to be a cabbage. The Bible reaffirms my opinion in Ecclesiastes 4:9-12 (NKJV):

> Two are better than one, because they have a good reward for their labor. For if they fall, one will lift up his companion. But woe to him who is alone when he falls, for he has no one to help him up. Again, if two lie down together, they will keep warm; but how can one be warm alone? Though one may be overpowered by another, two can withstand him. And a threefold cord is not quickly broken.

This scripture has proven to be so appropriate for me, and is even more appropriate when one of the partners only has one arm!

As to the names of people mentioned in this narrative, they are real. To those who made my road smoother with their help and kindness, I extend a grateful thank you.

> Blessed are the poor in spirit, for theirs is the kingdom of heaven.
> Blessed are those who mourn, for they will be comforted.
> Blessed are the meek, for they will inherit the earth.
> Blessed are those who hunger and thirst for righteousness, for they will be filled.
> Blessed are the merciful, for they will be shown mercy.
> Blessed are the pure in heart, for they will see God.
> Blessed are the peacemakers, for they will be called children of God.
> Blessed are those who are persecuted because of righteousness, for theirs is the kingdom of heaven.
> Blessed are you when people insult you, persecute you and falsely say all kinds of evil against you because of me. Rejoice and be glad, because great is your reward in heaven, for in the same way they persecuted the prophets who were before you. (Matthew 5:3-12, NIV)

I
RISKY BUSINESS

ROOTS

"For I know the thoughts that I think toward you," saith the Lord, "thoughts of peace, and not of evil, to give you an expected end." (Jeremiah 29:11 KJV)

My father was born on February 14ᵗʰ, 1889, on a farm in Coffee County, Kansas. He was named Valentine Jasper, since he came into this world on Valentine's Day and jasper was the birthstone for the month. He was one of six boys and three girls born to his parents. During his lifetime, he was simply called "Jap" Davis by all his friends. Perhaps when his mother called him Jasper, he knew he was in trouble. This name raised eyebrows during World War II as anything associated with the Japanese was considered suspect. Today, I highly doubt you would encounter this as a nickname as Japanese people find it offensive.

In 1907 when Jap was age eighteen, Jap's father and his family—with the exception of the eldest daughter, Maud, who had remained in Kansas with her husband—immigrated to Canada, along with the horde of homesteaders who came from many other countries—all of them wanting to speak English and proud to become Canadian. It saddens me that these do not appear to be the objectives of many immigrants at this moment—now when they come, they often bring their homeland problems as well as their own language with them and feel they are entitled to have everyone cater to their desires.

My father's family arrived in Nanton in 1908 along with all their household goods, family belongings, and livestock in five boxcars. Jap's father had purchased land near the town of Chinook and he and his six sons each applied for a homestead grant of land in the area. When they had built enough tar-paper shacks on their homesteads, the family travelled across country to their makeshift dwellings with all their belongings in a cavalcade of wagons, just as the early American settlers had in their wagon trains. It must have been quite a sight as they made their laborious way across the prairie to the land of their dreams. Jap's younger sisters, Grace and Nina, were part of the long trek. Nina, the youngest girl, told me that she hated the whole affair. To her, it was a nightmare as she had left behind her home, her piano, and all her friends. As well, her sister, Grace, was soon to marry and then move to Peace River with her new hubby.

My Aunt Nina told me that her brother, Art, drove a team of balky mules who resented the rigours of hauling a heavy load and once simply refused to move when they were leaving a farm where they had spent the night. In Nina's words, "Upon noticing that sadirons were heating on the kitchen stove, Art fetched one of them and stuck it under the mule's tail and they were on their way in a hurry." I cannot affirm the truth of this encounter, but who am I to doubt my elders? I am sure it would pose some problems to a knowledgeable mule skinner to use this method to get a team moving.

I had supposed the irons were called sadirons because ironing clothes with a hot iron was a real problem and a dreaded household chore. However upon investigating, I discovered that the prefix "sad" came from the old English word "sald," which meant solid. The iron first appeared around 1738, pointed on both ends with an attached metal handle. As it was heated near an open fire or on a stove, the handle unfortunately heated up too and had to be held with a potholder or heavy glove. The sadiron was heavy as the weight was as necessary as the heat to flatten material. One of the major drawbacks of these irons was that they cooled off fairly rapidly which would explain why the irons were sitting on a hot stove that morning.

Somewhere along the way, as Nina described it, in the middle of nowhere, they were visited by an old "Indian" who looked at Nina intently. Since our family had native blood—I do not now remember to what extent or from which side—Nina was dark-complexioned with high cheek bones, brown eyes and long braids. The old gentleman, with a knowing smile, declared majestically, "Me have wife in tepee just like her!" Considering the prejudice of the times, you can imagine Nina's consternation. Unfortunately, her older brothers would not let her forget the incident and they teased her mercilessly. A stop on the reservation became necessary when all the men developed snow-blindness following an early spring storm. There they were well treated until they could once more be on their way. The struggling caravan crossed the Red Deer River on the ferry as they neared their land of promise, south of Chinook. One freedom-loving steer bolted from the conveyance, never to be seen again. Perhaps someone was fortunate enough to come upon some free unbranded beef.

When World War I began, my father was at first exempted from Canadian military service for two reasons—as a farmer, food production was essential, and secondly, he had been severely injured when he prevented a hog they were butchering from falling. His badly-stooped posture stayed with him for the remainder of his 61 years. Later, Jap was allowed to enlist, though he never saw combat. Thankfully for me and my brothers, he did not become cannon fodder.

For some years, farming went fairly well for the entire family, though never easily as all was accomplished by four-legged horsepower or manpower. One fall near the end of the War, the family had a bumper crop. By not selling until the next year, they had hoped to make a great deal more money as they expected grain prices to continue to rise. However, the good years of the early 20th century ended with catastrophically falling prices following World War I. When the prairie farmers called for help from the federal government, their pleas fell on deaf ears. Thus, though the urban areas enjoyed the prosperity of the 1920s, the period was disastrous for farmers especially when one considers that they were no longer self-sufficient but had to pay in cash for machinery, seed, fertilizer and transportation as well as for consumer goods in spite of the fact that their incomes had fallen sharply. My family was caught in this downward spiral.

My dad left the farm to try to earn a living in Calgary. During this time (around 1920), my dad met and married Edith Webber Trask, who was a teacher at Victoria School in Calgary. He was driving a taxi at the time of his marriage. When that business folded, he worked for Imperial Oil, riveting huge oil tanks. My father and mother moved to Nanton, a town south of Calgary named after Sir Augustus Meredith Nanton of Winnipeg, who directed firms that offered financing for farms and ranches throughout the west. Nanton was established first as a village in 1903 and then as a town in 1907. Here, Jap had good friends, and by faith, rented a nearby farm and began farming again. By this time, Edith and Jap had become parents to two boys. My oldest brother, Don, was born in 1921 and was a real prince and my mentor. My next brother, Bill, who was born seven years before me in 1922, became my tormentor. This big bad belligerent brother battered me badly. I can really relate to the first Joseph who is mentioned in the Bible—cruel sibling rivalry is a reality even today in many families. I am the youngest and was born in Nanton, Alberta, on Wednesday, March 13th, 1929, having arrived just six months before the event that marked the beginning of an austere time in history—the stock market crash of 1929 which began in late October.

The Wall Street Crash signaled the beginning of a ten-year-plus Great Depression which only ended with the American mobilization for World War II at the end of 1941. This period shaped the destiny of people for most of their lives. People who owned stocks in mid-1929 and were able to hold them lived most of their adult life before getting back to even. The "Crash" followed a decade of wealth and excess called the "Roaring Twenties" when many believed that the stock market would continue to climb indefinitely. The higher share prices encouraged more people to invest; even ordinary people hoped the prices would rise further and thus borrowed money to buy stocks. By August 1929, brokers were routinely lending small investors more than two-thirds of the face value of the stocks they were buying. Soon over $8.5 billion was out on loan, which was more than the entire amount of currency circulating in the U.S. at that time. On September 18, 1929, share prices abruptly fell which led to a slow slide that on October 29th became a huge avalanche of lost hopes, lost dreams, lost fortunes, and in many cases lost lives, as those who had borrowed had no hope of paying the debt. The stock market crash and the economic crisis compounded the farmers' difficulties arising from overproduction and low prices. If this was not enough, unfavorable weather conditions appeared. Persistent dry winds during an extended period of drought blew away the nutrient-rich top soil from vast tracts of once-very-productive farmland. The terms "dustbowl" and "dirty thirties" were coined to describe the dreadful conditions. With no crops at all for three long years but a continuing obligation to pay the rent, my father's hopes once again perished, and he gave up the farm to move into Nanton.

Had the government acted upon the Palliser Report, a document by an early surveyor that recommended against long-term cultivation here, this area would never have been considered for farming. Though the soil is dark brown or black in color and very nutrient rich, the area is largely a semi-arid steppe region. At the start of the twentieth century, settlers began to move in with the intent to farm. The yields were high for a time, but dry conditions soon set in, helping to plunge Canada into the Great Depression and catching many farmers off guard. When the land dried out completely, they simply departed as did my father's family, leaving homesteads and dreams behind in the drifting soil of their fallow fields.

Though modern techniques and more rain have helped re-establish the area as an important farming region, it is still precarious and the farmers need government subsidies to deal with drought conditions. In 1983, I met a man who had farmed in the Chinook area years after my family departed. He remembered my grandpa well and the location of his homestead. This gentleman invited me to visit the farm he owned where his son now lived, offering to show me around. He said, "I am a small farmer, owning only twenty-five sections. In order to succeed around here, you need a whole township" (a township is thirty-six miles square). He took me on a tour of the area and showed me Grandpa's old homestead. Nothing remained of any previous habitation except the signs of a rhubarb patch and a caragana hedge. The farmer said, "I have ploughed many farmsteads under and that is usually all that is left." His basement was like a museum of homestead artifacts left behind so many years before.

My father moved to Nanton where he stayed, working as a carpenter framing houses for many years, and then finally as a janitor in the school, which I attended for twelve long distressing years. I recall days spent helping him after school, doing such chores as shovelling walks, sweeping floors, or taking out the garbage. Although Jap worked hard, often his employment was not steady. Of the rest of my grandfather's family, Nina married and lived in Ucluelet, Vancouver Island, British Columbia—where I later visited her often during the summers; a son also lived in British Columbia in a tourist house that appeared to be crooked but wasn't; Art went to Cochrane; and Les ended up in California.

At this time, my roots on my mother's side of my family shall be related. Although both of my parents' families came to Canada through the United States, my mother's history reveals a vastly different background. Edith Webber Trask, my mother, was born in Yarmouth, Nova Scotia, on July 7, 1895, into a family of six girls and three boys—just the opposite of my father's family. Some of them I got to know quite well.

My mother's sister, Alice, lived in Calgary and I was in frequent contact with her through the years. Upon returning to Alberta after graduating from college in 1958, I lived with her for one year.

Aunt Alice once told me a story about her dad. Her young brother, Sid, was singing loudly, "There's powder in the blood," from his memory of it having been sung in church that day. Grampa replied, "Yes, Sid, to see it on some women's faces you would think so." It certainly proved to be my Aunt Alice's habit. When travelling together, she would suggest, "Let's stop for tea." I thought, *"Why not tell the truth?,"* but I knew my question would not be very proper as she was every inch a lady, formed in the same mould as Queen Victoria. She powdered her nose regularly, in keeping with her station in society, just to prove it. She was a real dear! Aunt Alice died years later when my daughter, Beth, was about six years old. Beth admired her hubby, Uncle Sid (Alice's second husband).

In the fifties, while attending college in Boston, I was able to meet more of my mother's siblings—her brother, Stayley, as well as her sisters, Marion, Lou, and Delia. Aunt Marion had invited me to stay with her while I attended Gordon College but the result was a fiasco. During my college years, having travelled to Nova Scotia, I met my youngest uncle, Sidney Trask, of Trask Artesian Well Drilling Co., and often travelled back and forth in my trusty old '41 Studebaker to his home in Kentville. There was always a meal, a bed, and a worthwhile visit with him and his large family and a free tank of gas when I departed. Another uncle, Elkanah, lived in New England though I never saw him. As well, Aunt Eva Jane lived in Chicago—I had contact with her but never met her. My mother's family and my experiences with them will be expanded upon later.

Edith's father, James Logan Trask, began teaching, so I have been told, when he was just out of high school at age seventeen. He taught all his life, constantly improving his qualifications. When he died of a heart attack in his sixty-first year, he had apparently just been appointed to the position of

Deputy Minister of Education in Nova Scotia. My mother's family history goes back a long way.

Elias and Elkana Trask emigrated to Halifax from Dorchester, Massachusetts, because they were afraid of Indian attacks. In Halifax, they would have the security of its fort. They were buried in the church yard at Chegogon, the area where they had moved. James Logan Trask was the great-great-great grandson of Elias. I visited their graves near Yarmouth in the 1950s when I was a student, a summer pastor at Lake George, Yarmouth County. For this and other information about the Trask Family in Nova Scotia, I am indebted to the book, *Elias Trask, his Children and their Succeeding Race: the Trasks of Nova Scotia,* by Gwen Guiou Trask.

Further back in the Trask history, Gwen's book records that William Trask, great-grandfather of Elias, along with perhaps his brother Charles, set sail from Weymouth, England, on the Zouch Phoenix in 1624 for the New World. William allied himself with the Dorchester Co. on Cape Ann. He was an outspoken citizen, soldier, and petitioner for all sorts of causes. My mother must have retained some of these family traits as she also supported causes for good and was involved in promoting the Social Credit Party of Alberta in the 1930s. I was told that one of her causes was to stop the practice of dumping chamber pots in the alley behind the rooming house in Nanton of which she was the proprietor and where we all lived for a short time in the 1920s. Due to her insistence at Town Council, the practice was stopped, the mess removed, and new gravel brought in. I suppose the habit is contagious for I, too, have probably canvassed for every provincial and national candidate for the Conservative Party since the time of John Diefenbaker, even though after being elected he shot down the Avro Arrow, which really tarnished his image, and set back the progress of aviation development in Canada for many years.

SCHOOL DAZE
1935–1948

Just two events previous to my school days particularly come to mind. One day, when playing hide-and-seek around an old barn behind our house, I jumped from the hayloft into the well-rotted manure pile, landing on part of a broken bottle and almost slicing off my heel since my shoes were seldom worn in summer. Much later, when Mother feared that gangrene would set in, Dr. Keen came to the house, stretched me out on top of the kitchen table, applied chloroform, and then thinking that he had rendered me unconscious, began hacking away at my heel with what felt like was a very dull knife. As I did not cry out, he assumed I was under. However, that feeling of cutting through tough skin still causes me to wince when it is recalled today. Years later at age 21, a much more dreadful pain was to confront me.

Another fiasco took place after eating some buffalo beans that grew by the fence in our front yard. Unbeknownst to me, they were no relative of the garden variety, and I became deathly sick as they were poisonous. Mother's care in both of these disasters was most comforting. When it came time to attend school, I was not at all enamoured by the idea of ending my freedom and leaving my mother.

For a time, school did go fairly well! My first and second grade teacher, Miss McKay, was a pleasant and resourceful teacher. She enlivened the otherwise tedious chore of learning by rhythm band. We marched around the room, grating blocks of sandpaper, banging on jam cans, shaking gourds with pebbles inside, imitation tambourines—all to lively music, played on an old gramophone. She must have been a charming teacher because our new principal, "JT" Foster, married her shortly after his arrival.

Mr. Foster's first assignment was to restore order and discipline, which had been lacking previously. In next to no time, he accomplished this task as he was six feet tall and over two hundred pounds with the determination of a football linesman. He quickly became known as simply JT—both my hero and my fearsome antagonist.

At my young age, such misdemeanours as happened in school were minor compared to the non-school catastrophe which was soon to follow. In July of 1937, I visited my mother in the upstairs room of Dr. Keen's hospital in Nanton, shortly after the birth of my baby sister, Alice Fay. She was a beautiful bundle of joy with black hair and bright blue eyes. I could hardly stop admiring her, but, after a long, loving look, my mother called me to her bedside. After affectionately running her fingers through my characteristically unruly hair, she pressed a precious quarter into my hand, saying, "Off you go now and get a haircut at Tom Sawyer's. You can keep the dime." Little did I know then that it would be the last time I would see either the delight of my life alive or my newly-born sister.

While mother was sick, presumably fearing the worst, Dad had arranged for me to stay with the Burge family, who lived on a ranch, west of Nanton. My dad took me there in his boss' old car. Henry Gahn was so proud of and careful with his car that it remained in the garage next to his shop most of the time. He spent many of his daylight hours in his shop when he was between carpenter jobs. He would sit by an old wood-burning stove, smoking "Forest and Stream" tobacco in an old curved pipe. Henry's son had given him a huge, colourful parrot that held forth in a very large cage on the back porch during the summer. It appeared Henry was only welcome in the house at meal-time, when his wife would call him in a shrill and demanding voice, "Henry!" and he would immediately respond to the summons. This parrot had learned to mimic her perfectly. Often, at mealtime or not, Henry would hear the familiar order—a fact not well received by his cranky wife, as the food was not then ready nor did some task require his presence. This pesky parrot had an extensive and profane vocabulary which would curdle milk. He must have learned it at sea from a very volatile sailor. Occasionally, the bird would pour forth from the porch at the least provocation. At the time, the parrot's vocabulary appealed to me with the prospect of vastly improving mine—of course, swearing makes a man much more manly, or so I mistakenly thought!

The prospect of a summer holiday in the hills thrilled me when Dad explained where we were going. As we rumbled along, uphill and down, my dad spoke about how every machine, especially an automobile, had a point of harmonic balance at which they performed best and how your ears would tell you if you just listened carefully. "Just change gears to maintain that sound." Proudly, the thought filled my mind, "My dad sure knows what he's talking about." The conversation we had that day is forever embedded in my memory.

A hearty welcome awaited us as we came to a stop. Mrs. Burge was a good friend of my mother's. Her sons, David and Billy, were both older than me, but we had a glorious time riding horses and playing all kinds of games. No end of battles and rescues took place. I vividly recall one night at the ranch, all tucked snugly into an upstairs bed, when suddenly the silence of the night was shattered by a nearby, unearthly scream. I was petrified. In the morning, the boys' father simply said, "Oh, it was only a disappointed cougar that just missed a kill. It's nothing to be afraid of." Just the same, there was a new awareness of what kind of animals prowled the nearby woods.

Not realizing that my Robin Hood holiday was about to abruptly end, I heard the familiar sound of Henry's old car chugging up the lane around noon. "Why is Dad coming here now?" We had a long, quiet ride back to Nanton, but Dad did not advise me then that Mother had just died. However, later that night, he told me she died from pneumonia. The next day, with Dad in his best clothes, we were on our way to the Baptist church to attend my mother's funeral and mine. Something in me died with her.

My mother was lying in a casket in the entry as white as a sheet. I was completely devastated! Sorrow, confusion, anger and questions engulfed me. "Why did my dad not tell me on the way to town yesterday? Why did she have to die anyway?" That very night staring broken-heartedly into a star-studded sky, I raged inwardly. "If there is a God in heaven, why would He allow my mother to die? Since He did, I hate Him and all He represents. I hate cops, preachers and anyone in authority and especially teachers." The passing of my mother seemed to rip the heart out of our family and that traumatic, sorrowful event was to determine my emotions and reactions for many years. Later, I came to understand that I was not in control and must lean on God for understanding and know that my plans and desires were not necessarily His plans and desires for my life.

My newly-born baby sister had been adopted by a school superintendent from Edmonton, as arranged by my Aunt Alice, after considerable pressure according to my father. Five years later, my baby sister died following a failed appendix operation. Heartbroken, my dad said, "I don't think that would have happened if we had kept her with us." Unknown to me, I had played with her one afternoon at Aunt Alice's when my sister was three years old, as I was later informed. Her adopted mother and father had been visiting Alice.

Our family life was greatly disrupted by the loss of my mother. Since my brothers were both considerably older, I did not have much to do with them other than getting tormented by Bill. My father arranged for two girls to care for me as he was often away working. We had a lot of fun together. Both girls were named Mary, one of whom had a father who was the school's janitor. Once when Mary Zebedee decided that discipline was in order by means of a hair brush, I took it away from her and swatted her.

I don't recall what Christmases were like before my mother died, but afterwards the holiday, like our lives, was pretty skimpy. We did make each other small gifts to exchange, but our associations were not warm or close and our family was far from what one thought of as normal—any family relationships I formed were mostly with others. Dad, however, was a very good father. With Nanton being a small town of approximately 1,000 people, I would hear him calling me to come home for supper—"Ho, James, and don't spare the horses!" With him away working so much, there really was no opportunity to get to know him in any meaningful or deep way. However, once when arriving home while I was sitting on the front step, struggling to put spokes into a bicycle wheel, he sat down beside me and said, "Let's take a look." He found a 'four by nine' rule with the thirty-six spokes and we soon had the wheel repaired. Dad was a very practical man and often said, "If you can't make do, do without."

My dad worked hard to put food on the table and keep a roof over our heads. Over the years, we lived in several different places in Nanton.

One house was on a corner and my bedroom was in the garret. At night, every time a car turned the corner the shadow from the leaves outside my window looked like creepy, crawly hands reaching out for me. I was very superstitious and would hide under the covers, shaking like the leaves outside. Later, my dad built a house with his own bare hands, using nothing but a hammer and a saw, which he finished when I was seventeen. Since he could not afford plywood, he used cedar boards that were free of knots which he purchased at $30 per thousand. He ripped the boards by handsaw to make window frames and trim.

During the Second World War when gasoline was in short supply and rationed, he bought a team of horses to do the work that trucks had previously done. The horses were kept in a field across from our house. My dad built a makeshift barn in order to give them shelter and another small building to store the oats and hay he had purchased. He took wonderful care of the team, getting up at five in the morning to go to the barn where he kept them to give them oats, hay, and water and to get them ready for the day. Only then did he return home for breakfast before going off to meet his commitments by 8 a.m.

Once I recall a load of cement had to be delivered from the train station to Crown Lumber and I went along to help my dad. When the train arrived, the engineer shuttled the boxcar carrying the cement onto a siding much too fast and the bags of cement jammed up against each other, splitting and squashing some. We had to patch up the bags which had split open and straighten out others before we could load them. It was a frightfully cold day and working with the frozen bags of cement was a pain in the neck as the bags were frigid and hard to get a hold on. With fondness, I recall my dad taking off his gloves and holding his hands against the sides of my cheeks as he did not want me to suffer frostbite. It was one of the few times I remember him being so concerned and helpful. Following the war when gasoline was again in good supply, my dad sold the horses back to the farmer he had purchased them from.

Our family always had a dog. One consolation I had following the death of my mother was Bill's dog named Tang. The dog was just a mutt but I loved him and I found solace in him. Nevertheless, I continued to long for the comfort of my mother's presence and was forever searching out surrogate mother figures and families to fill the empty void and to ease the heartache and emptiness I felt within. Mrs. Rousseau, a mother of three, lived next door and was one such person. Once while I was building a rotary steam engine, it blew up and burned my hands badly—at least on one hand the skin was lifting off. After I ran next door, Mrs. Rousseau put cold tea leaves, which she retrieved from a pot on top of the stove, onto the burns, then wrapped my hands in a clean towel. My hands healed beautifully.

Following two years spent in the second grade, Miss Findlay became my grade three teacher upon my return to school that fall. Miss McKay must have been relieved when I entered Miss Findlay's class, as even by then I was a bit of a clown. Miss Findlay was the daughter of our next-door neighbour. That year, a very important lesson in life should have been learned which was not in the school curriculum. During "Show and Tell", Mary Patterson held out a shiny buffalo nickel, which, even then, was rare. When both the room and the hall were empty, I returned and pocketed the coveted coin. Upon coming back to class with no one having confessed to the crime, I was interrogated accusingly, since my desk was in front of Mary's. With me professing innocence, the teacher said, "Turn out your pockets." No coin appeared, but as I raised my arms, Mary exclaimed excitedly, "He's got it in his hand; he's got it in his hand!" Thus the culprit was revealed red handed, but with a look of feigned innocence.

My punishment was to write out for homework, "I will not steal" one thousand times. Since paper was in short supply, I chose closely-lined brown paper cut into page-sized sheets. As I laboriously wrote, my mind rebelliously repeated, "I will not get caught. I will not get caught." I dared not put it on paper as Miss Findlay would probably check my work carefully. This penalty took long nights and nights to finish.

The love of my life, pretty Patty Stafford, who sat in the screwed-down desk in front of me, proudly possessed long, red braids. When our tedious writing class was over, I screwed down the end of one of her braids firmly into the inkwell on my desk as others were putting the tops on their bottles. This did nothing to further my aspirations of her returning my attention. Neither she nor our teacher was impressed. Strap or not, my shaky reputation had just taken another tumble.

Miss Robertson became my fourth grade teacher. I regarded her as a reluctant old spinster who had missed out on marriage and took out her frustration on her students—especially boys. She ruled her class with iron authority, supposedly invested in her by a higher power. One day, the reason long forgotten, she grabbed me by my sore ear and proceeded to jerk me out of my desk. That was a bad mistake—Vesuvius erupted! Springing from my desk, I began kicking her shins viciously. Of course, the usual very thorough strapping by JT followed.

Ear infections from diving into the muddy creek water at the local swimming hole were a recurring problem. This particular time, I had just returned to school following an especially painful session. As we did not have a hot water bottle in our house, Dad heated a bag of salt in the oven. As soon as I could stand the temperature, I would lie on it for hours and have someone reheat it as required. The pounding in my ear seemed endless, but finally, with a screech, the drum would burst, the thumping stop, and the infection drain. Yanking me by the ear that day was not the best method for her to enforce discipline. Needless to say, I was not her favourite student either.

Sometime in 1939, the army came to Nanton to enlist able-bodied men to be trained to defend Canada's rights and freedoms. Brothers Bill and Don were eager to accept the challenge—Bill was 17 and Don was 18. The recruiting officer accepted Bill, even though the eligibility age was 18. My brothers joined the 14th Tank Battalion and were soon on their way to Camp Borden, Ontario, before shipping out to England. While still in Canada, a realistic mock battle was held between the 14th Battalion, which was made up of a rather mixed bunch of Westerners who were equipped with aging Churchill Tanks, and a group of Easterners, who were mostly blue collar workers equipped with the newer Sherman tanks—Bill told me, much to the surprise of all concerned, the Westerners licked the pants off their Eastern rivals. It may be noted that the Westerners were accused of not following the prescribed rules of combat for that exercise!

I'll just add a few comments about my brothers' war experiences before returning to my adventures at school. After arriving in England in 1941, endless months of training followed, with poor rations, housing that was not the greatest, and rigorous physical demands. Bill trained as a gunner, but forever after, he seemed to drive any vehicle as if it were a tank! Their big first deployment, Dieppe, was a fiasco. Fortunately, Bill's battalion was ordered back to England before they landed. Italy was Bill's next conflict. He told me that a jug of good Italian red wine was a provision second only to plenty of ammo. He survived the campaign in Italy, and served in the army of occupation in Germany after the war. He is to be remembered and honoured for his part in preserving the freedom and liberty of democracy in our country; however, when brother Bill joined the 14th Army Canadian Tank Core in 1939, I had told him in no uncertain terms, "If the Krauts don't kill you, I will. I will give you the worst beating you ever had when you return home!" (Bill died at age eighty, about fifteen minutes before I arrived at his bedside. Fortunately, he had apologized to me for being so mean when Trish, my second wife, and I visited him shortly after we were married.) As it turned out, although I practiced boxing and wrestling with determination while Bill was away, when he did return I was sick in bed with pleurisy. It would have been hard for me to lick my way out of a wet paper bag. Earlier, when the local druggist, Dr. Creighton, who made house calls in those days, came to see me, he dolefully removed his stethoscope and solemnly pronounced, "Your mother died of the pneumonia, and it sounds like you have it, too." Thankfully at a time with limited antibiotics, his diagnosis was incorrect.

No doubt, another disgruntled spinster anxiously awaited my arrival in grade five as most likely my reputation preceded me. Miss Dulmage was of a different sort, but she also had some queer habits. When upset by my antics, she would launch into a verbal tirade and the occasional spray of spittle would splutter from her mouth, whereupon I would extract a large red bandana from my hip pocket and ceremonially begin wiping my desk in my usual honoured spot at the front of the classroom. Naturally, this resulted in another condemning note and a trip to JT. As a measure of revenge, her exalted "degree" was inscribed by me on the back-alley fence she passed as she walked to school every day: "D.D.D.D." and in smaller letters—"Dippy, Dummy, Dopey, Dulmage." Soon, the principal summoned me to my appointed doom as, of course, there were no other suspects. A chilling and foreboding reception awaited me! "James, I see that you have been practicing your artistic ability on back-yard fences." Of course, the administration of the assigned discipline was generously applied again. Had he said, "James, we expect better things from you, paint them over, apologize to Miss Dulmage, and you may keep her company during both recesses for two weeks"—that would have been much more effective and would have achieved greater results than all the strappings he could administer. The cruel punishment only solidified all the hurt that already festered in my eleven-year-old heart.

Another reprieve from school came that summer—an invitation to stay with my favourite uncle, Uncle Art, who was really a diamond in the rough, with a heart for his errant nephew and more than enough ability to meet the challenge, having probably had a chat with my dad. I stuffed all my belongings into a twelve-pack beer bottle box, tied it up with binder twine, and set out hitchhiking all the way to Grand Valley, in the hills west of Cochrane, more than one hundred miles away.

While on the way to Calgary, a big, beautiful black car stopped and I was invited to sit in the back seat beside a lovely, little old lady who greeted me with a smile. She asked me a lot of questions. Just before getting out of the car, she pressed a shiny quarter into my hand and put her finger to her lips and pointed to her son up front. Taking a bus, which stopped at Aunt Alice's street, I spent the night at her house. It was probably then that the little girl who was actually my little sister was at my aunt's. The next day, I was on the road again. Uncle Art told me that he would meet me on Grand Valley Road. My last ride dropped me off quite a long distance from my uncle's place. I walked and walked a fair ways on that dusty valley road without one car passing me. The only house with a phone in my uncle's area was quite a ride by horseback from the neighbour who would inform my uncle that his nephew, James, was en route. It was so hot the shade under a bridge beckoned me and I sat there for some time before proceeding onward, one step after another and one more after that. After what seemed an eternity, a big man on a tall horse jogged toward me, leading a smaller horse. What a relief! He tied my beer-box suitcase behind his saddle and hoisted me onto old Babe.

After a long, hot ride, as we approached the pole gate leading to the house where he lived, the most uproariously loud belly laugh that I had ever heard filled the air—even the horses perked up their ears. The merriment had just enlightened me that Art's partner, May, had a good sense of humour. She would probably need it. Thus began the first of two long-to-be-remembered summer holidays in the hills that were criss-crossed with trails and boggy muskeg.

My first out-of-school lesson as a novice greenhorn cowboy was to catch Babe, the foxy old mare that had recently brought me to paradise.

After failing to catch her several times, and following some suggestions from Uncle Art, I set out with a bucket partially filled with some precious oats, a long modified wire used to catch chickens, and a rope under my shirt to capture the old mare. As I called "Babe!" she gave me a questioning look as she saw the pail put down. I backed up a few steps while still calling her in my most affectionate tone. She cautiously put her nose into the grain, grabbed a mouthful, lifted her head and eyed me warily. When her nose entered the pail again, I carefully slipped the widened hook behind her ears and commanded firmly "Whoa!," then carefully untied the halter rope and put it around her neck, gave her a pat and said "good girl." She then followed me with the oats to the hitching rail quite happily. Soon, other lessons were revealed to me, which thankfully, were not about school, either.

At first, I rode without a saddle, having been told to do so. *"No problem,"* I thought! Here came a very painful experience. Since Babe was an old mare, recently retired from the racetrack in Calgary, the love of running was in her genes which I happily obliged. One day, after a long, hot ride in the woods, my legs and behind were soaked with perspiration. To my great surprise and discomfort, I soon learned about sweat-scald and why cowboys are often bow-legged. It was quite some time before I was on a horse again and pleaded earnestly to use a saddle.

One day, I had unwittingly tied Babe to a wasp-laden willow branch before chasing the milk cows out of some boggy bush. The cows knew where to hide but I didn't. When I went back for Babe, she was frantic and the reason was soon apparent. Fortunately, having tied her with a special slip knot learned from Uncle Art, we were on our way instantly. Getting on a horse at a full gallop is not an easy task for an eleven year old inexperienced town boy!

Once, and not the last time, I took the wrong side of the trail and was immediately knocked off of my speedy mount by an overhanging deadfall. Another time, when a group of us were on a long ride through the bush to visit our neighbours and far from home, I went left when all the others went right, thinking I had outsmarted everyone and would soon be ahead of them all. Instead, I quickly became completely lost. Turning back was not an option. Babe was very uneasy, so trusting her to find the way home I loosened the reins and hung on for dear life. What a wild ride followed! We went crashing through the brush, with me shielding my face from overhanging branches as best as possible, all the while scraping my shins on tree trunks. Relief and a good bawling-out awaited me when Babe finally pounded up the lane. Uncle Art's adjectives need no explanation, and he finished by saying, "You were one so-and-so lucky kid because you were riding that horse." A search party had just been organized to go looking for me as darkness was approaching. Other antics too numerous to mention flood my memory of those happy and eventful summers in the hills with Uncle Art and his merry partner. These respites were a welcome relief to a sad and heartbroken youngster. Years later, my beloved Babe died one spring while trying to get up in the bottom of an old, rotted straw-stack—ice was underneath the straw and it was too slippery for her to get a footing.

In the fall of 1941, upon my disappointing return to "jail," Miss Shaw became my grade six teacher. She was also to be my grade seven teacher. We had to climb to the third-floor garret at the top of the stairs to get to her room. It reminded me of a tired old prison. Patches of loose brown stained plaster hung from the ceiling and only one large window enlivened the loft wall. Just the same, we began to have more fun in her room than we previously enjoyed. With eager anticipation, the boys excitedly looked forward to a new course in grade seven, called Industrial Arts, which we just called "Shop." We hoped it would be a change from the same-old, same-old.

The old coal bin in the basement had been empty since the conversion of the school to natural gas heating. It had been transformed into our new Industrial Arts Centre. One wall was adorned with a huge freshly painted green cupboard, with double doors which opened out to expose a glorious array of sparkling new hand tools. The long descent down four flights of stairs to the basement was accomplished in haste and hilarity, unless met by the ever watchful teachers along the way. Our eager anticipation soon faded, however, when we were required to sit on tall stools behind a heavy-duty bench. Once again, we were called upon to listen to endless cautions and rules, writing down the usual boring class notes. It was really frustrating. Finally, we were allowed to use the fascinating tools to make simple projects. The first was a so-called bench hook, which was supposed to hold your project steady while sawing, sanding, or chiselling—but it wiggled and jiggled just the same. The thought flickered in my mind, "Why bother with that contraption when each bench had a perfectly good wood vice?" My favourite tool soon became the coping saw which I used to make piggy-shaped cutting boards—one we used at home for a long time and others I sold in order to earn some money. Though our dungeon-like room had a low ceiling, no windows, and poor light, just the same, time in the shop ended much too quickly and you can be sure we did not ascend the "wooden hill" nearly so quickly as we came down.

Upon arriving in grade eight, I entered my first and only really enjoyable year at school. An unexpected reprieve awaited me. Miss Daley, a motherly-looking lady, greeted me in a very friendly fashion. Since she and Miss Dulmage had started teaching in Nanton about the same time and they were good friends, I feared the worst as she did not look like a teacher to be trifled with and I imagined that the echoes of my adventures in grade five probably had proceeded me as they always had previously. To my complete surprise, she told me that she had loved my mother's cooking while living in my mother's boarding house when she had first arrived in Nanton to begin teaching, which she did very well for over forty years. In fact, one school in Nanton is named the A.B. Daley School in honour of her; the other was the J.T. Foster School as JT was also admired greatly in Nanton for his achievements—the one who restored discipline and good order to N.H.S. I have my reservations about that acclaim!

Miss Daley told me that I was the little boy who came to her room, and asked, "Miss Daley, may I sharpen your pencils?" My mother would say, "Now James, you leave Miss Daley alone. She has work to do." Once again, I became her devoted helper. Woe betide anyone who said anything nasty about her when around me. On many occasions, especially if we had worked particularly hard in her class that morning or if it was a dull or stormy day, she greeted us with a delightful concert of classical music, played on an old upright phonograph, which, happily, I was given the honour to crank. On other similar occasions, we would sing songs until we were out of breath, often in rounds row by row or, with the class divided in half, singing in two part harmony. What a splendid surprise! It's been said, "Good music will soothe the sorrowing soul." Others claim that music will improve the growth of house plants. However, in my opinion, most of our so-called modern music would wilt even dandelions! For me, classical music was uplifting for a time, but my heartache always returned, no matter the welcoming interlude.

Though trying my best, arithmetic remained my worst subject. Miss Daley suspected that my problem was vision as the questions from the board were often copied incorrectly, even when sitting in my usual honoured position at the front of the room. A trip to Tom Attwood, the local eye-doctor, solved the problem, but the cost of all-too frequent repairs to my spectacles became my father's nightmare! Previously, I could not even hit a soft ball well though I had absolutely no trouble catching a football. Just toss me the football and we would make the third down every time, for which I was quite often rewarded by a foot on the head when attempting to get up from the bottom of the pile. As recess was never supervised by a teacher, our brand of football was a very rough-and-tumble game.

Upon entering grade nine, more subjects were added to the curriculum along with the teachers equipped to teach them. To my delight, our English instructor, Miss Frances, was also our home-room teacher. She was a young and very attractive beginning teacher. For me, the temptation to become the class clown was too enticing not to assume the role vigorously. Strangely, I had no opposition; after all, I was not running for a political office! Miss Frances was not much of a disciplinarian. One day, my punishment for some comedian act or comment was to push a peanut all the way across the front of the schoolroom with my nose. I don't remember how successful I was but she soon chose another method of attempting to correct my classroom behaviour: "Just go out into the hall and consider your ways!"

Since there was a huge dictionary under a light on a stand in the hall, I became engrossed in looking up meanings. As it was well illustrated, the time out of class was quite enjoyable. Except for being deprived of the opportunity to be an entertainer, I learned more there from those illustrations than anything she taught in class. Usually just about time for the bell to ring to change the teacher or the class for the next period, JT's observation of "James, you seem to be spending a lot of time in the hall these days" alerted me that he was on the prowl. I reflected, "Why doesn't he spend more of his time teaching or in his office?"

Toward the end of my grade nine year when all the class had long since memorized the required number of lines of poetry in English class, my quota was still far short. My only poetry was a memorable little piece which ended on a sad note. "How sad—I wonder what his problem was?" often flashed through my thoughts. It reminded me of my own upstairs bedroom. Occasionally, the writer's longing had momentarily crossed my own mind.

> *"I remember, I remember the house where I was born. The little window where the sun came peeking in at morn. It never came a wink too soon, nor back too long a day; but now I often wish the night had born my breath away."*

Reality arrived when our charming teacher, Miss Mary Frances, informed me in no uncertain terms, "Without it, you won't pass!" Waiting until almost the last moment when she was busy marking our final exams, I interrupted her progress to recite two epic dirges which would just meet the requirement: "The Yarn of The Nancy Bell" and "The Duel of James-Fitz James, With Sir Roderick Dhu." Though she no doubt was not impressed, they are included here for your enjoyment. As you can imagine, it took me quite some time to memorize these lengthy pieces. Since those early days, I have applied my memorization faculties to a much more valuable project, learning many Bible verses by heart, which has been a great comfort to me on numerous occasions.

The Yarn of the 'Nancy Bell'
by W. S. Gilbert (public domain)

'Twas on the shores that round our coast
    From Deal to Ramsgate span
That I found alone on a piece of stone
    An elderly naval man,

His hair was weedy, his beard was long,
    And weedy and long was he,
And I heard this wight on the shore recite,
    In a singular minor key:

"Oh, I am a cook and a captain bold,
    And the mate of the Nancy brig,
And a bo'sun tight, and a midshipmite,
    And the crew of the captain's gig."

And he shook his fists and he tore his hair,
    Till I really felt afraid,

For I couldn't help thinking the man had been drinking,
   And so I simply said:

"O elderly man, it's little I know
   Of the duties of men of the sea,
But I'll eat my hand if I understand
   How you can possibly be

"At once a cook, and a captain bold,
   And the mate of the Nancy brig,
And a bo'sun tight, and a midshipmite,
   And the crew of the captain's gig."

Then he gave a hitch to his trousers, which
   Is a trick all seamen larn,
And having got rid of a thumping quid,
   He spun this painful yarn:

"'Twas in the good ship Nancy Bell
   That we sailed to the Indian sea,
And there on a reef we come to grief,
   Which has often occurred to me.

"And pretty night all o' the crew was drowned
   (There was seventy-seven o' soul),
And only ten of the Nancy's men
   Said 'Here!' to the muster-roll.

"There was me and the cook and the captain bold,
   And the mate of the Nancy brig
And the bo'sun tight and a midshipmite,
   And the crew of the captain's gig.

"For a month we'd neither wittles nor drink
   Till a hungry we did feel,
So we drawed a lot, and accordin' shot
   The captain for our meal.

"The next lot fell to the Nancy's mate,
   And a delicate dish he made;

Then our appetite with the midshipmite
    We seven survivors stayed.

"And then we murdered the bo'sun tight,
    And he much resembled pig,
Then we wittled free, did the cook and me,
    On the crew of the captain's gig.

"Then only the cook and me was left,
    And the delicate question, "Which
Of us two goes to the kettle?" arose
    And we argued it out as sich.

"For I loved that cook as a brother, I did,
    And the cook he worshiped me;
But we'd both be blowed if we'd either be stowed
    In the other chap's hold, you see.

"I'll be eat if you dines off me," says Tom,
    'Yes, that,' says I, 'you'll be,'—
'I'm boiled if I die, my friend,' quoth I,
    And 'Exactly so,' quoth he.

"Says he, 'Dear James, to murder me
    Were a foolish thing to do,
For don't you see that you can't cook me,
    While I can—and will—cook you!'

"So he boils the water, and takes the salt
    And the pepper in portions true
(Which he never forgot) and some chopped shallot,
    And some sage and parsley too.

"Come here,' says he, with a proper pride,
    Which his smiling features tell,
"Twill soothing be if I let you see,
    How extremely nice you'll smell.'

"And he stirred it round and round and round,
    And he sniffed at the foaming froth;

When I ups with his heels, and smothers his squeals
   In the scum of the boiling broth.

"And I eat that cook in a week or less,
   And—as I eating be
The last of his chops, why, I almost drops,
   For a vessel in sight I see!

"And I never grin, and I never smile,
   And I never larf nor play,
But I sit and croak, and a single joke
   I have—which is to say:

"Oh, I am a cook and a captain bold,
   And the mate of the Nancy brig,
And a bo'sun tight, and a midshipmite,
   And the crew of the captain's gig!"

The Duel of James-Fitz James, With Sir Roderick Dhu
(from *The Lady of the Lake*)
By Sir Walter Scott (public domain)

Ill fared it then with Roderick Dhu,
That on the field his targe he threw,
Whose brazen studs and tough bull-hide
Had death so often dash'd aside;
For, train'd abroad his arms to wield,
Fitz-Jame's blade was sword and shield.
He practiced every pass and ward,
To thrust, to strike, to feint, to guard;
While less expert, though stronger far,
The Gael maintain'd unequal war.
Three times in closing strife they stood,
And thrice the Saxon blade drank blood;
No stinted draught, no scanty tide,
The gushing flood the tartans dyed.
Fierce Roderick felt the fatal drain,
And shower'd his blows like wintry rain;
And, as firm rock, or castle-roof,

Against the winter shower is proof,
The foe, invulnerable still,
Foil'd his wild rage by steady skill;
Till, at advantage ta'en, his brand
Forced Roderick's weapon from his hand,
And backward borne upon the lea,
Brought proud Chieftain to his knee.

XVI

"Now, yield thee, or by Him who made
The world, thy heart's blood dyes my blade!"
"Thy threats, thy mercy, I defy!
Let recreant yield, who fears to die."
Like adder darting from his coil,
Like wolf that dashes through the toil,
Like mountain-cat who guards her young,
Full at Fitz-James's throat he sprung;
Received, but reck'd not of a wound,
And lock'd his arms his foeman round.
Now, gallant Saxon, hold thine own!
No maiden's hand is round thee thrown!
That desperate grasp thy frame might feel
Through bars of brass and triple steel!
They tug, they strain! Down, down they go,
The Gael above, Fitz-James below.
The Chieftain's grip his throat compress'd,
His knee was planted in his breast;
His clotted locks he backward threw,
Across his brow his hand he drew,
From blood and mist to clear his sight,
Then gleam'd aloft his dagger bright!
But hate and fury ill supplied
The stream of life's exhausted tide,
And all too late the advantage came,
To turn the odds of deadly game;
For, while the dagger gleam'd on high,
Reel'd soul and sense, reel'd brain and eye.
Down came the blow—but in the heath;

The erring blade found bloodless sheath.
The struggling foe may now unclasp
The fainting Chief's relaxing grasp;
Unwounded from the dreadful close,
But breathless all, Fitz-James arose.

School ended with me passing English by the skin of my teeth. Miss Frances really had been a nice teacher and I often dreamed how wonderful it would be to marry a lady like her. She did not stay in teaching for long but married a well-known radio announcer from Lethbridge. Years later, I unsuccessfully attempted to contact her and apologize for my actions in her class.

Before the story moves along, I would also like to tell you about my experience with the subject taught by Miss Tanner, our young typing teacher. She had a problem—too many students and not enough typewriters, resulting in the need to take turns. One day, JT visited our class to assess the situation. As he watched my awkward attempts at typing, he said, "James, put your hands on the keys." When I obliged, he proclaimed, "Your hands are too big to ever learn to type! Let someone else use your typewriter." Thus, my hope of learning the skill ended. Such is life. Weeding out typing students was one way to solve the equipment dilemma and those who apparently were not good prospects were expendable. After all, clowns don't need to learn to type!

About this time, an employment opportunity arose with a man who made and repaired shoes. John Kotelas was my boss, friend, and mentor. When the Russians invaded Budapest in Hungary and the streets were filled with tanks, John thought it was time to leave the country before it was too late. Fortunately, he was able to emigrate to Canada. Upon arriving in High River, he worked for Lou Bradley, repairing shoes and learning to make cowboy boots. Later, even though he had learned very little English, he decided to move to Nanton and start his own business. He told me once that "cornflakes" was one of the first words he learned. He said, "I ate so many boxes of cornflakes, I never want to see another as long as I live." Since my shoes often needed repair, I asked John if I could be any help to him. All the wonderful things that happened at the back of his store attracted me. I soon became his ardent understudy, discovering why cowboys found it necessary to get their boots repaired and becoming adept at removing the mud and manure from the boots to get them ready for John to half-sole. After John stated, "Job accomplished," I could proceed with more pleasant tasks. My favourite task became the repair of binder canvasses for which both John and the farmers were most grateful. John could work more on making new cowboy boots and the farmers avoided an oft over-looked, tiresome repair.

My boss became known for much sought-after beauties that would complete the attire of many a would-be bronc-rider, especially at the Calgary Stampede, where it's likely that many contestants admired boots made by John Kotelas. Some were ordered from as far away as Australia. Unfortunately, none of John's three sons decided to follow in their father's footsteps, and John's business folded soon after his long-overdue retirement. At that time, I worked for John every day after school and on Saturday, which kept me out of my new stepmother's hair, a fact she surely appreciated. My cobbler career ended when my road in life abruptly took another turn.

My dad had married Tena two years previously and all was not well on the home front. My attitude toward my stepmother combined with my frustration in school produced a volatile situation. Tena was good at heart but I considered her to be a bit lacking mentally—as the saying goes "one brick short of a load." She often talked to herself excitedly while repeating our most recent altercation. Since most of my spare time was spent in our basement fixing bicycles for friends, I would prop the trapdoor open just enough to watch her footwork as she walked from counter to stove, rehearsing the report of our latest dispute that she would deliver to my dad at the end of the day.

Evidently, Dad married Tena to serve as his companion and housekeeper, and as a replacement mother for me. Perhaps he hoped it also might provide a solution to my lack of application to schoolwork, but in my mind, no one could or would ever replace my mother—not even Mother Teresa herself! I often wished that my dad had married Tena's sister, Nellie, who was friendly, funny, and artistic. No such luck, but Nellie did supply us with plenty of fresh farm eggs free of charge. Years later, a friend told me, they had a picture that was painted by my mother, who was quite a capable artist. I said, "No way!" Examination later revealed it was painted by Nellie DeVries, my step-mother's sister.

One day, upon arriving home from school at noon, as I was washing my hands at the top of the stairs (the trap door having been left open) I tauntingly asked in a very knowing voice, "So, what's for lunch?" She responded, "Soup and eggs." Whereupon, I said along with some colourful parrot talk, "Woman, don't you know how to cook anything but soup and eggs?" As I glanced in the mirror, I saw a pot of hard boiled eggs flying at the back of my head. The pot, the eggs, and the boy disappeared, all tumbling down the stairs together. Though I do not now recollect exactly what happened afterwards, it became apparent that leaving home would be a very good idea.

Relief from my distress with school and with my well-meaning step-mother arrived from a very unexpected source. With it, my hatred of schools and any other authority as well as my quarrels with my step-mother came to an end. It also alleviated the very distinct possibility of having to go to Reform School, as my recent encounter with the local Justice of the Peace had indicated as a very real possibility, following my entering one of the elevators and stealing their stamps. Because of my many scrapes with the law due to general mischief and vandalism, this suggestion had been recommended by George Ellis, the town cop, who had arranged the recent visit to the JP. For riding illegally on the sidewalk, my bicycle was often confiscated and kept in the jail. When George was away, I would slip into the jail and take it for a spin, returning it before George noticed it missing. My reputation among the populace of the town was not one of "high esteem." If anything went wrong about town, people just naturally blamed it on "Jamesey" Davis. "Any attention is better than no attention" seemed to be my motto. George Ellis lived next door to us and was a very nice neighbour. One time, he dared me to eat a huge purple potato from his garden. I told him it would be no problem—but as it turned out, it was too big for even my appetite!

One day, Joan Burrows, a class-mate of mine, communicated that her dad might be in need of help on the farm. Perhaps I would like to ride my bike out to their place and have a chat with him. When school finished that day, Lulabelle, my beloved bike, took me out to their farm in double jig time. Joan had told her parents, "I don't think Jim is a bad kid at heart. He just needs some re-directing." Also, in 1943, most able-bodied men like my brothers had long since gone to war. Consequently, my five-year apprenticeship as a farm-boy began. My only disappointment was that my shoe repair stint with John Kotelas was over, but I was relieved to end my fiasco with Tena.

On the farm, my jobs included: milk the cows, run the cream separator, feed the pigs, churn the butter, gather the eggs, chop the kindling, bring in the coal and water, take out the ashes, and empty the slop pail. In summer, chores increased to include: weed the garden and the flower bed, trim the hedge, mow the lawn with an old push-mower, and all too soon, run the John Deere tractor with any of the equipment it pulled, mend fences, and in general fix things around the place as needed—all for $20.00 per month, plus room and board and learning to be a farmer as well as free lessons on protocol and manners, which were sadly lacking. Often, Joan practiced classical music on her beloved piano, while I worked nearby. Chopin was her favourite composer and it was a real challenge for her to play his difficult works perfectly. Reg was a good father-figure and a no-nonsense boss. Just for fun, we always manufactured petty bets for candy bars, which I mostly lost, while still learning a great deal about farming.

My dad always said, "You grew up just like Topsy." After reading *Uncle Tom's Cabin*, I understood what he meant. My new mother-figure was a no-nonsense, lovely red-head. As you can imagine, growing up with two older rough-and-tumble brothers and no mother to rein us in, I was not a shining example of manners or decorum. For example, while attempting to lick my knife before sticking it into the peanut butter, I was kindly but firmly informed, "Not in our house, you don't!" One morning as Georgia, Joan's mother, was about to put a shovelful of coal into the stove, she absent-mindedly opened the lid of the reservoir, whereupon I laughed. She promptly warned me, "If I had done that, you would be the one to clean it out and fill it again before breakfast." Another time, when Reg and I were chopping pig feed—a very dusty job—we wanted to finish before the noonday meal, so Reg said, "Go ask the War Department when lunch will be ready." So I obeyed word-for-word and received a rather curt reply, "You tell him that it will be ready as usual, and he better be in here on time." Lunch that day was very quiet. When Reg returned much later, looking a bit sheepish, he said, "Don't you ever say that to her again!"

As the farm tractor usually sat on the driveway, I often tried to start it. Previously I had asked Reg, "When can I drive the tractor?" He replied, "Just as soon as you can start it by yourself." Even then it was an old tractor and it was one of the first John Deere D's to have the metal lugs replaced with rubber tires. As it needed to be started by hand, it took some effort to turn the flywheel. One day as Reg came out of the house, he witnessed me trying strenuously to turn the motor of the tractor over. He suggested, "Why don't you open the petcocks?"—which was a necessity. I had frequently watched my dad as he started the huge old Rumley engine which was used to run the separator when threshing grain. Both were started manually and were of a similar design. Following my boss's suggestion and Dad's example, I was relieved to hear the familiar pop, pop sound of the two-cylinder engine coming to life. Thus began my long love affair with this durable, old tractor.

One of my first jobs on the farm was to learn how to operate the binder. It required knowing what to do with all the confusing levers and exactly when to dump the bundle-carrier, leaving the bundles in long, continuous rows. I soon surmised why Reg was on the tractor and I was on the binder, as it was almost impossible to trip the bundle-carrier when it was heavily loaded (which happened all too often). As the task should have been easily accomplished that evening I investigated and saw the reason why it was so difficult—the end of the pipe on the bundle-carrier was badly bent. After supper, I managed to remove the pipe, pound it back into shape, then drive a smaller pipe into the once crooked end. I was exhilarated with the result and Reg was sure surprised to see the carrier dumping the bundles with just a touch of his toe on the leather strap of the trip mechanism. Now, he wanted me on the binder for sure. Adjusting all the levers in order to tie perfect bundles was both a challenging and satisfying task.

One day, having just come off the bus, I spied Reg disking the hog pasture and rushed out to see if I could help, while still in my school clothes. As Reg was busy turning, I attempted to lift the depth-control lever. However, my foot slipped and was immediately caught under one of the discs. Yanking with all my might—with my other leg still on the hitch, I got myself free. Just in front of the heel, the sole of my shoe was cut all the way through, but fortunately my foot had not even been touched. You can imagine my relief! Since Reg was busy turning, he did not realize what had just happened and you can believe I didn't tell him or anyone else of my foolhardy exploit.

In the fall, swathing became my favourite assignment. We still used a well-worn sixteen foot, bull-wheel driven swather, which under good conditions laid down a well-supported snake-like windrow. As we frequently had to stop for repairs, I asked Reg if I could rebuild it following harvest that year. On one occasion, I had a heart-stopping accident with the swather before its restoration. It was a wonder that I was not killed. While transporting the huge machine to our north field, I accidently drove into the ditch, with two wheels on the road and two in the ditch. It required standing in the ditch to shut off the fuel, as there was no other off-switch on a John Deere. With every pop of the engine, I expected the tractor to roll over. Fortunately, the weight of the swather hitch held the tractor wheels on the ground. When Reg came looking for me in his new, 1946 Ford truck, he produced a shovel and said, "You dig a trench ahead of the front wheel, and we will see if we can get back on the road again." Thankfully, he started the tractor this time. Much to my relief, we were soon back on the road. Reg gave me a good dressing-down because instead of paying attention, I had been watching a flock of geese flying south.

The next fall, having rebuilt the swather completely, I waited with eager anticipation to see how my handiwork performed. Reg said, "I'll make the first round." Since it required driving around the field in the reverse direction, I was relieved as it meant cutting close to the fence. Standing on the back of the tractor watching, I was ecstatic to see the swather cutting quietly and cleanly. Suddenly the tractor barked as the wheels dug into the dirt. The end of the cutting bar had snagged in some partially buried hog wire and the cutting bar was instantly transformed into a rainbow. I burst into tears, crying despairingly, "It will never cut another straw! It's ruined! It's ruined!" The beautifully rebuilt old swather did not cut any more grain that fall. Reg gave the useless swather to his very patient brother who, years later, repaired it for his own use.

That fall, Reg's neighbour cut his grain with a new-fangled, power take-off, end-delivery machine, which simply dumped the swath in an unruly pile. The swath stuck to the ground when it finally dried out after the first fall snow, making the swath almost impossible to pick up. Reg was really disappointed as his old relic was designed to prevent that problem. It was a center-delivery machine—as the stubble was being cut, it bounced upright in such a way so that the swath was held high and would support a considerable amount of snow without even touching the ground. Also, it greatly lessened the chance of picking up rocks, which could really damage the combine.

The old, worn-out '29 Ford truck—a three-quarter ton with a grain box—was used exclusively for farm work, mainly hauling grain from our old combine to the grain bin. I had graduated from pushing the grain to the back of the bin when almost full, to driving the truck from the combine to the bin. It was a relief to be rescued from shovelling inside the bin where my knuckles often got ripped on the points of the shingle nails sticking through the roof. Sporadically, the old contraption would die on the way to the bin when a tube in the carburetor dislodged because of the bumpy trail. On these occasions, Reg became a bit grumpy because I would usually be delayed getting back to the combine for the next load. Since the cab was so rickety, the floorboards caused the motor to run wild every time you turned left. The cab shifted from left to right or vice-versa depending on which way you were turning. The truck had a big bulge on the front left tire—as big as half a grapefruit. Reg said, "You don't ever need to worry about a blow-out as it has a ten-ply boot inside." One can only imagine how anxiously he waited to be able to buy a new truck after the war rationing was off.

J. J. Dalki's Wildlife Show had just visited Nanton. One Saturday while attending the show, my curiosity was interrupted by a very firm arm-lock being applied to both my appendages. Two voices declared in unison, "You're coming with us!" The circus barker called out, "Take a chance—wrestle the bear and win ten dollars." Whereupon, my friends shouted, "We dare you!" Of course, since I always accepted a dare, I was game. The bear's first trick was to climb to the top of a six-foot step ladder, drink a bottle of sour milk and then descend. Meanwhile, I was hustled into a pair of well-worn coveralls and introduced to my eager opponent to the delight of my determined challengers. I'm convinced that they doubted that I would win, and they would enjoy a good laugh at my expense. No doubt the bear was taller than me when he stood on his hind legs. A plan emerged as he eyed me nonchalantly. I backed away cautiously, then suddenly charged the bear, hitting him solidly, with my right foot firmly locked behind his out-stretched leg. Down the bear went. Though he bounded up quickly and charged me with a look of defiance in his eyes, it was too bad for him. It was the first ten bucks that I earned from my part-time, soon to be short-lived occupation, and I gloated over successfully defeating the big brute.

Not long after, an invitation came to join the circus and wrestle the bear regularly. The new barker now invited the crowd insistently, "The Boy and the Bear Wrestling Match. Come and watch the boy and the bear wrestle." J.J. Dalki also had an old 1925 mile-long Dodge touring car of which I would be the proud chauffeur. Oh boy, that would be living! However, my last encounter with the bear somewhat dampened my enthusiasm. The bear was fitted with a strap over his nose, which was supposed to be reconnected after descending the ladder. On this particular occasion, that important feature was accidently omitted. As I charged the bear, he leaned forward and engulfed me in his 'loving' embrace and attached his wet, sticky nose to the side of my neck. I suddenly felt an electric-like shock as he tried to bite me. Instantly, with what must have been a good shot of adrenaline, I pushed him away with all my might and he landed flat on his back. Believe me, I was one relieved would-be bear wrestler.

My lack of motivation to return to school was dealt with in the usual red-headed fashion. Georgia Burrows was not one bit impressed with my grandiose hopes of joining J.J. Dalki's Wildlife Show. She immediately informed me in no uncertain terms, "When Monday morning comes around, you will be on the bus to school. You will forget all about J. J. Dalki and his Wildlife Show." And it was so. My supposed hope of an idyllic life with the circus fortunately perished. I have many more fond memories of my time on the farm that are too numerous to mention. Having come from a very dysfunctional situation following the death of my mother, suffice it to say, the farm was a place where I enjoyed stability and experienced life in a normal family situation—one in which I received love, encouragement, and guidance.

While on the farm, we travelled to and from school on a Fargo truck, which had been modified into a bus by a skilled carpenter to accommodate about twenty students. They were remarkable hand-crafted vehicles—a far cry from today's big, yellow monsters. The rear of the three-quarter ton Fargo truck was turned into a seating area. It was enclosed with wood and equipped with two rows of narrow seats, each beside a window. They were well-made by a town carpenter, nicknamed Clubfoot Smith.

One day on an extremely muddy track from the main road down the badly-rutted zigzag course to the farm, I decided to move up to the front since the bus was nearly empty. The vehicle suddenly lurched violently sideways and my behind shattered the glass in the window beside the seat into which I suddenly crash-landed. The jagged pieces of glass did a job on my rear end and, for long afterwards, small shards sought eviction from my behind. I said nothing to anyone and nothing was said to me. However, I sat down gingerly for quite some time.

My school was named the Nanton Consolidated School, because it had absorbed all the little rural schools which were scattered throughout the school division at the rate of one per township as required (a township is six miles by six miles).

During my years on the farm, I regularly visited home to see my father and step-mother. By this time, they were parents of a little girl named Ann, my half-sister. Tena did my laundry and often popped the buttons off my shirts with the wringer—thankfully, she always sewed them back on. Nanton had no water system at that time, but my dad had dug a hole at the corner of the house in order to collect rain water from the roof. He installed a pump, which delivered water for washing after it was primed.

During my stay in grade eleven, another great change took place in my life. Billy McLuskie, the new pastor of the Nanton Baptist Church, entered my life in a very sudden and unexpected manner. One Friday night, I attended the regular Young People's meeting at the church as an excuse to get a ride to town with a friend so that I could attend the Friday night dance with my new girlfriend. While fleeing the premises by the back door, I was met face-to-face at the bottom steps by this little Bantam-rooster-like preacher, who blocked my way, frustrating my intentions. After some discussion, he suggested, "Why don't you go over to the house? My wife Audrey has a cup of hot chocolate ready for you." Since my life was one of a bold front with a broken heart, I thought, "What have I got to lose?" When I told Pastor McLuskie about breaking my date, he simply said, "Oh, she has probably been stood-up before, and she will be stood-up again. Don't worry about that!" Thus, a mentor of a different sort entered my life.

Pastor McLuskie became my very good friend. Receiving Christ as my Saviour that night began the life-long transformation of a hurting and confused *sinner*, one who knew his sinfulness to be all too true. When I was ten, I had made a confession of faith at a Baptist's Boys Camp but it was not until now that there was any change in me. The first time I attempted to revert to my parrot-talk vocabulary, including taking the Lord's name in vain, it was as though a dagger pierced my heart. To my knowledge, I have not done so in all the years since then. My parrot lingo vanished overnight. I realized instantly that I was indeed a new creature in Christ.

Until I went to the farm and experienced kindness and a reason to reform my ways, I had often wet my pillow with my tears; but by day I was Mr. Macho, unafraid of anyone and a terror to bullies and to those who tried to torment me or others. The happy-go-lucky show, however, was all a facade. My hurt and anger came out in many ways. Upon returning to school and being taunted repeatedly, "Jamesey's got religion. Jamesey's got religion," I put my fist under my tormentor's nose and replied, "You better be glad, or your nose would be one very bloody mess."

Sometime during grade twelve, I also toiled for a very short interval at Magee's Dairy in Nanton. The dairy man had several attractive daughters who did all the work. Some of the girls had become ill with the flu and I came to their rescue. As well as milking the old cows which were hard to drain, it was my job to bring in the green feed for the next day, as well as extra feed on Saturday and Sunday. As the dairy man was a Seventh Day Adventist, I worked both Saturday and Sunday. To my utter dismay, when I went out to the field to bring in the bundles to run them through the hammer mill, the field was nearly bare. There were more than enough bundles in a slough, except they were frozen almost half-way up to the bands. What to do? I went back to the barn for a shovel to chop them off. This did not solve the problem since the mice had eaten the binder-twine bands. The pitch fork would not pick up the loosened green feed, so I returned to the barn for a manure fork. Now, another problem arose—the wind blew most of the loosened straw to kingdom-come instead of staying on the bundle rack. When I turned the bundle-rack down wind, I was able to get about enough loose straw on the back of the bundle rack for one night's feeding. Then, I had to hitch the little tractor to the hammer mill and chop it up and blow it into the haymow, and then proceed with the milking.

Was it really worth all this just to be a helper to a guy's family, when most of the time he was away on other matters? Was a little smooching with his daughter Joyce worth it all? I think not, but I continued on with the daunting task. Then, too, the barn was always in need of cleaning. That meant using a scoop shovel and a wheelbarrow and a trip to the riverbank and a ho-heave-ho and over the bank she goes. I had levelled out the path earlier by dumping the stuff along the way from the barn and the going was much easier since by the next day, my road repair was frozen solid. Quite often, the wind blew so hard that the wheelbarrow would actually fly through the air like the daring young man on the flying trapeze, but it was very difficult to control.

There were mornings when I thought the stars above were still in the same place as I had left them the night before. Each morning I went with the dairy man to deliver milk door to door. He did the driving and I did the running. Sometimes I thought I was nuts to stay. The family must have been quite sure that I would marry their daughter and soon become an ardent Seventh Day Adventist, as they constantly invited me to join them at services. When I informed Billy McLuskie that I was considering their request, he appeared at their house one day as I was on my way to supper, and he commanded, "Get your stuff! You are coming with me—now!" I had endured more than enough exposure to the reality of this dairy farm episode and S.D.A. propaganda that a little smooching with Joyce along with minimal wages was not enough incentive for me to stay any longer. All the girls were well now and there was no longer any reason to continue the struggle. I hurriedly got my stuff together during supper and soon after left with a very hasty, short apology. I departed more quickly than I came!

One day in class, when we were attempting to learn the periodic table of atoms, I quoted 2 Peter 3:10 to JT—"*The elements shall melt with fervent heat...*"(KJV). He simply replied, "Everyone knows that atoms are the smallest particle known to man and they cannot be split." I wonder what he thought after atomic fission was discovered. Scientists say that the world probably began with a big bang. If that is true, we can ask the scientists, "Who then made the powder and lit the fuse?" Conversely, we know that the world will end someday with a big bang when the elements "shall melt with fervent heat." As the Psalmist declares: "*A thousand years in your sight are like a day that has just gone by, or like a watch in the night*" (Psalm 90:4, NIV). No one knows when that day will be, for we are very plainly told in Matthew 24:36, "*...about that day or hour no one knows*" (NIV). As Mr. L. E. Maxwell, the principal I was to meet during my post-secondary education, would say, "Plan like you will live forever and live like you will die tomorrow."

My memory of the events which took place in school from grades ten to twelve is foggy. However, JT is still my most well-remembered protagonist. As my conversion from clown to a prospective saint was still very much a work in progress, I still managed to find myself the object of his undesired attention. The method of the ringing of the bell, both to end one class and to start another, was not automatic as it is today, or as closely controlled as it probably would have been on an assembly line in an automobile plant. Usually, JT would stick his head into the classroom door which was nearest to him and push the button. One afternoon on one such mission, JT's thinning hair was nicely parted by a piece of chalk, which I had aimed at a student sticking his head around the cloakroom corner. A moment of sickly silence abruptly ended the war and I headed for my seat. JT arrived at my intended destination at the same time. I heard the familiar accusing voice, "James, you know better than that!" While the principal gave my hair a very thorough rough-up, you could hear my adversary, Bill Greig, snickering in the cloakroom. I assumed that JT was probably teaching that period as I was spared from receiving his usual administration of justice. As soon as JT left the classroom, and before our next teacher arrived, I tore into the cloakroom and fired my rubber boot at Bill Greig for snickering at me. My boot missed him and crashed through two panes of glass, landing on the ground two stories below.

In gym class, which JT taught in a dusty old room in the basement, we practiced the usual calisthenics—some tumbling, spring-horse vaults, and diving through hoops, as well as the occasional boxing match, in which I thought I was really showing off my supposed ability. Unknown to me, a grade twelve lad by the last name of Greig—but not related to Bill—was asked by JT to take the wind out of my sails, which he did in no time flat. As I approached him, flailing my arms like a broken windmill, he stepped back and landed one solid blow on my chin. Instantly I found myself lying flat on my back, wondering what happened. Laughter erupted from the boys in my class. After that, I was a bit more humble when proclaiming my successes as a prizefighter.

Since I had decided that application to learning in school was not my cup of tea as homework had been replaced by farm work—which I considered much more productive—matriculation was not currently my objective. I paid for that dearly later as I had standing in only five grade twelve subjects. In math, I never did learn the difference between a permutation and a combination, nor which was which when attempting to find out how many licence plates could be produced from such and such combination of letters and numbers. My question was always, "How does this apply to real life?" Later, you will see some of the problems which arose from my not having succeeded in high school. However, the four years of Industrial Arts with a very capable and friendly shop teacher, Mr. Hoover, who always appreciated my efforts and my well-done projects, were most enjoyable and appreciated. This success was to prove to be a comfort during much of my lifetime.

The English teacher, George Ryberg, was also a teacher of a different sort. He was a very sensitive, intelligent, and caring person, for whom I had the utmost respect. It is sad that many students—mostly boys—take advantage of such teachers. Later in life, most of us regret the lost opportunities caused by our indolence and indifference, as well as the disturbances inflicted on such teachers. It is also very sad that these able teachers often leave the teaching profession prematurely, while lesser beings, "the eat, drink, and be merry" boys who bend over backwards to impress the principal, become those who adorn the profession and teach simply for the assurance of tenure and the extremely good pension they will receive at the end of their career.

Enter a new teacher into the seemingly endless progress in learning. Since I had achieved all the allowable credits in Industrial Arts, along with several other boys, we were allowed to take Home Economics for credits, which must have been a violation of the regular, endless belt of education requirements. Furthermore, this new teacher was both young and attractive. She was a no-nonsense teacher of Ukrainian ancestry and immediately informed us, "Boys, we can be friendly, but not familiar," and so it was. We soon completed heavy-duty aprons, which did double duty for both Shop and Home Economics. We also learned how to prepare simple, tasty, and economical meals.

In finishing this oft-interrupted tale involving a nearly complete school failure, you will be surprised to hear the account of an unforgettable graduation present from my very-well respected and fearsome adversary, JT Foster. Towards the end of my twelfth year in what seemed like an endless education process, a young lad from elementary school arrived at the principal's office, accompanied by an accusing note from his teacher. JT excused himself from our class to attend to the assigned task—the appliance of justice. As we clearly heard the whack-whack of the strap being carried out, the girls began to wince noticeably. When JT returned, having applied the cure effectively, one girl asked, "What is it like to get the strap?" If any girl had been punished in like manner during my time in the doldrums, I was not aware of such. When he asked, "Do I have any volunteers?" Foolishly, I raised my hand. Here begins an encounter which will never be erased from my memory, though it has been more than sixty years since that sadistic experience. Again, he excused himself and returned with the strap, holding "Big Bertha" authoritatively. There were two "Berthas" with whom I had been acquainted over the years. The smaller sister was a two foot section of pump engine belting, in foreboding black with a white stripe down the middle. The older sister was much superior— much wider, longer, and heavier with a stripe down her middle as well. I had expected to see the younger sister as it would still be warm from recent use. However, such was not to be the case.

JT removed his jacket from his substantial frame and ceremoniously rolled up both sleeves, spat on his right hand and called me forth to demonstrate the application of so-called corporal punishment. Alarmed and amazed, thinking, "This cannot be real," I was soon proved very wrong. I dared not pull my hand back early as the application of that manoeuvre had proven fool-hardy when trying to avoid the inevitable. He rose to his full height, just like the bear in J. J. Dalki's Wildlife Show, and "Bertha" descended from upon high with a crack like thunder. My surprise will only be exceeded by the events at the "End of the World." As usual, he ordered, "Now, out with the other hand!" A very wild and foolish notion suddenly crossed my mind, as I recollected the blow from the Greig lad that landed me flat on my back: *"When JT raises his arm to maximum height with the offending instrument of torture, I will smack him under the chin so hard that he will land flat on his back."* Fortunately, a more reasonable decision interrupted this silly notion: *"Do you really want to go down in history* [my favourite subject] *as the clown who was half-killed by this now-famous specimen of humanity?"* Better sense saved me from such a disaster, but the absurd process continued. I received six solid blows on each hand. Even with my poor math, that added up to an even painful dozen.

Some of the girls were crying and all the boys were probably thinking, "I am very glad I am not the recipient of that demonstration of justice!" What a graduation present that proved to be! There was no apology offered. Badly shaken, I asked for permission to leave the room, whereupon I descended to the dusty old basement washroom and held both of my burning hands under cold water 'til I thought the cows would come home. That night, back on the farm, Reg probably had to milk the cows for me, as my swollen fingers would hardly close. My evaluation of the supposed process of education was not elevated by that terminal encounter. Needless to say, I was very relieved that school was about to end (or so I hoped). However, I was quickly and firmly informed on several fronts that further education was a requirement for any worthwhile success in society. Little did I know then that the length of the following process called *post-secondary education*—college, university, or such-like endeavour—would just about be as long as its predecessor. My rewarding life on the farm came to an end upon the termination of my haphazard affair with school in June of 1948.

Junior high and high school are a combination of military precision and the endless belt of an automobile assembly line, which is supposed to produce a cookie-cutter, professional product upon graduation. It only takes twelve years to produce the supposed result! Any change in the process was considered anathema and any teacher who questions the process is treated accordingly. Unfortunately, success here is only used to promote further education called post-secondary—actually often more of the same.

Though my memories of my time in high school are a bit fuzzy, let me share some suggestions, which, if applied, will greatly reduce the high rate of school-dropout, especially among boys. Girls are anatomically designed to sit in desks for longer periods of time than boys. The mind absorbs only what the seat can endure. Thus it is not very motivational to demand—of boys especially—a response to these instructions: "Turn to page 195. Do questions one to ten in class. If not finished by the end of class, do them for homework!" Nonsense! Also, give some consideration to the personal circumstances surrounding each student's life. Many behaviours and learning problems are the result of what the child is enduring in his personal life outside of school. The devastating loss of my mother at a young age was only exacerbated by the tortuous treatment I often received at school, especially at the hands of those in authority.

> Bless those who persecute you; bless and do not curse. (Romans 12:14, ɴᴋᴊᴠ)

Poor Boys' Institute
1948–1950

The Spirit of God shining on
The Word of God reveals
The mind of God to
The heart of man.

Prairie Bible Institute of Three Hills, Alberta, is an evangelical post-secondary Bible college which began with eight students on October 9, 1922, on the property of the McElheran family farm. Its precursor was a local Bible study group led by J. Fergus Kirk, a central Alberta Presbyterian farmer. L.E. Maxwell, who became the school's dynamic principal and later president, was a graduate of the Christian and Missionary Alliance Bible Institute in Kansas. He was invited to come to Three Hills to develop a structured curriculum. Under his leadership, the school—one of the first Bible training institutes in Western Canada—grew to become Canada's premier missionary training center with international influence among evangelical Christians. In addition to the Bible school in Three Hills, another Bible institute was established in the north at Sexsmith, Alberta, and a Christian academy was added on the Three Hills campus in the 1930s. Maxwell, the Kirks, the McElherans, and other local families saw the school attain an enrollment of over 900 students by 1948 and become Canada's largest Bible college, a position it would hold until 1984. Although initially wary of outside alliances and influences, PBI was officially incorporated and eventually accredited to award degrees in divinity through provincial legislative acts and amendments. After 58 years, Maxwell retired in the spring of 1980 near the age of 85. After his death in 1984, two more post-secondary schools were created to train missionary pilots and professional tradespeople. Today, as many as 900 students study each year at one of these five schools founded or influenced by L.E. Maxwell. The current president of PBI is Mark Maxwell, the grandson of L. E. Maxwell. The school has a large body of alumni, many of whom attend the annual reunions.

In the fall of 1947, I had joined a group of young people from the High River Baptist Church, who were having a wonderful time skating on the canal which runs through town (and feeds the Little Bow River to the south). While warming my hands at the fire beside the canal and entertaining the assembled gatherers, attending Bible school became the topic under discussion. I scoffed about the school, of which I knew little except that the "Jews" had no dealings with the "Samaritans" according to a recent revelation (the boys were the Jews and the girls were the Samaritans, and never the twain should meet). I complained bitterly about this anomaly in my bantering. Lorna Rowland, a girl I knew very well along with other members of her family, and who attended another church also pastored by my friend and advisor, Billy McLuskie, interrupted my tirade with this goad: "I dare you to attend PBI. You would not last long. They have rules there, you know." The results of my recent conversion were obviously not yet in evidence. Of course, my immediate response was to accept the challenge, finishing my grandiose speech with a further elaborate complaint: "Farewell, cruel world—welcome those grey stone walls." How could I ignore such a taunt, in the presence of so many grinning witnesses? In that instant, I had committed myself to four years of post-secondary education, which, as it happened, only proved to be an interlude in the long road to my ultimate chosen career—and unbeknownst to me then, one of several in my long crooked road through life.

Not long afterward, word of my plans to attend Bible school reached the ears of my worthy antagonist, the Honourable JT Foster. To my utter surprise and amazement, he was not the least derogatory. He simply said, "Why don't you look up my brother, Ed, when you get to Three Hills? He is the mayor of the town." Once again, another interlude in my scholastic endeavour earned me a very rewarding friendship. Upon completing grade twelve that year and working my last summer on the Burrows farm, I joined the Prairie Bible Institute in the fall of 1948.

Although I don't remember how I arrived at that worthy institution, I rather think that it would have been my pastor and mentor, Billy McLuskie, who took me there, as he had recently become the proud owner of a new Chevy car, having replaced his old, unreliable relic much to his relief. His old car had a six-cylinder side-valve motor. I had made many trips from Nanton to High River with him as he was pastor of churches in both towns. Quite often, one or two of the valve keepers would dislodge and the motor would sputter and miss. One Saturday night when he was trying to replace the valve keepers—a difficult operation—he, in a fit of frustration after he had banged his head on the hood, fired the pliers at the big door at the end of the garage, proclaiming bitterly, "Bah, humbug, this crazy old car is trouble enough to be human." You can well-imagine his relief and pleasure then when he purchased his beautiful new blue Chevy. My first encounter with him and his new vehicle happened on the first day he became its proud owner. He rolled down the window and invited cheerfully, "How would you like to go for a ride?" Of course, I would! If it was he who took me to Three Hills, I know I would have been very relieved when he offered to transport me and my meagre belongings to Prairie Bible Institute, which was to be my new home for the next four years. It was often referred to as "Poor Boys' Institute" or "Prunes, Beans, and Indigestion" as they were a part of our regular fare.

Having spent twelve years in which I had not paid a great deal of attention to schoolwork (though I should have), I soon began looking for a worthy diversion. JT's recommendation came to mind instantly, thus beginning a fond, four-year friendship with his brother's family, which I enjoyed immensely. Since Ed Foster was the mayor and Commissioner of Oaths, learning where he lived was easily accomplished and I quickly found my way there. Of course, I chose to accomplish this when it was the Prairie girls' day to be allowed to go downtown. Why choose girls' day? Well, the scenery was much better, and the possibility of being reported to Uncle Ernie, the boys' supervisor and administrator of infractions of the rules (as Lorna had informed me), was less likely, so I decided to take advantage of this clandestine escape. As I fled confinement, I felt much like a prisoner of war escaping captivity in Germany during World War II.

Upon arrival at the mayor's home, I introduced myself as one of his brother JT's admiring students. There was no mention of the reality of the actual relationship. Whether being funny or just uninformed, I asked Mr. Foster what was wrong with wheat and barley, since I had been told that he was also Commissioner of "Oats." Of course, my ignorance was laughingly corrected. At the same time, I became aware that he was also a no-nonsense official, worthy of respect. Actually, my friendship with his wife, Josie, and little daughter, Caroline, formed the better part of my relationship with the family. Since coffee, a tasty snack and a good visit were the basis of the former, and the fun of playing with Caroline healed some of my heartache over the loss of my lovely little, blue-eyed sister, my visits were pleasant interludes during the time of my academic endeavours. As it would turn out, for more than one reason, my anticipated graduation was not reached on an easy road.

Fortunately for me, Poor Boys' Institute had a policy whereby the cost of attending was somewhat reduced. This policy was known as *Gratis*—perhaps a short form of gratitude—which required that the student perform certain duties that contributed to the school's operation. Therefore, I was assigned to kitchen duty, which included some part of the preparation of meals, serving, and doing dishes, and hopefully the opportunity to arrange some contact with the "Samaritans"! Enter my contact (literally) with one Elaine Cashman, who, being rather plain, was not the object of my expectations. The dishes were loaded into big carts and wheeled to the kitchen when the meal was finished. Whether real or imaginary, I fancied that her occasional sidelong glances were an indication of interest. Wanting to discourage her hopes, I slightly bumped into her behind (quite accidentally of course!) as she bent to pick up some cutlery. She immediately responded with a very angry scowl.

Not too long afterward, the Director of Gratis, Mrs. McLennan, a lady who disapproved of any such contact, summoned me to her office. I was informed you were in big trouble if she spent quite some time stroking her pencil from top to bottom repeatedly along with a furrowed brow. Since the process took quite some time, followed by a definite clearing of her throat, I expected the worst. Just how bad, I soon learned. The sentence was meted out with dignified authority, "You will report to Bill Thornton tomorrow morning at five o'clock in front of the Dining Hall." Bill's job was to keep the sidewalks clean, along with another unspecified task, which remained a mystery. Consequently, Bill instructed me to report to the rear of the first female dorm at midnight.

No explanation was made of my new-found fortune, and my assignment seemed somewhat puzzling. Since the long row of dormitories then lacked plumbing, the end of the necessities of life were deposited in five gallon pails in a secluded room at the end of the hall on each floor of the building. My instructions were simple: enter the top floor first, quietly announce, "Man on the floor," and proceed with the malodorous contents to the waiting contraption behind the dorm, known as the "Honey Wagon." I very soon exercised a very fervent prayer: "Please, Lord, may the pails never be too full." My prayer was not always answered positively, as an unobservant or otherwise careless depositor had taken no notice of how full the pail was. That person may even have planned to afflict punishment on the "Jew" who was unfortunate enough to be assigned the chore. Once again, another prayer was avidly uttered: "Lord, please don't let me slip when I ascend the ladder to the tank and don't let anything splash on me when I finish the task!"

The schedule of the undertaking is now forgotten, but such was my tour of duty until the end of my first year—sidewalks, "honey," or whatever. Bill Thornton was a very fine fellow who must have graduated at the end of my first year as I don't remember him afterward. He humbly accepted this job as essential and appreciated—a job he ably performed. We had many chuckles and times of teasing through thick and thin and all types of weather—snow, blow, or cold. When we were finished, we descended to the kitchen for a cup of hot chocolate and a piece of PBI pie—a slice of bread topped with cornstarch pudding and fresh farm cream. If we were not too late and our work had been accomplished quickly, we visited with Pop Gowdie, who was in charge of those who had volunteered to patrol the campus periodically during the night. Then it was off to the dorm room K32 for whatever was left of the night.

Pop Gowdie had wonderful stories to relate of the events of his long life. Pop's account of God's love and care and of His protection may well have been the seeds which have persuaded me to put mine down in written form. I trust that my experiences will also interest others. Pop became a very good friend of mine as I often did extra assigned turns of duty, substituting for others who preferred to study or have uninterrupted sleep.

As the halls were patrolled regularly, late night study was accomplished by hanging a blanket over the door in order to conceal any tattle tale glimmers of light. Given that the halls were dimly lit, the floor boss often did not detect anything amiss. It was his duty to prevent late night affairs, often referred to as "study" if caught in the act.

I was never found guilty of such an offence nor of the "up-grade" in which K32 often participated. Some students occasionally received a care package from home. Since my room was at the end of the hall, it became a café for such shared arrivals. The dear ladies from the Nanton Baptist Church had beautifully restored an old patchwork quilt, which my mother had made years before. When hung carefully in place after the last recipient of the invitation to attend this appetizing feast had arrived, it served as both a sound suppressor and a blackout curtain. Someone always sat right near the door to listen carefully for the squeaks in the floor. Another watched for the finger to his lips, warning us of the nightly inspections. Floor bosses—who took their job too seriously—had been known to approach quite noisily, then retreat a few steps, and likewise tip-toe back later to apply their ear to the latch. If caught, we could resort to bribery. However, our plan must have worked well, as I do not remember ever being discovered—but then, absolute silence was maintained until we were very sure that the immediate danger had passed.

Now, let me assure you of my steadfast intention of graduating by applying the method of Bible study called "Search Questions." This program had been prepared and revised by a knowledgeable theologian and from what I learned later, I assumed it must have been one Miss Millar, who had been earlier involved with a similar Bible school. In all likelihood, Prairie was probably organized according to this pattern. It worked very well: read the assigned portion of the Bible, study carefully, thoughtfully answer the questions, and attend class for discussion. Prairie was staffed with great mentors and gifted instructors. I greatly appreciated C. T. Poulson, our False Cults teacher. His teaching remains with me to this very day as it was and is still very true: "False cults are like concrete—hopelessly mixed and permanently set." As my daddy would say, "There are none so blind as those who will not see." How true. I also loved Mr. Maxwell's lectures. His observations were full of both humour and wisdom.

Occasionally, when Mr. Maxwell took his daily walk north of town, falling into step beside him, I asked "May I join you?" He never seemed to mind, although he probably preferred being alone with his thoughts. Many of his insightful and challenging sayings have often bounced into my mind over the years. Two of which repeatedly come to mind: "Disappointments are His appointments," and "Don't ask why me. Ask why not me?" It is so easy to trust God and remain happy when all is well. It is much harder to do the same when all seems otherwise. Because of these wise and dedicated teachers, I learned to stay happy regardless of the circumstances.

The three distant bumps on the skyline to the north, from which Three Hills acquired its name, were frequently my destination when out for a hike. One day while out walking, I saw one Mrs. McElheran chopping kindling, so I offered to help the elderly lady. As a result, I learned that she had three nice young ladies living with her—Edith, Nora, and Pearl. Since she was so much older than the girls' mother would have been, I suspected she was their foster parent, who had come to their rescue as the result of some unfortunate experience unknown to me. We remained in friendly contact long after my graduation, which proved to be very satisfying.

At this time, a new friend, example, and mentor entered my life at Prairie, and long after. Don Smith was the pilot who flew "L.E." (as he was affectionately referred to by the students) and the "Janz Quartet" all over North America promoting the school. The Anson aircraft, a relic left over from World War II, became a familiar sight to me as its hanger could be seen easily from my dorm window on the third floor. For my entire time at Prairie, I monitored the plane's comings and goings as often as possible. It was not just an old training aircraft, but one which was especially modified for transport of officers and V.I.P.s during the war. It served the school very well, but it was a gas guzzler.

On one assignment when flying high over Kansas, Don asked L.E., "Didn't you live somewhere around here?" Just then, I was told, he looked out the window and replied, "Yes, right down there!" He asked, "Do you think that you can land in that nearby pasture?" Don's response: "Let's give it a try." Completely unknown to L.E., they arrived in time to join a family gathering. As L.E. was perhaps the only convert among them, he had had no personal contact with his family since leaving to teach the scriptures to a few students on the McElheran farm. Before leaving for Canada years earlier, he had said, "I may drop in again some time." How prophetic that proved to be! Since they had just appeared out of the sky so suddenly and so unexpectedly, you can imagine L.E.'s relatives' surprise. I am sure that his family received a hearty injection of the gospel, and perhaps a song or two, from that very famous and long-lived quartet.

During my very enjoyable friendship with Don, I went with him on two flights, neither of them in the noisy Anson. At first, Don flew a Piper Cub for fun and for shooting coyotes. He had removed what I called the joystick for safety, so if a passenger panicked, they could not cause an accident. As we were flying along nicely, I put my thumb in the empty control socket and felt its gentle motion, so I pulled back slightly. To my surprise, the motor roared, the stump came all the way back, my stomach tensed, and we abruptly did a loop. When we were level once more, Don looked over his shoulder with his usual sly grin. I then concluded that I better just let him do the flying!

Another time, Don offered to take me with him to Calgary to pick up and return the speaker for our annual Spring Conference—Mr. Theodore Epp—and what a fine fellow he was! On the trip in, while sitting up front in Don's recently acquired Stinson Voyager, I noticed what I called the steering post slightly rising and falling. When I questioned him as to why it was loose, a foolish and ignorant question, Don pushed the wheel forward and I was suddenly facing the ground, which was rising fast, and then, he pulled it back and I was looking at the sun. Once again, he flashed his playful grin.

Now, I must tell you a bit more of my contact with Don and his family. Because Don was often away flying and busy with other commitments, my new "gratis" assignment was being boy-Friday to his family with all the interesting duties that came along with it. One was to replace the big stone pillar by the front porch steps as it had recently collapsed. My response, "Sure, I'll give it a try." I had mixed mortar for my dad on many occasions: "Three shovels of sand, one of cement, and a dash of lime, and mix it stiff." Since the mortar between the stones had nearly all crumbled, I removed the stones, mixed the mortar, and rebuilt the pyramid—such satisfaction! Beware of pride! When I returned on Sunday morning to inspect the

'Tower of Babel', it had completely collapsed. It turned out that it had been built too quickly and the mortar was too sloppy so it could not hold the weight. As a result, I learned to take my time and re-erected the pillar in stages. Finally, it was finished successfully and the pillar lasted until the house was moved to make way for a new gas station years later.

Another task required removing all the little poplar tree suckers that were migrating into the lawn. Borrowing the little D II Caterpillar from the school and a logging chain, I proceeded to extract them. The task itself was easy, but on my first try, I was presented with a real unexpected problem. The tractor snorted and the tracks began to cut through the sod and pile brick-sized pieces of sod behind each tread. The chain had been hooked too low on the trunk of the tree. By chopping off most of the roots at the base of the tree and raising the chain, the job was finished and the sod, which fortunately remained exactly the length of the track, was neatly replaced.

Don's wife, Alta, and their two younger and two older children also became good friends during my four-year stint at Prairie. Believe me, I enjoyed many tasty Sunday dinners in their home. One day, David, the younger boy who was just over two years old, disappeared completely. No one could find him, and Alta was in a state of panic. As a last resort, I opened the door of the long unused back house, to see David sitting quietly with both feet dangling down the hole. After all, he was just hiding as little kids often do. I carefully retrieved him and thankfully returned him to his distraught mother.

I'll record one last encounter during my time amid these grey stone walls in isolation from the "Samaritans." Between JK dorm where I lived and the Smith house was an old barn with a lean-to on the west side which was used for storage. One night during a wild chinook, the shed roof came loose and began pulsating in the wind. With great effort, Don and I worked feverishly to fill an old round bath tub with rocks and thus managed to save the roof. Evidently, the barn was also badly shaken. One of my last jobs was to put two huge braces on the east side of the barn in order to prevent its demise if another such storm arose. The base, as Don instructed, was to be anchored with a two-foot by two-foot concrete slab with metal plates and anchor bolts.

Nothing Don Smith did was haphazard. In fact, he had been the engineer who designed Prairie Tabernacle, which at that time boasted the largest auditorium west of Winnipeg (with a capacity for 4,300) and was the location of the school's very own campus church, the Prairie Tabernacle Congregation. The fellowship met there for more than fifty years. Remodeled and renamed in 1985, the Maxwell Memorial Tabernacle was Canada›s largest religious auditorium. In 2005, the building was demolished—in my opinion, unnecessarily—so that a new multipurpose facility, the Maxwell Centre, could be built. The new structure will continue to bear the name of Prairie›s founder and will house a chapel that will seat 1,200. The dorm, the barn, and Don's house are all gone now. When I visited Prairie not long ago, I noted that the lot between is now a parking lot. The Prairie Tabernacle Congregation purchased its own property and plans to erect a church independent of the college facilities.

The next cog in the process of obtaining post-secondary education was the opportunity to be a summer worker, one of many who stayed at the school until the next year's study began. In return, we received tuition, plus board and room. On the night I entered this program, part of the process was a rewritten, familiar hymn with the words altered accordingly: "A volunteer for Jesus, a workman true, others have enlisted, why not you?" Not being afraid to rise to any challenge, I joined up too, since it could hardly be more demanding than the initiation to my "gratis" duty on the Honey Wagon. When most of the students, both "Jews" and "Samaritans," fled to freedom for the summer, I remained, greatly anticipating my new assignment and continuing to nurture the close family relationships I was developing in Three Hills.

You can decide if my summer employment was for better or worse. One of my first tasks was to repair any leaks in the tar-paper roofs on campus, of which there were many. Such was the task of "Tar Babies." Climbing up and down ladders with buckets of tar in the scorching summer sun was not much better than carrying pots of you-know-what downstairs in the middle of the night in winter. It surely was the other end of the scale. After the hot, smelly task was quickly accomplished (along with much good-natured banter and teasing among our motley crew), I was assigned to Sandy Hanson's bunch, which was a job I grew to dearly love. Sandy was Top Dog on the construction crew and Stan Firth, Captain of the carpenter shop, was to be my supervisor. He was a very diligent and godly man, but like all of us, a project under construction and always bent on saving time and money for Prairie.

My first assignment was working on the nearly completed fourplex which we called the "Janz Quartet" Manor. Although a so-called budget project, it was to be completed ASAP Each aspect of the job was finished accordingly. I had a brief part early in the process by helping to nail the rafters, which were to be toe-nailed to the plate securely—remember the roof on Don's barn! The west side crew was led by a zealous proper Prairie prospect, while our crew was considered to be of lesser status. The west side was finished far ahead of ours and we received much taunting from "Marvellous Marvin" and his gung-ho companion. If anyone could toe-nail faster than Sam Reid—he was my ruddy, red-headed hero—such a person was not to be found on the west side of this building even though I regarded myself as being no feather-duster at banging in nails. Long after the building had been completed and following another strong west wind, it was discovered that the rafters on the west side were not secure as they had not been fastened properly with only about half of the required nails having been used. The roof simply lifted off and set sail for Winnipeg, landing almost one hundred yards away from the building.

In the shop, my first task was to get busy making the cupboards for the fourplex, which led to many interesting discussions with Stan. He would say, "Cleats and nails on the cupboard doors," and I would suggest urgently, "Screws and glue." He would respond, "The Lord is coming soon—nails and cleats will do just fine." How I won over a determined Englishman is still a marvel to me! Since four finished cupboards were the target, I suggested, "Let's do all the cutting for each stage at once," only to be met with his fear, "What if we cut them the wrong size?" My response: "If they fit the first one, the parts will fit them all." Again, Stan reluctantly agreed. Apparently, all were eventually finished to his and Sandy Hanson's satisfaction.

During my second year, my assignment continued to be working five days a week in the carpenter shop, learning a great deal at the same time. One incident underlines how to avoid a very real danger when using a table saw. Upon ripping a narrow strip off a long board, the finished cut caught in the saw-blade and shot out of the saw like an arrow from Robin Hood's bow. It smashed through the wall of Stan's office and only stopped when it hit the outside wall. Fortunately, he was not in his office. At the end of my second year, work on a farm near Nanton during the summer break beckoned me. It would be a nice break from Prairie and give me an opportunity to pad my meagre bank account toward my future endeavors. Unknown to me, I would soon face a most devastating injury.

DISASTER–1950

I met "Baldy" Larson when home from Prairie during the Christmas holiday of the second year. While out for a walk north of Nanton, I kept hearing a distant, perplexing rumble. After walking northwest for a mile and a half, I saw a farmer trying to do his chores while using crutches. Upon inquiring about the noise, he told me, "That's a gravel crusher working in my field about half a mile north." After helping him with his chores, I went to investigate. His field must have been underlain with rocks of all sizes. This iron dinosaur ingested them at one end and spat out a stream of uniform road-sized gravel at the other. An endless belt dumped them on top of a huge pyramid-like pile.

Baldy Larson seemed to be a likeable sort. I was not then aware that his reputation for generosity in Nanton was not the best. He told me that it had been a long time since he and his family had had a real holiday and that they were hoping for one that summer. Because working for him during my second summer respite might earn me enough money for my third year, I accepted the offer of employment from him. We agreed accordingly. Little did I realize what the consequences of my decision would be. When June came, I moved my meagre belongings into the little old house which had been the first one built on their farm. The day would start when I heard the yard-gate bang as Baldy made his way to the barn to call in the cows. I would hurry to be there before he began milking. Breakfast came later.

The morning of July 26, 1950 started off typically enough. After finishing cutting the last of the roadside hay and clover bundles for enough dry silage to feed the cows for most of the winter, the family would be off on their long-anticipated holiday (their little English Vanguard car had just been fitted with a heavy-duty box on the roof and the trunk was already full of their belongings).

In order to produce the silage, Baldy would toss a forkful of dusty road-side hay onto the feeder. It was my job to be sure that no metal or otherwise objectionable material entered the "Blizzard," which was the name of the beast. It chewed up whatever entered and spat it up into the hungry haymow. With my summer jacket on to protect me from the sharp-pointed clover bundles, I was inspecting the hay carefully when the "funny-boy" neighbour lad fired such a missile at my alluring mid-section. There was a release mechanism on the long, chain-driven feeder trough to stop the feeder in order to remove foreign materials. However, when I pressed the lever to pull wire out of the hay, nothing happened. I sent Baldy an enquiring look, and yelled that the machine needed to be fixed, so he stopped the tractor to investigate and take a short rest. The one inch cotter pin had broken and consequently had fallen out, followed by the four inch main pin. It would have required only seconds to fix but Baldy simply said, "It's almost lunchtime so keep going, just be $#@#$ careful!" A minute of time may have saved me a lifetime of disability but who was I to question my boss? In his eyes, I was just a twenty-one-year-old hired boy to do his bidding.

Soon the belt-driven Blizzard began its fearful roar and I was again pressing the bundles down flat before cutting the binder-twine with a curved knife. I was wearing a new pair of "Work King" cotton gloves just bought for the job. I left my right hand on the bundle a fraction too long and, suddenly, my arm was being drawn into that horrible monster with such force that Superman himself would not have been able to drag it out. Realizing what was happening, I braced my leg against the feeder and pulled with all my adrenaline-loaded might. Chop, chop, chop—one inch at a time.

As my arm was slowly and unrelentingly being torn to shreds, Baldy jumped off the hayrack and hit the belt with his hip. He then grabbed the pulley on the Blizzard and fought like a tiger to stop the machine.

Just as I felt my arm leave the socket, I pulled my shredded sleeve out of the machine and looked where once my good right arm had been. Horrified,

I saw only four inches of white bone protruding from a tattered sleeve. The thought flashing across my mind was, "*Mmm, this is interesting. It looks like a good sized leg bone from the butcher shop.*" To my surprise, blood spurted out just like from the neck of the old red rooster when my dad had chopped off his head. The pain was excruciating. I later told Baldy that I thought I was hollering at the top of my lungs, as it felt like my arm was being lowered into boiling oil. He said, "You never made a sound."

Unknown to me at the time, the clover hurler had fled the premises. Sue, Baldy's wife, heard the commotion and came to see what was happening. Baldy yelled, "Bring me a dish towel." The laundry had been hung out that morning in order to be ready for their expected departure right after lunch. He picked up an old, dry poplar stick, and using the towel, hurriedly applied a cleverly-devised tourniquet. Putting his arm around me as we headed to the car, he asked, "Do you think you can hold that stick?" I said, "Yes," being very aware of why it was there. My head spun round and round like a drunken man, and I felt as if I was falling sideways as the world whirled round and round at a steep angle. I felt strangely calm and did not panic, nor could I believe what was happening.

Soon, we were headed to the High River Hospital, twenty miles north, at top speed. Enter another death-defying challenge. The Vanguard was designed for economy, not speed. As we pulled alongside a Greyhound bus, with our horn full blast, and with a long line of traffic approaching on the old narrow two-lane highway, our hearts were in our mouths. The bus neither slowed nor moved over. Our bumpers nearly kissed as we finally pulled ahead just at the last possible moment before a head-on crash. With gasps of relief, we sped on our way! With the heavily loaded box on the roof and a tightly packed trunk, this little car could hardly make seventy miles per hour, even if it had been running on airplane fuel. Since Sue had called the hospital, the head nurse awaited our arrival. She held the blood-soaked tourniquet on one side of me with Baldy on the other, as we made our way to the Emergency ward. Thus began my interesting, all-too-short stay in hospital.

The doctor told me later he saved as much of my arm as possible as he thought skin-grafts inappropriate for me. I was left with a six-inch stump, which later proved very useful, but not long enough to properly use an artificial arm. (Later, I will tell you of two abortive attempts to do so which were both humorous and unproductive.) My good friend, Gertie Fowler, a ward aide, was called upon to clean up the operating room after my surgery. She was sent home as she could not handle the mess when she learned who had been the occupant.

Upon coming out of anaesthesia in the middle of the night, I found myself wrestling with a pretty little red-headed nurse in a white sweater, while the bandage on my once-upon-a-time right arm was swinging round and round on the end of a long piece of adhesive tape. The nurse untangled herself, straightened her sweater abruptly and declared, "Well, I'm glad that's over." Much later I thought, "Too bad I was not awake in order to enjoy the tussle."

My next stop was a four-bed ward with other patients. As I lay there, the awareness of the loss of my good right arm suddenly dawned upon me with devastating reality—would life even be worth living now? Anger and desperation crawled through my body and mind. A black cloud of deep anguish beyond description engulfed me as I stared at the ceiling with feelings of gloom and doom. Questions and thoughts flowed through my mind. The first three days, I felt absolute despair, spending much of my time singing the blues to all who would listen.

To my surprise and pleasure, later on the day of the accident, Don Smith from Three Hills was the first to turn up at my bedside, looking very concerned. Bad news travels quickly. After a few attempts at humour, he seemed to relax, especially when I told him that bone meal and hamburger did not make good cow feed. He told me that the school was shocked by the news of my accident. They wished me well and expressed sympathy and assurance of their prayers. I do not recall how they had learned about the accident so soon.

Shortly before dark, my brother Don and his wife arrived and asked how and why this horrible accident had happened. They told me later, "You sue that so-and-so for every dime he has!" Later, when I visited the town lawyer and told him how the accident happened, he told me, "I would entertain a lawsuit in the amount of $20,000, and be sure of success." After considerable thought, and having read Romans 12:19, "'Vengeance is mine, I will repay,' says the Lord" (NASB), I decided not to take Baldy to court. This was ultimately a bad decision from a human perspective. I told Baldy, "After I finish PBI in two years, if you will pay all the expenses that I cannot pay for the next four years when I attend Gordon College, I will not take you to court." He gladly agreed and we shook hands, but, unfortunately, did not put it in writing. Foolishly, I took him at his word.

In the hospital, it became a real challenge to put one of Mr. Maxwell's maxims to the test: "Disappointments are His appointments." Finally, I surrendered to God and confidently said, "I am sure You can handle me losing my arm, too." So He has. To me, the loss of my arm was more than just a disappointment, it was a real disaster, but even in this, I knew deep down I could trust God to be my helper. *"However will I manage now? My arm is gone! I can't do one thing about that! However, I do not need to lose my sense of humour, and my trust in God. Just make the best of this new truth."* Conference ended!

When I had at last decided to give God a chance to change my life at age seventeen—as I was still blaming God for allowing my mother to die—Isaiah 26:3 became the anchor of my soul, *"Thou wilt keep him in perfect peace, whose mind is stayed on Thee"* (KJV). Simply put, "'Let go and let God." This was the verse that inspired Frances Hovergal to write, "Stayed upon Jehovah, hearts are fully blest, finding as He promised, perfect peace and rest." Since God's word had brought peace of mind when I decided to depend on Him four years earlier, the assurance of Isaiah 41:10 and 13 came to my mind:

> So do not fear, for I am with you; do not be dismayed, for I am your God. I will strengthen you and help you; I will uphold you with my righteous right hand...For I am the Lord your God who takes hold of your right hand and says to you, Do not fear; I will help you. (NIV)

This, too, became my confidence and never was a truer verse ever spoken in my case. I was soon to learn that others were more than helpful when I complained, in mock sincerity, "I am just a poor man with only one arm, and I need all the help I can get." It still works wonders, when I swallow my pride and quit trying to maintain my stubborn independence. I soon learned to tie my own shoe laces, much to the surprise of marvelling onlookers who would ask to be shown how.

The other patients in the four-bed ward were also recovering from surgery, and they, too, were not sick. The fact that all of the tendons in my right arm had been pulled out during the accident contributed to the presence of excruciating pain at the slightest movement—even rubbing my tummy really hurt. So-called "phantom pain" was to prove to be the greatest problem that I had to deal with regarding the loss of my arm. Trying to always present a brave and nonchalant face while in the hospital, I would adopt my Napoleon stance and hold my stump firmly to ease the intensity of the throbbing, having decided that humour would keep my fears at bay while brightening my situation. A flock of visitors were soon to descend and a cat-and-mouse game with the nurses began.

One day a set of very friendly visitors arrived with plenty of cake and watermelon. My bed was pretty well-surrounded with a host of friends. A rather hilarious party followed. The next morning a rather busy cleaning lady began a hasty clean-up of a rather sticky floor with a dust mop. Dry puddles of watermelon juice impeded her progress. Much to her chagrin, she announced, "Well, I just have to get a wet-mop and clean this whole floor." I am sure that the antics of this ward were well-known. I feel badly now that we were such a troublesome lot.

Surgery patients were monitored regularly (for fear of infection, I suppose). Frequently I was left with a thermometer protruding from my mouth like an all-day sucker. On one occasion (the first and the last), I rubbed the instrument on the leg of my pyjamas. I did not ring the bell, but waited impatiently, lolling on the pillow with my eyes crossed. When the nurse retrieved the offending instrument, she nearly jumped out of her uniform, but suddenly responded with an exasperated, "Oh, you again?" She shook the thermometer violently and returned it to my mouth with a wily grin. Upon re-examination, she came back and applied a shot of penicillin in my rear end with what must have been a very dull needle—applause erupted from my room-mates.

I soon learned that I could almost predict who was coming down the hall by the sound of their footsteps. One was a frail, old arthritic gentleman whom I referred to as Mr. Step-and-a-half. The swish-swish of his paper slippers were easily identified. Once he stopped in front of the doorway to our ward. His pyjamas had fallen and he could not bend down far enough to pull them up, so I rang the call bell, whereupon Gertie arrived. Not seeing the old gentleman's predicament, she demanded, "What do you want now?" I said, "Oh, Gertie, that poor man in the hall cannot pull up his pyjamas. Will you help him?" She cautiously approached from behind, shut her eyes tightly, pulled up his PJs and tied them in front (once again to the applause of our ward).

The last of many such incidents was of a very different nature. I must tell you first, that the head nurse was by no means unattractive, and probably well-informed about our ward's shenanigans. Since no one had responded soon enough after I rang the bell, I impatiently went looking for a nurse at the station. The door to the inner sanctum was open and I beheld my doctor engaged in a very affectionate embrace with the head nurse. I departed quickly though I am convinced that my unwelcome presence was noted. However, no mention of such an observation was ever made. I had been told that I could be discharged from the hospital as soon as the stitches were removed, but it was best for me not to rush that much-anticipated release. Suddenly, there seemed to be a change in my doctor-friend's attitude. When I asked him, "When could I possibly leave the hospital?," I was told that I could leave as soon as someone could come and get me, but actually, I should stay longer as it was only one week since my distressing arrival. We both knew I would leave ASAP!

Following my discharge from the hospital, I hurriedly retrieved my stuff from Larson's without seeing any of them as far as I recall. Before returning to Prairie Bible Institute for my last two years, I stayed with my dad and step-mother in Nanton. I remember entering Dad's house and seeing him sitting on his upholstered chair which was beside the stairs going up to the bedroom. He looked really shook up and was simply devastated by what had happened to me. All animosity toward my step-mother had long since evaporated and I did little but rest.

My stitches still needed to be removed, which took place in the Nanton doctor's office. I recall sitting on a tall stool, watching him pull a mosquito-like stitch out a little, snipping it loose with tiny scissors, then drawing it out. Much to my surprise, I fainted suddenly and fell flat on the floor. Soon after that when out for a long walk, dizziness overtook me and I had to sit down by a telephone pole and wait until the same lightheaded, spinning sensation that had filled me during the accident abated and I was able to walk home. I felt like a dishrag. Before long, I accepted the offered hospitality from both of my brothers and stayed with each of them for a short time.

The left hand is the weaker hand and supports the right. Until my right hand was gone, my left hand had a limited role. Now I had no other choice. I had to use my left hand for everything. Learning how to use my one remaining arm and hand when I had been always right-handed proved to be much harder than I anticipated. Having to relearn everything I had previously been able to do while using my weaker hand was frustrating, and I was very clumsy doing many of the tasks I had done without thinking before the accident. However, I did learn and became quite proficient.

In my attempts at rehabilitation while staying with brother Bill and his wife on a farm on the outskirts south of Calgary, I practiced driving the little Ford-Ferguson tractor for something to do, which later proved to be very helpful. Not wanting to wear out my welcome, I then stayed with brother Don until returning to Prairie Bible Institute. While there, I painted windows with small panes which were a real pain! I became quite proficient, much to his satisfaction. This, too, was to prove to be a very useful experience when, many years later, I was hired to paint for two years for another boss, who is still one of my many best friends.

It is interesting to note that the Larsons never once came to the hospital to see me, nor as far as I am aware, even enquired about me. After these many years, it suddenly dawned on me that Baldy Larson, to my knowledge, did not pay a cent of my hospital expenses. Perhaps I had some wages coming—even that I do not now remember. I had very little money, but the people of Nanton rallied to my immediate needs and paid all of the approximately seven-hundred dollar hospital bill. There was no such thing as publicly-funded healthcare then. Neither do I recall how my school-expenses for the last two years at Prairie were met, but evidently they were.

My dad was very saddened by the fact that he was not able to help with my school expenses. He simply apologized for that fact. By that time, he, Tena and Ann were living in a garage-like shack, which he had built on our property, and struggling to live on the income from the rent from our house on the same lot. His dwelling was the size of a single garage, with living quarters on the main floor and sleeping quarters on the second. He said, "If I can, I will try to send you fifteen dollars a month while you are in school." Though I did not, I should have learned from his example and begun preparation for retirement then, which would have been such a benefit in my senior years and made my life so much easier.

Behold, an hour is coming, and has already come, for you to be scattered, each to his own home, and to leave Me alone; and yet I am not alone, because the Father is with Me. These things I have spoken to you, so that in Me you may have peace. In the world you have tribulation, but take courage; I have overcome the world. (John 16:32-33, NASB)

FINISHING AT PRAIRIE 1950–1952

Upon my return to Prairie, I received a very encouraging welcome. At my next interview with Mrs. McLennan, no pencil appeared (nor did it appear later). I asked to be allowed to return to the Carpenter Shop with Stan Firth, to which they both reluctantly agreed.

My first job involved window panes of a different sort. It required chiselling out enough wood to allow the glass to fit properly, followed by puttying and painting them. Thankfully, I was not there long enough to finish the painting. It was a trying enterprise though it would have been no problem with a mallet, two hands, and a sharp chisel, but I struggled valiantly onward. One day, thinking it would be easier if this wide chisel was really sharp, I proceeded to hollow grind it carefully and hone it until it was razor-sharp. Having accomplished the task to my satisfaction, I put it in my back pocket, sharp side up, and began walking back to my tedious chore. As I passed the thickness planer, I felt a pain in my remaining arm. Upon investigation, once again blood was spurting. This time it was decorating the pile of shavings behind the planer.

Enter Stan Firth. He immediately thought, "*Horrors, he has caught his arm in the planer.*" That would be impossible, but he feared it had actually happened. Thankfully, no such disaster. I don't know how the bleeding was stopped, but I had a deep three inch gash. When I went over to the school infirmary, I figured with just a few stitches all would be well. The school nurse applied a few butterfly stitches, assuring me that they would hold the incision shut. Unfortunately, that was not the case and I have a nice canoe-shaped scar to remind me. The shock of the incident convinced Stan that he would rather I was not working in the shop.

Upon returning to Mrs. McLennan for reassignment, I wondered, "Whatever can a guy with one arm really do?" They already had a one-armed mailman with whom I soon became acquainted. He had fallen through a garage window while painting. Gangrene had set in, necessitating the amputation of his arm. Because of the nature of his loss, he was not bothered by so-called phantom pain, which in my case was no laughing matter. Imagine the pain you would have in the arm you lost, especially the hand. Believe me, it is very real—both a constant vice-like constriction, accompanied by an unannounced spasm.

After a period of thoughtfulness and with my uncertain future in mind, Mrs. McLennan replied, "We have been having some trouble with our second vegetable crew." I was soon to learn why. She asked, "Would you like to be their supervisor?" I asked no questions and simply replied, "Yes." Her instructions were, "You will report to Mr. Shepherd, the head cook, and he will fill you in." Thus I was given a very interesting and challenging two year assignment, which was a great advantage to me much later: "Eye the spuds when peeled, dice either beets or turnips into three-quarter inch squares, and put them in water in the metal-lined cart. Your work starts at five a.m. in the morning in the vegetable room. By the way, there is to be no talking while you work. As well, examine each sack of beans and make sure you find all the pebbles. Mrs. McLennan recently broke her dentures on one."

Imagine the sick sensation I felt as I descended the stairs the next morning to see the last project I had finished in the carpenter shop waiting at the bottom of the stairs. It was a long dicing table made from three long fir two-by-tens, which had been painstakingly planed by hand and joined together with half-inch maple dowels and water-proof glue. I was especially proud of my efforts. Now, it only mocked me.

I knew all my fellow workers' names, but not their faces. As I took attendance, I attempted to evaluate each one. After prayer, I asked, "What do we do here?" (Of course, I knew.) "What do you like? Are there any problems? How can we do things better?" It seemed that Joe was the spokesman, and he answered all my questions. First problem, "We have to wait too long for the vegetable peeler to do its job. We don't like sorting beans. It's too hard to dice the turnips!" (Except for the navy beans, the school grew all kinds of vegetables.) The "Extra Vegetable Crew," as our assorted menagerie was called, described a unit composed of *"...the poor, and the maimed, and the halt, and the blind"* (Luke 14:21, KJV) (although fortunately no one was without sight), and I had been assigned to join them accordingly. None of them seemed to fit in elsewhere and now I was included as their captain.

Once again, another very demanding but encouraging and pleasurable duty began, now early in the morning, and this time with only one arm. My elevated assignment was to be the *supervisor*, with the instructions: "Avoid accidents and quarrelling, and keep the cook, Mr. Shepherd, happy." Mrs. McLennan never found another pebble in her beans under my watch.

When the vegetables erupted from the peeler, Joe, the original operator, would dump them on the other table which sported a long, metal top with raised sides, where they were inspected for any defects in the peeling process. This occupied about half the crew. When finished, the vegetables were spread out on the dicing table, where a certain skill was required to avoid cutting off any fingers. They were then deposited into a large metal tank, ready to be wheeled into the kitchen to be cooked later. Our first problem was to get ahead of "The Eye Doctors," as I called the first crew, but the potato peeler was much too slow, as the abrasive plate was completely worn out. I pleaded for immediate repair. While waiting, I asked Joe, "Can you come in early, and have enough vegetables peeled to get that crew working as soon as we are all here? Then you can leave as soon as I arrive." Joe had been the problem talker, so this solved two issues.

While the peeler was being repaired, I waited anxiously as it had taken longer than anticipated to get the job done. Once we were underway again, we waited the usual amount of time for the potatoes to be peeled. When Joe dumped the spuds into the tub, we were first astonished and then jumped for joy while laughing hilariously. The spuds had almost vanished: they tumbled out not much bigger than peanuts. "Mr. Spud" could hardly believe his eyes. We quickly learned vegetables needed much less time in the peeler than previously. Peeling vegetables was never a problem again.

One lad with hands that had fingers which reminded me of the potatoes he had tried to eye found the "Eye Doctor's" job difficult, so I asked him, "Would you like to be an inspector?" He readily agreed. Under "Mr. Bean's" steely eye and rubber fingers, no pebble in the beans ever went undetected, and no crew-member had to tackle that tedious task again. Whenever he found a pebble, we all joined in his triumph with shouts of joy and "The Inspector" was allowed to leave early that day. Mrs. McLennan could now eat her beans with confidence that her dentures would not suffer any repeat damage.

Let me introduce an educational theory which would have made a great difference in enrolment at Prairie in the years that followed had it been applied: assign students to professions which have economic return in the real world, both in Canada and as missionaries around the world. What a boon such would be to both aspiring Christian workers and prospective foreign missionaries. Such a program would serve the school, as it did in their "gratis" program. Costs to the school would be reduced and students would be prepared realistically for immediate employment in the real world upon graduation. Although a diploma from Prairie would not rate with public vocational institutions, it would be accepted on the basis of the skill of the recipient. Workmen of many professions came to Prairie to fill staff requirements: nurses, secretaries, seamstresses, mechanics, boiler men, carpenters, cooks, dairy men, pilots, bakers, clerks, truckers, welders, painters, electricians, and even farmers. The school, not Mrs. McLennan, would enroll the student in the profession of their choice and assign them to the appropriate expert, like Mrs. McLennan's husband, an artistic welder who fashioned beautiful, heavy duty bumpers for the fleet of trucks which the school used to transport supplies to and from Calgary to meet their many needs.

To their loss, such a program was never implemented at the institute—with one exception, which was probably inspired by Don Smith. Their pilot program has become its most productive course. Such is life. My hopes for Prairie's future is rather dim. To my knowledge, there is now no "Gratis" involved, and all of the above aspects of Prairie are as extinct as the dinosaur, the dodo bird, and the carrier pigeon. Since the school now has a policy which declares that tuition fees will be paid for completely by students—board, room, and tuition—"Poor Boys Institute" is no longer an appropriate nickname. However, since I attended in the heyday of the school, my memories are simply fantastic and I have no regrets.

I had many extra-curricular activities as well as my studies, with a few of particular interest. Along with my devotion to the Smith family and occasional visits with the mayor's family, I maintained contact with Mary Pratner, who had some association with the students. Mary was confined to a wheelchair, but was an excellent seamstress and managed to eke out an existence in this way. Since my right arm had been amputated, I decided that the right sleeves on my clothes should also be amputated. I traced the wing-tip of a Spitfire aircraft on a piece of cardboard for a pattern and she accomplished the operation at very little cost.

Upon scouting out the surrounding town, I visited a dairy where some "Samaritans" milked the cows. I became an occasional welcome visitor. Care of cows had been a part of my job when I had worked at Magee's Dairy in Nanton. Memories of the fiasco there came to mind when I first visited Davidson's Dairy near the school. There was an attractive Samaritan in that establishment as well, but smooching with her never entered the relationship even though I became friends with both her and her family. Here the method of putting milk in bottles was only a distant relative of my former introduction to the process. Ample feed awaited the cows as they eagerly entered their own stall. A mechanical milker did the job without any manual effort and manure was removed at the push of a button. Wow! It fascinated me just to watch this modern mechanical marvel in action (and that was more than half a century ago). How the complexity of this modern dairy farm contrasted with methods of the one in Nanton almost defies reality! There was simply no comparison then, and probably much less now!

The summer of 1951 following my third year at Prairie, I volunteered to be a missionary at a Metis reserve near Lac La Biche (Lake of the Elk). The word "Metis"—pronounced May-tee—comes from the French language, meaning "of mixed blood," and so they were. They are descendants of the marriages between First Nations girls and the fur traders who were mostly French or Scottish. Since eligible white women were very scarce during the early settlement of the West prior to the later period of mass immigration, fur traders enticed local women, usually younger attractive specimens who were often relatives of the chief, which enabled their acceptance into the tribe and the assurance of female companionship. Usually a few well-placed trinkets or trade goods facilitated the arrangement. Unfortunately, the children of these unions were not readily accepted into either society and not every fur trader remained true to the "contract."

This assignment by the CSSM, the Canadian Sunday School Mission based in Three Hills, appealed to me, especially as it would give me the opportunity to follow the missionary tradition of PBI as well as the added adventure of caring for myself in a somewhat wilderness environment. It certainly did prove to be challenging. I do not remember that my instructions were very specific or detailed; since it was a Sunday School mission, DVBS (Daily Vacation Bible School) sessions for the children were arranged and I also pastored the adults on the reserve as opportunity arose.

Ed Klingenberg, a fellow PBI student, got in touch with me and agreed to assist me as required. Ed's family lived near Lac La Biche and he had been the former CSSM missionary on the reserve. He said I could use the "accommodation" which he had occupied the previous summer. Ed offered to take me and the "Caboose," the trailer I would be living in, along with my stuff from the town to the reserve. Before coming, he suggested that I should buy "down south" what I wanted to eat before leaving by bus for my summer's assignment. Accordingly, I gathered my bedroll, an old suitcase containing suitable clothes for the adventure, and a big gunnysack full of staple provisions—which included lots of canned beans, veggies, and fruit. The bus drivers were not at all pleased with the latter as it would have bent a camel's back.

Ed met me at the bus stop in Lac La Biche and took me and my stuff to stay with him until departure for Kikino—some miles south by way of a very questionable road. He informed me that it wound its uncertain path over hill and dale through muskeg. Even in late May, it was too early in the spring to be passable by car. However, we stood a pretty good chance of making it while pulling the "Caboose" with Ed's family's Fordson tractor. We travelled by night while the frost was still in the ground. Since I had practiced driving on such a tractor while staying on the farm with brother Bill, I pleaded to be the driver. With permission reluctantly given, all my stuff was safely stowed under the bed in that improvised trailer—merely a home-made wooden box, about six feet by ten feet with a sheet-metal stove and a little table and chair. This very primitive environment would serve as my home for the summer.

Ed unenthusiastically entered the "Caboose," I triumphantly established myself on the tractor, and we were off on our midnight ride to Kikino. The tractor had a hand-operated throttle and, as steering required all the effort of my good left arm, you can imagine my decision to travel full throttle and high gear all the way—probably about twenty miles an hour in the dead of night. Moonlight shone on the glittering, snake-like ruts as we sped on our way, with the "Caboose" swinging madly from side-to-side. The lights shone directly on the trail up the hill; however, coming to the top of a hill, the trail seemed to disappear. It was just a guess where the pathway had gone until the nose of the tractor brought the none-too-bright lights down onto the trail again and it once more became a road instead of someone's imagination.

When we arrived at the end of the road in a little grassy field, Ed staggered from his prison like a drunken man. Ed had been thrown around inside the "Caboose" like a ping pong ball. Upon regaining his composure, he told me that while far back in the woods, he had opened the door and yelled, "Slow down," and was almost thrown out the door. His plea for less speed was lost amid the roar of the motor. I apologized profusely and Ed again retreated into the "Caboose" to gather his wits. Had he fallen out, it would have required a return trip back to town to find him, minus the "Caboose" of course. For that, we were both grateful.

Suddenly, as we sat reliving the wild ride, there was an insistent pounding on the door, and a loud, anxious voice called out, "Come quick. Mrs. Lightning needs you!" We both ran to a nearby house where all the lights were ablaze. A group of bewildered men and women gathered around the lady's bed. We discovered that she had recently returned from the hospital following a miscarriage. Since the people had expected our arrival, they must have had assurance that Ed would somehow know what to do, which turned out to be the case. Ed quickly ordered, "Get ice from the well, put it in glass jars, and pack them around her. At first light, put a mattress in the manager's pick-up and get her back to the hospital as fast as you can!" Their lethargy turned into decisive action, and the plan was soon under way. They were able to chop chunks of ice from the nearby dug-out well, which was fortunate indeed.

Just as the sun began to peek over the horizon, the manager's Dodge pickup arrived. Its long running boards were lined with willing men. In next to no time, Mrs. Lightning, with two ladies attending her, was on her way down the long, soggy trail to town. Overnight frost had not done much to make the going any easier and there were several impassable places. I was later told that in these spots all the men jumped off and practically carried the pick-up so they could continue. Fortunately, the group arrived safely and in time.

Mrs. Lightning survived and soon returned home, though the doctor stated that she almost died from loss of blood. I do not know how many transfusions this lady had, but on her return, she no longer looked like she was mere inches from death, as she had at the time of our appearance. No wonder the Bible records *"the life of the flesh is in the blood"* (Leviticus 17:11, NASB). Furthermore, to Christians, the blood of Christ is precious as declared in 1 Peter 1:18, 19—*"For you know that it was not with perishable things such as silver or gold that you were redeemed from the empty way of life handed down to you from your ancestors, but with the precious blood of Christ, a lamb without blemish or defect"* (NIV). Acts 17:26 tells us He *"hath made of one blood all nations"* (KJV). As a result, the blood of anyone—whether red, yellow, black or white—may be used in transfusions regardless of the recipient's nationality as long as it is compatible. Calling transfusions cannibalism as some do is just plain nonsense. Had George Washington been given a transfusion, rather than many sessions of blood-letting as reported by history, the record of his death would not read, "At the last, his blood came forth, thick, dark and muddy, and he died." What a wonderful contribution to modern medicine Doctor William Harvey made in 1628 when he discovered that our blood circulates through the body. When we breathe in, oxygenated blood is returned to the heart and ultimately pumped to every cell in the body. Venous (deoxygenated) blood picks up carbon-dioxide from oxidation in the cells and returns it to the lungs where it is expelled as we breathe out. Man breathes out carbon dioxide and green vegetation produces oxygen. Such a marvellous creation could not possibly be the result of evolution. No wonder David declares in Psalm 139:14, *"I am fearfully and wonderfully made"* (KJV).

Ed's quick thinking had certainly saved Mrs. Lightning's life. My arrival with him paved the way for my welcome to the Kikino Reservation. After Mrs. Lightning returned from hospital, her family more than welcomed me into their home. Not having a radio, television, or even a mouth organ or Jew's harp for amusement, I enjoyed many evenings in their comfortable home. Entertaining their children became a pastime both by day and night. Their two little boys never tired of horsey-back rides, though I must admit

I did—often, I had to call it quits, all too soon for them. One evening after the boys were tucked snugly into bed, Mrs. Lightning told the older girls, Ala-Joy and Dorothy, "off to bed now," after a good-night kiss. They looked at me inquiringly, and I said, "Can I give you a kiss, too?" I promptly gave them each a loud smack on their cheeks. As Ala-Joy, the younger one, climbed the "wooden hill" as my father would say and as their mother watched, she proudly declared to all, "Now, I taste just like a preacher!"

Trying to arrange Daily Vacation Bible Classes on the reserve got me nowhere so most of my days were occupied by preparing meals, Bible study, and visiting homes in the area. With the roads drying up and becoming passable, pulp trucks resumed hauling wood to Lac La Biche and I often rode into town where I became acquainted with an older CSSM worker and her attractive, much younger assistant. Because the lady's husband had left their car in Lac La Biche and she did not drive, she asked me to be their chauffer and to help them conduct the DVBS programs which they had already arranged in schools in the area. I gladly accepted and, as a bonus, the missionary workers offered to do my laundry, which was really appreciated. The arrangement worked very well, much to my satisfaction.

Along with doing my washing, the workers also regularly sent delicious "goodies" of home baking back with me. One day, however, I decided to try my own baking skills on the little tin stove in the Caboose. The stove always seemed to be red hot, smoking, or just plain out. Following the biscuit recipe carefully and using the chicken fat which I had been given as a shortening produced encouraging results, and I looked on the biscuits with pleasure as they came out of "Mr. Temperamental." They were quite tasty when hot, especially buried in butter and strawberry jam, but when they cooled and I tried to bite into them, they were harder than hockey pucks—so ended my baking episodes.

Between times, I became friends with the manager of the reserve, enjoying many good visits with him, learning as much as I could about all its inhabitants and where they lived. Attempts were made to visit as many as possible, leaving Christian literature with them, witnessing to them about Christianity, reading the Bible to them, and praying with them if they wished. On one occasion while visiting the manager whose name I no longer recall, I showed him my mother's picture of several teachers with their principal taken at Victoria School in Calgary. To my great surprise, he told me that his wife knew the teachers and could probably confirm which one was actually my mother. He offered to show it to her when he had time off and told me he would return it to me as soon as possible. He did as promised, and his wife knew them all and confirmed which one was my mother—Edith Webber Trask.

The picture had been taken prior to my mother's marriage to my father. The manager did not tell me when the picture was taken but he did tell me that the principal was Ralph Speakman and that he, too, had only one arm. Later, while teaching in Calgary, I attempted to contact Mr. Speakman, only to learn that he had recently died. Disappointment filled me as I was convinced that he would have been able to tell me interesting stories about my mother, as I had all too few. Almost everything I knew of my mother came from my father who often said with a hint in his voice which I did not understand, "Oh, you are just like your mother, Ede!"—a fact which caused me to wonder if their relationship as husband and wife was not always sunshine and roses. Strangely, I have always considered myself more like a Trask than a Davis; being a teacher was my greatest delight and satisfaction, which in all probability was inherited from the Trasks and had an influence on my feelings.

The activities at Kikino more than filled the hours of the day and the week. Nevertheless, time was still found to drive the two CSSM workers to and from their DVBS assignments in the area and assist them with arts and crafts as well as games, which required me to go back and forth from time to time on the logging trucks.

All too soon, and much to my surprise, CSSM home office got word to me to return to Three Hills immediately. Just as I had feared when sent to the principal's office during school days, I wondered "What's wrong now?" All seemed to be going very well and I was having a very enjoyable time. I considered myself remarkably resourceful living with only one arm in a somewhat primitive environment. My knees, covered with a dish towel, served to hold potatoes when peeling them. Though opening tin cans had its difficulties, the little hand can opener with its quirky handle worked well if used carefully. Then, too, empty cans proved useful for many purposes, confirming my daddy's saying, "Where there is a will, there is a way." Leaving suddenly was devastating.

Simply leaving the Caboose where it was parked, I packed up my belongings, said a hasty goodbye to my newfound friends, and hitched another ride to town on a pulp truck. I explained to the CSSM workers in Lac La Biche that I had been ordered to return to our home office in Three Hills ASAP. The same message was given to Ed Klingenberg. He assured me that he would retrieve the Caboose with its cranky stove and my leftover food supplies. Before long, I was on my way back to Home Office. Upon arrival, I was informed that my association with the CSSM workers in Lac La Biche was inappropriate as it had been reported by a supposed well-meaning Christian in the area. However, as the married worker was my chaperone and I had never even so much as laid a finger on her helper, this revelation came as distressing, shattering, and disappointing. The irony of it was that later the CSSM supervisor was fired because of an affair with one of his workers.

My dilemma was "What to do now?" With school opening still some time away, it was too late to be a summer worker at PBI. Once again, friends came to my rescue. Because the summer camp east of Okotoks was still in session, they welcomed me as a camp counsellor and the Kerfoot family extended an invitation to stay on their farm, a mile west of the town. This proved to be a very rewarding long-term relationship, and a fulfilment of the promise, *"when my father and my mother forsake me, then the Lord will take me up"* (Psalm 27:10, KJV).

While at camp, I developed a severe case of tonsillitis. When the flood of infection drained into my system, I was actually sicker than when I lost my arm. Mrs. Kerfoot noticed that I was not at all well and suggested that I see a doctor. He recommended immediate removal of the offending tonsils and that was quickly accomplished. This time, there was no time for monkey business with the nurses and very few visitors came during the short hospital stay. Lucy Kerfoot suggested, "Stay with us. When you are well, we can use your help on the farm." Percy, her salt of the earth hubby, was employed as a surveyor for Calgary Power and was only home on weekends. Upon returning to the Kerfoots' farm, I was not strong enough to fight my way out of a wet paper bag and felt so sick I was completely useless. Just enough energy could be mustered to come to meals but little more; then it was right back to my sleeping quarters and to oblivion. For the entire time that I spent in bed upstairs, the sun hardly shone and it rained almost every day. But none too soon, my sense of usefulness returned and I was able to return to a somewhat normal life.

The farm had previously been a pig farm and then later a market garden. There were little tributary creeks on both the north and south sides of the property. A potato patch was near the north creek and I happily set out to find it which I eventually did. It had never been weeded and the sight was daunting: the weeds were taller than the spuds. The task looked insurmountable. "How to chop out all of those pesky weeds, with only one arm?"

Although I had often hoed and hilled potatoes in our garden in Nanton as a boy, this was a much greater challenge for me as a one-armed person. I found a ring and harness and snap with a slot for my belt in the shop. With the hoe sharpened and the blade cleaned, I tackled the discouraging chore. When I put the hoe handle through the ring and began an earnest chop, chop, chop on the obstinate mile-high stinkweeds, they reluctantly began to yield. Soon, however, my knees began to tremble and the sweat ran into my eyes. With only one long row of weeds lying in a twisted, green tangle to show for my efforts, I retreated to the house to recover and report my lack of progress. I was scolded for going at the job so hard so soon after my operation and told to quit and not to return to the undertaking until it was cooler and I was feeling better. The repercussions from tonsillitis had taken more out of me than my accident a year earlier. I finally finished chopping down the weeds, and though not much of a potato harvest resulted it gave me some satisfaction—again fulfilling my dad's assurance, "If there's a will, there's a way." Still, I can't scratch my head and rub my tummy at the same time—not really a severe limitation for only having one arm!

In the fall of 1951, I returned to Prairie Bible Institute for my final year. Just before I graduated in 1952 (two years after losing my arm), my dad died at the age of 61. He had suffered a heart attack, had been wrongly diagnosed as insane, and taken to the mental facility at Ponoka, Alberta, where he passed away. This was another sad and unfortunate cog in my story. Adding to my anguish, my brother, Bill, stripped my stepmother's home of all the furnishings he felt had belonged to our mother. It was most distressing to see my stepmother living out of the cardboard boxes which she used to store her belongings. At the time, due to my own miseries in dealing with the loss of my arm as well as my lack of financial wherewithal,

I was in no condition to help her. Tena continued to live in the remodelled garage behind their house, living off the rental income and her small old age pension. Before I married, I sometimes stayed with her on a day off. We remained friends until her death. Sadly, my dad did not live to see the remarkable progress I made and things I accomplished—he would have been impressed.

Prior to graduation, since I found writing very difficult, I recruited a high school student to type my completed final, major assignment—*A Commentary On The Book Of Romans*. During the day, the papers were slid under the door of his room and he provided me with very professional results. "Thank you very much" was all he would accept as payment. Before graduating, along with regular class attendance, I volunteered to be a part of our class committee, which created the class motto for both our Junior and Senior Classes. First, we chose "Behold, I Come Quickly," and then, for our last year, "Even So Come Lord Jesus"—even then, the Second Coming seemed imminent. Now, more than sixty years later, it is yet more true, as it was expected even before the death of Jesus and especially since the resurrection. Even then, the disciples asked, *"Lord, are You at this time going to restore the kingdom to Israel?"* (Acts 1:6, NIV)—they did not understand what the kingdom was and thought this action would bring freedom from the tyranny of Rome and paying taxes.

Our graduating class was given the opportunity to decorate the dining room for their Graduation Banquet. Amazingly, both boys and girls were a part of this committee, so at long last, the "Jews" began to have dealings with the "Samaritans"—of course, contact was allowed only while working on the task at hand. We were very proud of the results, as the decorations in the dining hall, with the miles of accurately measured streamers which hung in huge, overhead, fan-shaped patterns in alternating class colours, were very attractive. Imagine, boys and girls could actually work together at Prairie to complete this exhilarating task. The big beautiful class mottos were hung year by year in the old underground dining room for all to see. Each time upon returning to Poor Boys' Institute, I admired them and concluded that ours was among the best.

Upon graduation, Mrs. McLennan once again summoned me to her office. I thought, "Oh, boy. Whatever for now? I am such a good boy!" No pencil appeared as she rose from her official position and extended her hand and said, "I am very proud of you, Mr. Davis. We never had another problem or complaint with 'The Vegetable Crew' under your care. Thank you very much." You can imagine my surprise! I thought, "*Usually, you only go to her office for discipline.*" Had she known the other aspects of my clandestine life at Prairie, it would have hardly merited such a hearty commendation. I had discontinued my late-night watchman's duty with Pop Gowdie, and missed his very interesting stories about his life when he was a boy. Upon completion of my time at Prairie Bible Institute in June, I returned to the Kerfoot farm. Soon, my plans to attend Gordon College were set in motion.

GORDON COLLEGE
ROUND ONE–1952

At last, my-long anticipated desire to attend Gordon College in Boston, Massachusetts, was about to be realized. In 1889, the Bible school was opened to train Christian missionaries for work in the Belgian Congo in the basement of Pastor A.J. Gordon's Baptist church. Later it was moved to the Fenway into a building given by Martha Frost and renamed the Gordon College of Theology and Missions.

Confident in the promise from my former farmer-boss to pay all I could not for my four years in college, and with all essential arrangements having been made, I was soon on my way by bus with sincere good-wishes from my new-found family. All my earthly possessions had been stuffed into an old half-size steamer trunk, including some books for study purposes along with Percy's old graduation tuxedo, which he said a promising young lad should have when in staid Boston company in case of an appropriate occasion. He had not worn it in years and said he probably never would.

Little did I know the problems the heavy trunk would inspire along the way. At each transfer from bus-to-bus, every driver complained bitterly, asking, "What do you have in here that weighs a ton—lead?" As it turned out, I did have a very enjoyable use for the tuxedo, but the trunk nearly denied my entry into the United States as it probably indicated that I intended to be much more than a temporary visitor, which, of course, was all too true. I did not know then what effort four years of college would entail; nor that my stay at Spring Creek Farm would bring an interesting interlude in my objective to be a missionary in Africa.

Even though my entry visa gave no permission to work or to go to school in the United States, I was admitted to Gordon as a student and all my earthly possessions arrived at 51 Prescott Street in Everett, Massachusetts. My Aunt Marion had invited me to stay with her and seemed to be pleased with me upon my arrival. To reach the college on the Fenway from Everett, a mishmash of public transit had to be taken. The back and forth journey by tedious forms of transportation was to become an odious and tiring chore. First a trip early in the morning by street car to the underground, which became the squealing elevated train, and another jaunt by street car to the college. At the end of the day's classes, back to Everett in reverse order.

All began well enough. Most of the time, I was alone, as Aunt Marion was a very, capable palliative care nurse and a favourite caretaker. She was regularly employed by children who paid to have their rich elderly Jewish parents cared for in their own homes. She provided services far beyond the usual expectations: she nursed them much to their satisfaction as well as meeting their other needs, such as cooking, mending, and companionship. I imagine she was probably very well-paid and her gratuities amply expressed her clients' appreciation. Though my aunt had a very unpredictable schedule, she always returned to her own home between jobs and on her days off.

I began to wonder about the reason for Aunt Marion's generosity and later concluded that she had asked me to stay with her because she was concerned about all those "foreign immigrants who were now infesting Everett and ruining the whole city," as she put it. On a Tuesday, when I had the delight of her company, she demanded that I scour the back alleys of stores in the area to find discarded wooden boxes which were needed for kindling to fire up "Beelzebub," my aunt's name for the cranky old coal furnace in the basement (who never revealed his secrets to me), and she demanded undivided attention to her stories of much better times from long ago. Her nursing compassion, however, was revealed on at least one occasion when I arrived back on an unusually cold night after trudging through deep snow in clothing which was not nearly warm enough. I was greeted by a very warm and welcome Scotch toddy. I never knew its origin or looked for its hide-away, but it sure felt good. As my dad would say, "Better felt than telt."

Since Beelzebub was so unreliable, the kitchen had an oil-fired heater to assist it. Marion warned me, "Be sure to light the wicks as soon as the oil reaches them and be sure to close the kitchen door!" When I finally remembered the warning, the reservoir was already nearly full. Thinking, "Awe, shucks, I'll light it anyway," much to my horror, it began to roar as the flames leaped higher and higher. With no fire extinguisher, the only recourse was to shut off the supply valve and pray earnestly. Much to my relief, it finally died down. Believe me, I never attempted to light it again, nor did my aunt discover my error. Horror of horrors if her house had burned down due to my negligence!

In regard to living with Aunt Marion, one of the last straws broke one Sunday afternoon when she was home. Friends of mine from Gordon College found their way to 51 Prescott Street and invited me to join them for a car ride. I was particularly intrigued by a very young, attractive lady in the back seat, whom I had seen before but never met. I was smitten at first sight. Memories of that brief encounter and all that followed during the next six years have stayed with me—even until today, as will be made very clear later on. Going into the house to tell Aunt Marion of our plans, I was immediately met with an angry tirade: "You ungrateful wretch! After all I have done for you, do you think you are going to leave me here alone and go off gallivanting all around the countryside with your friends?" Imagine my disappointment and humiliation. I do not now remember my response, but my hopes of meeting the attraction in the backseat died along with my self-esteem. I was crushed. When I returned to the car, I simply said, "Thanks a lot, but perhaps another time."

My will to stay any longer with my overbearing aunt finally died in a very unusual way. My Uncle Stayley, whom I had not yet met, arranged a Sunday dinner at a very posh, upscale restaurant in the area and invited all his New England relatives to join him. I'm sure the occasion cost a king's ransom. He was one very generous relative. He arrived in a mile-long black (Packard) Lasalle coupe to drive us to our destination.

Upon arrival, I was introduced to Aunt Lou and her three children. Lou was a soft-spoken widow, who was totally involved with the welfare of her own family (as it should be). Her daughter, Jane, was a real out-going charmer, while Dot appeared to be a potential spinster. Little Jimmie, who was much younger than his sisters, seemed to be a bit of an attention-seeker—having gone through many operations on his clubbed feet, he had become accustomed to being the center of attention in his family. Nonetheless, he was a perfectly delightful young lad. Both girls married—Dot much later than Jane. I kept in touch with them both for years.

I had already met my Aunt Delia, who had given me a cool reception when I visited her earlier in Fall River, Massachusetts (although at that time, I did have fun with her daughter and fiancé). Delia informed me when I left that she could not offer me any financial help as she and her hubby lived on a very small pension (he was unable to work). The comment seemed unusual to me, since I had made no mention of my financial need, assuming it had already been met. My purpose for being there was simply to meet her and learn more about my mother, of whom my memory was fading.

During this dinner, we appeared to have a very nice time and when we arrived back at the house, Uncle Stayley dropped off Aunt Marion and took me for a drive. He told me that Aunt Marion was avoided by all her sisters because no one could get along with her—they must have shared my unfortunate experience! Uncle Stayley enlightened me that Aunt Marion had informed them that she was bearing the cost of keeping me, and that they should help her financially since I was now living in their area without monetary means to pay for my tuition and board, explaining Aunt Delia's earlier remarks. My relatives had simply replied, "You invited him here; you can take care of him!" I had assumed when Marion generously offered to provide board and room free of charge while I attended college, she did so in exchange for having her house secured by my presence when she was not there.

Uncle Stayley also told me that he did not think that my mother had received her fair share of the inheritance from her father's estate and that he would gladly pay my college expenses, including board and tuition, when I returned the following year. I was greatly relieved for this added promise in spite of Baldy's assurance to me regarding college.

My stay with Aunt Marion had already become unbearable. Along with being travel-weary, my scholastic success was beginning to slip. Not long after my run-in with Aunt Marion, I developed a case of colitis and decided to seek guidance from Goldie Stocker, the college student councillor. She strongly suggested that I live in the dorm and avoid the long ride from

Everett and the stressful interaction associated with Aunt Marion. She also advised me to seek medical help. When Aunt Marion was informed of that decision, her apparent generosity evaporated immediately and she curtly told me, "Don't you dare show your face around here looking for help from me unless you can pay your own way!" Believe me, I was relieved to comply with her farewell wishes!

Upon taking up residence in the college dorm which also housed the administration offices and classrooms, my future immediately began to improve. The colitis disappeared and even a work permit was issued quite speedily, which was very rare. No more running up and down back alleys after dark on garbage nights to find kindling to fire up Beelzebub. No more arriving back at the house after dark, trembling and half frozen.

When I applied for employment, the manager of Filene's Department Store in downtown Boston was very friendly and obliging, contrary to my expectations. I had been warned that Bostonians were very cold and indifferent to strangers. One supposedly must be properly introduced before being received into a cautious friendship. The exact opposite was true in my case, having experienced nothing but genuine acceptance and offers of help. On becoming a part-time employee in Filene's Bargain Basement, I discovered having only one arm seemed to offer unique advantages. My job was "Joe Boy," working with three or four ladies who managed the refund desk. They were a close-knit, friendly group, who took the razzle-dazzle nature of their task seriously but with good humour. Frequently, there were long lines of frazzled, displeased customers, some of whom were artists of deception. At other times, the patrons just waited and waited patiently. Being my clownish self, I regularly entertained them.

Each garment to be returned to the store for refund had to have a securely-attached original tag. If there were any disputes or questions, it was my responsibility to take the article to the supervisor of that department to have the refund certified and then return it to the desk ASAP. You can imagine the resulting problems. The gals really appreciated my part in the process. As well, when the ladies ran short of cash, they gave me an authorization slip. I hurried upstairs to come back with a huge bundle of cash in a brown paper bag, having been approved to do so by my trusting manager. I never had any problems.

Toward the end of my first year at Gordon College, unable to make ends meet or pay for my next year's tuition, I wrote and asked Baldy for some money in the sum of $316. Much later, his wife wrote back to say, "We have all our own expenses to care for." Simply put, "We have no money for you." My demanding schedule and the time spent on tedious travel to my work, trying to earn enough for transportation tickets and any personal needs, and not having the necessary funds for my second year overwhelmed me. It was difficult to find the time and strength to keep up with the many assignments. In the end, as I am a very slow reader, the huge amount of material that had to be digested caused my downfall. I had never read that St. Augustine believed in reincarnation, and I failed a test as a result. I did a real snow-job on the beliefs of the fathers of the faith. Trying to learn Greek and Hebrew was another total disaster.

> Repay no one evil for evil. Have regard for good things in the sight of all men. If it is possible, as much as depends on you, live peaceably with all men. (Romans 12:17-21, NKJV)

ALBERTA BOUND–1953

I lift my eyes to the mountains—where does my help come from? My help comes from the Lord, the Maker of heaven and earth.

He will not let your foot slip—he who watches over you will not slumber; indeed, he who watches over Israel will neither slumber nor sleep.

The Lord watches over you—the Lord is your shade at your right hand; the sun will not harm you by day, nor the moon by night.

The Lord will keep you from all harm—he will watch over your life; the Lord will watch over your coming and going both now and forevermore. (Psalm 121, NIV)

Having little choice in the matter, I returned to Alberta in the hopes of earning enough money to pay my outstanding debt. My heavy metal steamer trunk stayed with Aunt Marion, and my first attempt at graduating from what was affectionately called "Gordon College of Theology and Matrimony" became only a fond memory. The lady who had been in the back seat of the car at Aunt Marion's was a nurse at the Massachusetts General Hospital and gave me no hope of continuing our relationship. We had become friendly, but she said upon my departure, "Don't you think that there will be a candle burning for you in my window when you return!"

On the lonely, uneventful bus ride to Alberta with many stops along the journey, there was plenty of time both to remember the enjoyable times and lament the double-barrelled disappointments of my first year of study and work while attending Gordon College. Evidently, I had failed in both.

Aunt Marion's neurotic tirades and tyranny under the guise of friendly hospitality were gladly now a distant memory. Uncle Stayley's promise of financial help to attend Gordon when I returned next fall was a great consolation. Unfortunately, it was not to be as it was almost two years before I returned. By that time, my uncle had died, and, evidently, had not named me in his will. As Mr. Maxwell often said, "Disappointments are His appointments." They have frequently punctuated the pattern of my life.

Since the leaden trunk no longer accompanied me and I was returning to my own country, I passed through customs easily. As the bus sped along, the anticipation of my arrival back in Alberta increased as the miles decreased. Nostalgia washed over me when my beloved Rockies appeared in the west as we turned north toward Calgary. My Alberta sense of direction returned: the mountains signalled the west, so the other directions were easy to deduce. The long, wearisome journey ended none too soon. Upon arriving at the bus station in Calgary, I phoned Mrs. Kerfoot that the bus was on time as I had written her by letter. Since Okotoks was under an hour away from the terminal and city traffic was far less congested than today, no sooner had I finished a cuppa and a snack than Lucy appeared. Her familiar face was a joy to behold, and our reunion after a very trying time away in Boston was more than overwhelming. Somewhere, there is a shoebox full of letters I received from Lucy Kerfoot while at Gordon. Her encouragement was the "Rock of Ages" to me amid my trials during that first year, especially those with Aunt Marion.

We arrived home not long before Lucy's children came racing up the lane. It was quite a long way from where the school bus let them off. I suspected their agility had arisen from my anticipated arrival—another occasion for a joyful reunion. What a change a year can make in the growth of young people—they had shot up like weeds. It was an absolute joy to once again be with Alec, known as "Red," little sister Tannis, and Jean, the aspiring nurse who was soon to graduate from nursing school. After fond greetings, I wondered, "*What awaits me now? Will I ever be able to return to Gordon? Will I just fail again?*" In spite of being welcomed like a conquering hero upon returning to Spring Creek Farm, feeling like a dud overpowered me as all the hangovers from the past seemed to cloud my future.

As I had been in contact by mail with Hilmer Jacobson, the Chairman of the Board of the Okotoks Gospel Chapel in town about two miles east on a dirt road, it was my hope to come to an agreement as to salary and expectations as a student pastor. My expectations were soon realized. I was overjoyed. Kerfoots confirmed that board and room would be supplied at no cost in exchange for "Joe Boy" duties at Spring Creek Farm. From that moment forth, my time as a farm-boy pastor was filled and my welfare assured. It did not promise a quick build-up of funds to enable me to return to college in Boston, but since I still expected to rely on financial help from Uncle Stayley that did not concern me terribly much. I considered him to be one great guy and very generous as well. His company, Trask Artesian Wells, seemed to be doing well in New England.

Percy Kerfoot arrived on my first Friday at the farm. Lying flat on my back under the belly of the old farm tractor applying the last of a new coat of sky-blue paint in order to spruce it up a bit, I heard the Calgary Power truck come to a stop, but I thought, "I'll just finish this job and then rise to the occasion." By then, Percy was standing beside the tractor. He made a strange remark as he bent over to examine me, asking, with a twinkle in his eye, "How's your liver?" Later I thought, I should have responded, "I haven't inspected it recently." Percy had a very wry, Scottish sense of humour which was very pleasing.

Percy gave me a list of the jobs that he never seemed to have enough time to get done. "Perhaps you can have a go at some of them," he said, almost apologetically. Since Hilmer had stated that I would be taking the morning and evening service on Sunday, prayer meeting on Wednesday night, and the young people's meeting on Friday mornings, it entered my mind that the summer would be just as busy as the months were at college in Boston, perhaps even more so. The latter proved to be all too true.

The first big job on the farm was to remove the hog wire and trash from the bush on the south side of Spring Creek which divided the almost twenty acre parcel of land into a one-third, two-thirds ratio. The creek ran west to east not far from the front door of the house. The south side was, thankfully, smaller. Percy Kerfoot said, "There are several pig sheds lying around out there. We can use what's left for firewood. Would you like to see what you can do about it? The kids can help you after school and on Saturdays." What appeared at first to be a little job began to require much more time and effort than anticipated.

I pulled an old hayrack across the little homemade bridge with the freshly-painted little tractor and parked it near the brush. A tussle with weeds, wire, and wood ensued. The south side had been a badly neglected pig pasture covered with trash. The tangled wire on the hog pens had long since been taken over by vegetation. Cutting weeds and bushes in order to remove the twisted section of wire was a daunting task. It was necessary to clean up the mess before headway could be made. Once the wire was free, I hooked the tractor to the hay rack and proceeded to attack the problem. It required driving over and through brush to get near enough to load the remains of our meagre success and return the load to the wood and trash pile. Taking the dilapidated sheds apart and carrying the results of my labours to the hayrack took lots of time and energy. Occasionally, the kids would help me. It soon became apparent that no cleanup had ever been attempted. Evidently, the previous owner had abandoned raising swine long ago. When the hayrack was full, the contents were unloaded onto the woodpile near the house and the wire on another pile of trash. Although I thought our achievements were small, each time Percy returned from his survey job, he inspected our work. Almost always, he announced his cheerful observation with his oft used expression, "Splendid!"

Percy had feared that their blind cow would get trapped in the hog wire as she occasionally found green grass when she wandered over there—how I do not know. Once in a while when Shep, their faithful Border Collie, was told to get the cow, he would sound his departure with a loud bark as though seeking the cow`s location. The cow obligingly shook her head, and her bell would ring. Shep would find her quickly and herd her to the barn where he expected to receive Percy's praise: "Good boy, Shep." If Percy failed to do so, the dog with his tail between his legs would slink back to his spot under the steps. He seemed to be saying, "He didn't even say thanks—no appreciation," or "Guess I didn't do that right".

Another task on the farm ended successfully while fortunately avoiding a near disaster. This job required two people working together, cutting up the assortment of accumulated wood. My part was to place a jumble of wood, piece by piece, onto the platform in such a way that it would be cut into uniform lengths for firewood when Percy raised the pivoted platform in front of a huge circular saw blade which was hooked to the tractor by a belt. There was no guard on the saw blade. Being an age-old way to saw firewood, it was not considered dangerous. Unfortunately, I lost my balance while trying to pull a long, heavy rail to put on the rack which would hold it in place while Percy fed it into the exposed saw blade. Tripping, I flung my arm out as I fell toward Percy, trying to catch myself when I suddenly realized I was falling into the rapidly spinning blade—another amputation seemed unavoidable. In a split second reaction, Percy lunged, grabbed my belt, and pulled me out of harm's way, preventing a disaster. Had he not done so, my other arm would have surely been cut off. You can imagine my relief and thanksgiving to our Lord. It took me quite some time to regain my composure. My gratitude to Percy was inexpressible. Life with only one arm was enough of a challenge for me. Percy said, "That's it for today." I gladly agreed.

I do not remember the degree of completion of the sawing project, but not long after my near mishap Percy called a halt in order to care for a more pressing problem which had arisen. Once, the north side of the creek had been a market garden, and that venture, too, had long been abandoned. There was a huge half-decomposed, half-buried root cellar which resembled an old rotted haystack covered with weeds. The makeshift structure consisted of an old poplar pole frame covered in earth. As the roof had begun to collapse, Percy feared a disaster because children often came out from Okotoks and played hide-and-seek inside. Percy said, "Fill it with trash and I will hire the municipality to smash it down with their bulldozer." I was happy to oblige.

One Saturday afternoon after dumping an array of garbage down through the roof, Red—Percy's young son and heir—and I decided to haul an old car body to its grave in the cellar. We planned to drive over the top and then dump it through one of the big holes where the roof had already fallen in. We put a chain through the window pillar opening in the area that once housed the dash board and headed across the field. Suddenly, Red shouted, "Look out!" We had not realized that the front of the old car body was digging into the dirt. Suddenly the old vehicle was airborne, flying through the sky with the greatest of ease. The stubble and dirt had piled up in front of the car body, causing it to gracefully take flight. Fortunately, the chain was long enough so that the top of the car body smashed down on the tractor hitch just as I pulled the clutch and leaned as far forward as possible, ducking down beside the steering wheel, missing my head by inches. As Alec had been riding on the fender, he jumped free and was spared, too. Had the chain been inches shorter, it would have landed right on top of us. We would, in all probability, have been instantly killed. We were both badly shaken. Young and inexperienced would describe us, but I learned a valuable lesson never to be forgotten—be careful how you hook the chain to whatever you plan to pull behind a tractor. We proceeded to hook the chain differently, drove over the root cellar and gladly pushed the car body through the hole. We were relieved to see the last of it. Fearing the car would be an even greater attraction to the children, Percy now had an added incentive to entice the municipality to send their bulldozer to squash the old structure. The huge beast soon arrived and demolished the treacherous trap, turning it into a gentle harmless mound. I was grateful to have escaped another close call. God was certainly looking out for me—*"the Lord is my helper, I will not be afraid"* (Hebrews 13:6, NIV).

A new problem arose. To my surprise and dismay, the two trips with the heavy bulldozer over the little homemade bridge nearly destroyed it. Going over it with our little tractor and a load of firewood or trash had never been a problem. The municipality took no responsibility for the damage and Percy would not be home until the weekend. I did not know who to ask for help so it became my responsibility to repair the damage by myself as no one could get in or out until it was serviceable once more. The job needed to be done as soon as possible.

The first step required removing all the cross timbers which were three by ten inch planks (to use a sensible measuring system) and then to drag two huge timbers into place to raise the level of the bridge bed before pounding spikes through the planks. Two supporting logs were raised and moved slightly west. Now, another dilemma awaited my efforts—how to drive those pesky enormous spikes through the planks into the logs? Holes needed to be bored into the boards in order to get the spikes started. An attempt to pound the spikes into the planks with a claw hammer met with no success. Once upon a time, I could drive two and one half inch nails into place in about three blows. Now, using my left arm, I often missed the spikes completely. They just made an annoying ping. What to do now? To my surprise, an old sledge hammer with a short handle and a heavy iron head was discovered in the shop. I went back to the bridge and began to hammer steadily. On this very hot and sunny afternoon, the sweat began to trickle into my eyes. Often I stopped to wipe it away and rest my aching arm. Even a small sledge hammer is intended to be used with two arms.

Determined not to quit until the job was done, I kept on pounding furiously. My predicament reminded me of the task in the potato patch long ago. For several days, I hammered vigorously with perspiration continuing to be a problem. A savage urge impelled me on to finish the job. Finally, one day near supper-time, the last spike was driven in, bringing to mind the satisfaction Sir John A. MacDonald felt when the Trans Canada Railroad was completed high in the Rocky Mountains. I gladly and triumphantly headed for the house—all else to be done could wait until tomorrow. I believe that was the only time since losing my good right arm that my hand almost refused to come to my mouth when it came time to eat. Falling into bed early that night in my little garret bedroom upstairs was a real relief. Sleep was seldom sweeter even though the job was not yet finished.

With the pounding complete, I arrived back at the bridge the next morning and it was time for the surface work. The driveway to the main road was full of ruts and pot-holes—hence another opportunity to try my skills. Using an old assembly which must have been left behind by some oil company, I attempted to level the road. The 'road grader' consisted of several six inch pipes about six feet long welded in a grid with space between each pipe—I surmised that it must have been some sort of cooling system for an oil well. I chained it behind the tractor, 'Old Faithful', in such a way that it was pulled at an angle with the front slightly lifted. At the right distance and the right angle, it was just the contraption to use in place of a grader. With the road still damp from a good rain, I loosened enough gravel to fill the ruts and potholes, then packed it down again with the tractor. Though previously, I had crossed the bridge several times with a hayrack full of wood and wire, now as I drove over the repaired bridge, I feared it might collapse again but thankfully it did not.

With some adjustments, my attempt to copy the action of a road-grader worked fairly well. Because of a shortage of rocks, I dragged enough loosened gravel from the road to fill in the approaches. I was euphoric with the result and the fact that I had managed to accomplish the work with only one arm. The repaired bridge and road turned out to be a big improvement, which were much appreciated by the family. With the work complete, it was possible to go for groceries, get the mail, and attend church regularly and I could also get back to my own church work. My weary arm soon recovered. When Percy arrived and was told about the bridge disaster and completed repair, he was most grateful that we had managed. He responded with his usual appraisal of both jobs, "Splendid!"

Now another venture on the farm arose. The cow barn had long been considered much too small. Percy apologetically suggested, "Would you be interested in making it bigger?" Since I always prided myself on taking a dare, this challenge was welcome. Plans were soon made and material purchased from Mr. Jacobson's lumber yard in town and the project was quickly underway, all while trying to keep up with the church assignments which had priority. The existing barn was probably sixteen feet square with a peaked roof.

I do not remember how the foundation was extended, but with Jean's occasional help, the edifice began to rise. The logistics of the framing came as a result of watching my father, who had been a framing carpenter, and his boss putting up wooden grain bins in just a day or two. They used only handsaws and hammers—no power tools. The walls were assembled and sheeted with plywood. The end wall with the peak attached was moved aside. Finally with all the walls in place, I made sturdy rafters with the same pitch as the other roof and assembled them on the barn floor. Raising them became a challenge with Percy available only on weekends. How the roof was shingled, I do not recollect. The floor was made of two inch planks with a wide gutter at the end. An electrician hung a light bulb from the ceiling with a switch beside the sliding entry door. Lastly, the outside was finished with inexpensive cedar siding which thankfully did not need painting. When Percy saw the results of all our efforts, his usual "Just splendid!" was delivered with more emphasis than his normal grateful appreciation.

My exploits on the farm were many and demanding, with some being most enjoyable, such as rebuilding an old bicycle which had been given to Alec ("Red"). It was just the right size for the ten year old, but in deplorable condition. Since repairing old bikes in our basement when I was a boy had prevented me from getting into trouble sometimes, this task was an appreciated change. When finished, the bike was painted a fire-engine red for Alec in keeping with his nickname. Alec really enjoyed his "new" bike.

He often attempted to see how many pieces he could slice out of a freshly deposited cow pie.

Repairing the bike reminded me of my favourite bike, which I had called Lulabelle. When Alec's bike was ready for the road, I reminisced about my first midnight trial ride which almost ended in disaster. Riding full-tilt down the highway after dark, I was zig-zagging back and forth when an old car passed. I foolishly crashed into the side of the car, and Lulabelle was suddenly snatched out from under me. The old style door handle slid under the handlebar of the bike and I landed in the ditch while the bike disappeared for a second before immediately falling off the car's handle. Dazed and shaken, I retrieved the bike and fortunately we both escaped in one piece.

One of the extra (but most desired activities) on the farm included the care of and love for the purebred Sheltie dogs that Lucy bred and showed. Her dogs were registered with the Canadian Kennel Club. Many of her dogs won local and national awards and prizes.

Another venture I undertook on the farm with much anticipation hoping to earn money to return to Gordon College failed miserably. Someone told me that there was money to be made raising rabbits as some people who had immigrated to Canada liked rabbit meat. My brother, Don, gave me a rabbit apartment which was about sixteen feet long and eight feet wide, divided into smaller cages, one on top of the other. Enough rabbits, Flemish Giants, I think, were bred to ultimately fill all the cages on one side. When they were ready to take to Calgary to sell, I decided to honour the rabbits with their "last supper," and so it was! An adequate amount of green clover was cut to give each cage of rabbits a tasty supper. What a shock awaited me the next day!

In the morning when I went to fill the waiting chicken crates with the rabbits to take them to market, they were all dead. Since they had previously been fed only on rabbit pellets, the tasty green clover on which they had feasted caused bloat. What I had dreamed would augment my meagre bank account ended in disaster. Since the old root cellar had been filled in not long before, I decided to bury the rabbits there. Thankfully, the dirt was still quite soft so, digging by hand, I laid them to rest. Robbie Burns would say, "The best laid plans of mice and men gang aft aglee." So it was.

During all this time, my church assignments carried on concurrently with my job on the farm. Busy does not adequately describe my scattered schedule. Mr. Jacobson ("Jake") was Board Chairman of the little church and was also the local Justice of the Peace as well as the manager of the only lumber company in town. He was a man of integrity with a no-nonsense character. He had a deep bass voice and the authority to go with it. His wife, a very pleasant lady of Victorian virtue, sang sweetly, and was well able to play an aged auto-harp musically. My reaction to the man of the family was much the same as it was to my once-esteemed principal—both caution and respect were required.

Before my return from Gordon College, the chairman of the board was both chief cook and bottle washer in the church. With my arrival as a student pastor, I assumed a myriad of duties, becoming the preacher, the youth pastor, man in charge of the weekly prayer meeting, responsible for having a children's story in the church each Sunday morning, as well as dealing with all the interruptions and extra assignments that go along with the job of a parson. Since Mr. Jacobson's business was in Okotoks on the way to the church and his job was similar to a fireman—much too busy or not busy at all—I often stopped by for his advice or counsel. Since he was also the local justice of the peace, I really paid attention and watched carefully in order to not displease him.

As calling on church members or prospects was one of my assignments, visiting was high on my list of priorities and one which I enjoyed immensely, especially with the elderly. "Keep it short" was the aim of my preaching but visiting did not follow the same pattern, especially as it often ended with coffee and cake! I frequently went to see one of our most active members, Alice Halstead, who lived only a block or two from the church. Her home became one of my favourite stops as she happened to be very hospitable as well as a marvellous cook. She also knew a great deal about the church and the town. Alice became my confidante. I appreciated her understanding and counsel when discussing church and personal concerns. Thus, I had two excellent and insightful sources of information.

Many years after I left the church, it became a part of the Evangelical Free Church in Okotoks, where Alice then attended. More than fifty years later, when she was wheelchair bound and still in very good spirits, I was frequently present at the monthly "Young At Heart" luncheons, which she also attended regularly. I often sought her for a chat and kneeled in front of her wheel-chair, looking her eye to eye and remembering the "good old days." As my first wife, Betty, was wheel-chair bound for several years in the latter part of her life, the disadvantages that the chair presented were no mystery to me. Betty repeatedly told me, "I am so tired of looking at people's tummies, I could cry," and "I often examine belt buckles." Also, she said when people spoke to her from behind the wheelchair, she seldom knew who was talking to her. Having experienced this with my first wife, I now kneel in this manner in front of wheelchair-bound people when speaking to them and visit whenever possible.

My opportunity as a student pastor fared reasonably well, but not without its problems relating to time and ability and all that accompanied the charge. Sunday School began before church on Sunday morning. Some children were well-behaved and some were class clowns, which I was very in tune with from my own school days. Somehow, I always managed to regain their attention. Church followed immediately afterwards. We began with prayer and then singing the old familiar gospel hymns, followed by announcements and any special prayer requests, then another hymn or two, a children's story, and perhaps a special number. From time to time a duet by Jake and me and the sermon completed the service. Almost always during the week, the topic would present itself with sudden inspiration like a light bulb coming on during a visit or a story in the news with a related textual message. The Bible and concordance were my only tools and what I trusted was God's still, small voice. I believe the congregation appreciated my efforts (some said they did, anyway!). If Jake spoke from time-to-time, I do not remember. Occasionally, we would have a visit from a missionary such as Jacobson's son, Ralph, who was a grad of PBI, as was his brother, Herb.

Preparing a sermon which informed and encouraged the adults and deciding what to do in Sunday school and with the youth group demanded time, energy, and talent—all of which were in short supply. Hence, Lucy Kerfoot came to my rescue once more. In those days, a method of teaching called flannel graph was of interest to little kids. Adults enjoyed it, too—probably more than my sermon. It was as popular as television is now. Lucy laboriously prepared the characters each week and I placed them on the flannel board as the story unfolded Sunday to Sunday. Our church chose John Bunyan's immortal *Pilgrim's Progress* as our first presentation. I particularly remember Pilgrim in the slough of despond where "Apollyon laid on him many a blow with his grievous crab tree cudgel." I, too, shared his plight and related to his distress, and of course, to his rescue. We seldom think of depression in that vein today. The children especially sat on the edge of their seats as they watched and constantly asked for more at the end of each session. Each week as Pilgrim faced another trial, the children demanded, "Tell us what happened!" My staunch reply "Come back next Sunday," always annoyed them. I often yearned for my sermons to be received with the same interest, especially by the young people. Prayer meeting was very simple. We sang a song or two, read scriptures and prayed which required little preparation on my part.

Since I was only a recent Bible school grad, my experience as a Student Pastor was sadly lacking and hardly qualified me for the task at hand. Often, the order of the day consisted of being interrupted, and then interrupted again, from the task at hand. Having studied the Bible for four years, I was comfortable depending upon what I had learned. Since I enjoyed preaching, it was always my objective to relate the history of the Bible and the events recorded within in order to apply them to our daily life amid its trials and temptations. My method was topical and textual rather than expository. With sibling rivalry having been so devastating after my mother's death during my early childhood, the Old Testament example of "trust and obey" by Joseph was most encouraging, and my admiration of Daniel, as we sang every week in Sunday school, "Dare To Be A Daniel," was a close second. Daniel's friends followed his example—they would not bow or bend and they did not burn.

Young People's meeting on Friday night was enjoyed by all. We had a short devotional first, followed by games of all sorts—though most often it was scrub softball. Since a short lesson was promised if they paid attention, interest was usually good. Mostly, I told them Bible stories somewhat dramatically. Since Friday night was free from homework, attendance was encouraging.

While learning about the sinner, the publican, and the Pharisees, the young people suggested producing their own puppet show. They chose their own part to play and fashioned the costumes for their puppets accordingly. The costume of the high priest—the supreme religious leader of the

Israelites who made the atonement for himself and the people for all their sins committed during the year, later replaced by Christ's once-for-all-time sacrifice on the cross for all sin—still lingers on the sticky side of my mind. He was truly majestic and resembled royalty. The program was announced for a Friday night. The church and the public were invited. By today's standards, it was not much by way of a dramatic presentation, but those attending very much enjoyed the show. The ladies provided refreshments and everyone had a great time. Years later, the same method was used while teaching my Special Needs students and proved that they were not "slow learners" in every respect.

A few words about the chairman of the church board are appropriate here. Since following his example and suggestions was my objective as his name appeared on my meagre pay check, I often stopped in at his place of business. Strange what we often remember about people. He was extremely frugal. As we talked, he would cut used business envelopes into scratch-paper sized pieces to be used for making quotes. As well, when I asked him about an odd contraption on one of the storage racks, he told me, "That's how I ease my back pain." A sheet of plywood was placed over a sawhorse and attached to ropes with loops at one end. He could pull the main ropes until he was almost hanging by his heels—a forerunner of a machine currently available for spinal decompression, which had me thinking, "Rigorous back therapy." When we occasionally sang a duet during the church service, I attempted to hang onto the melody while he sang bass. His voice booming out, "There's power in the blood," still rings in my ear. Recalling all these events and from this vantage point, it is hard to believe that more than fifty years have passed since I was a student pastor in Okotoks. How time flies!

BACK TO BOSTON OR BUST!
GORDON COLLEGE
ROUND TWO–1954

The fall of 1954 arrived, and all too quickly it was time to return to Gordon College. The question once again arose as to how I would accomplish this objective. Despite attempting to pad my bank account since leaving Boston a year previously, my hope of going back to Gordon College looked dim. Had it not been for the timely gift of an old car, which enabled me to depart on time, I may not have had the courage to return to college at all. Mr. Jacobson's son, Ralph, and his lovely wife, Doris, were returning to Ethiopia, where they had been missionaries for some time. They no longer had need of their old 1941 Studebaker Champion coupe, a well-worn relic ready for the scrap heap. On a visit to Okotoks to say goodbye to his parents, Ralph offered me the car, saying, "You can have it when we leave Calgary by train on our way back to Ethiopia." Not inclined to say "No" to any gift, I gladly accepted.

At the time of their departure, I met Ralph and his wife at the station in Calgary on the appointed day to accept my new car—my very first one. Accordingly, I arrived with great anticipation. After a short visit, Ralph turned over the keys and registration and told me to check the oil level before leaving Calgary, adding, "There is a five gallon can of oil in the back seat." As I left with keys and registration in hand, I thought it a rather strange remark, "Why not in the trunk?" Yes, the can of used oil was in the back seat but upon lifting the trunk lid—no key required—I was surprised to see only the rear axle as there was no floor. My heart sank as I realized my hopes for a usable set of wheels was going to be a challenge. Ralph's comment, "The car uses about a quart of oil every hundred miles," was not very encouraging either! The car did not need more oil and I was soon on my way south to Okotoks, a distance of about thirty miles. Upon my arrival, I did not hear any shouts of glee so I promptly hid my new chariot in the willow bushes south of the creek. It could wait there until there was time to attempt to repair the tired-looking old timer, which I feared might be a costly undertaking.

My planned departure date was announced, allowing time both for the necessary repairs to the car to be accomplished and to travel to Boston before the school year began. Upon telling my oil problem to my blacksmith friend in Okotoks, he said, "Bring her in and I'll see what I can do for you." As soon as the opportunity arose, I took the car to his shop—a garage would have been too expensive. When I drove the car into his shop, he did not look on the old relic with distain, as I expected, but saw it as a test of his ability. My friend put a piece of newspaper under the motor and said, "Let her run." After he examined the paper, he said, "It looks like the oil pump is leaking". He easily removed the part and made a new gasket from the top of an old boot from under the work bench, and proudly announced, "Problem solved!" After that repair, the car never required additional oil, even between oil changes, for as long as I owned it. As the gas pedal was broken, my friend bolted an old strap hinge from a screen door under the pedal to keep it from wandering, an annoying habit, and once again declared, "Problem solved!" I replaced the trunk floor with a piece of plywood and added a padlock hasp to secure the expected contents.

Not long after, I decided to take the car for a run even though it had rained for several days. The road from Okotoks to Longview had just been improved, but lacked the final coat of gravel. The three inches of oozie-goozie mud challenged the trip. Since the new pair of winter tires that came with the car had been sold for twenty-five dollars to help with my expenses, I had replaced them with a pair of oversize six-ply tires that I had been given and which were still usable. As the car slithered south, the smell of burning rubber reached my nostrils. My hopes for an operational vehicle had just hit another snag—what now? Upon later inspection, it appeared that the body of the car had broken loose from the frame. Again, it was back to my blacksmith friend. He removed the rusty bolts and fitted a six-inch piece of iron strap from the rim of a wagon wheel over the holes and bolted it back into place on the frame. He once again announced, "Problem solved!" Feeling smug about our efforts, I asked my very helpful friend, "Do you think this old car will take me all the way to Boston?" He laughingly replied, "Do you mean Boston, Massachusetts? With only seven pounds of oil pressure, I would not even drive it around the block." However, not to be deterred, I christened my new-old car LULABELLE in honour of my first beloved bicycle. Now it was Boston-or-bust. I was confident we would make it safely, in spite of my friend's discouraging prophesy. From paint left over from the old farm tractor, a coat of non-matching sky blue paint was added to cover up the many rusty spots. The evening before my departure, all my belongings were stowed in the trunk before retiring for my last night's sleep in my cozy, upstairs garret.

Early the next morning before the kids left for school, I bid the family a poignant goodbye, and with many hugs was finally on my way to the land of my dreams and ambitions. With the family waving a last fond farewell, Lulabelle and I headed out with mixed emotions—sad to leave but anxious to return to college again. My plans, made in advance, were to stop with friends and family along the way as much as possible, having previously written to each of them asking for hospitality for a night or two and giving them an approximate date of arrival. One invitation was to a PBI student's wedding in upstate New York, not far from Boston and my final stop before the dash for Bean Town—the place of origin of Boston Beans, any brand of which were fine with me. No matter what, I intended to be at Gordon College before the fall semester began.

The first stop on day one was Shaunavan, Saskatchewan, to spend the night with the Hunter family who lived near Gravelberg in southern Saskatchewan. They were the parents of the sons who later became known as the "Crazy Canucks" of downhill skiing fame. "Much easier said than done," as my dad would say. Lulabelle sailed along at 70 MPH and gave a sense of flying low as she was equipped with free-wheeling, a design to save gas and any back pressure on the motor. Taking my foot off the gas pedal at the top of any hill, especially on a steep incline, the car moved on her own, picking up speed all the way to the bottom. I never bothered to touch the brakes and that may be why somewhat later I became known as the "Flying Parson." I sang heartily at the top of my voice as I flew along, "When the roll is called up yonder, I'll be there," "Power in the blood," and other gospel hymns as we passed much finer looking specimens along the way—only a few cars passed me, most of them shiny sports models. All went very well until I reached the border into Saskatchewan. My cheerfulness soon ended.

The new road was under construction and my journey turned into a muddy dash, similar to my first test drive in Lulabelle. The "Under Construction" sign soon became one of destruction. The car swung from side to side, not unlike my ride to the Kikino Reservation driving the little Fordson tractor. Steering became very difficult as we slithered along. When I turned south toward Shaunavan, the country road from Gull Lake was not much better. It was now late in the day and though my first day's travel was soon to end, a new problem arose—the whole area was flooded which was very unusual for this part of Saskatchewan when harvest-time was approaching. Guessing where to drive, I steered by attempting to stay half way between the fence posts on either side of the road, all the while hoping to soon see the Hunter farm. Suddenly with no warning, the car slid off the road and became better acquainted with the ditch—it was stuck fast. Fortunately, a farm, which I hoped was the Hunter's, was not too far away. As there were rubber boots in the trunk, the farm was soon reached and proved to be the place I was seeking. Upon hearing my distressing story, the Hunters' huge tractor soon rescued Lulabelle. They parked the car near the barn, and we went inside as it was almost suppertime. How old their boys were then I do not now remember, but their parents, Lloyd and Peggy, were glad for my safe arrival, explaining that when the road was flooded, they drove on higher ground across their fields from the main road.

When told, "Boy, that car is hard to steer in mud and is like herding a pig on ice," Lloyd responded with, "I will take a look at it in the morning." After a welcome night's rest and a hearty dairyman's breakfast, the chores were completed with the cows being milked mechanically. Next, Lloyd investigated my car and said, "No wonder, your wheels are badly out of line and need to be adjusted." The Hunters, in true farmer fashion, measured the distance between the front of the wheels and the back of the front wheels and brought them back into alignment. The task was quickly accomplished.

Anxious to resume my journey, soon I was on my way back to the good, old Trans Canada Highway, but this time across the field.

On day two, my aim was to get to my Aunt Alice Docksteader's home in Winnipeg. I had spent time there two years before on my way to Boston by bus. The roads were more of the same—mud, mud, and more mud. Soon, the motor began to overheat which required stops occasionally to let it cool down. Overheating and running out of oil were two problems that had to be avoided. However, I did arrive safely late in the day at my second welcome stop. The next morning, upon discovering that the radiator was partially blocked with mud, the garden hose was used to solve the problem. I think I stayed that day despite wanting to get to upstate New York without further delay. Soon, however, I was back on the road again for the longest leg of my journey by faith.

Chicago was my target that day. Entering into the U.S.A. as a student became my chief concern. Having been allowed to cross earlier under suspect conditions, I hoped to do so again to continue my studies after my year-long interruption. With just a glance at my belongings, I was allowed to enter. To my great relief, I had successfully made it into the United States. I am sure that the agent at the border wondered how this derelict contraption had already almost crossed half of the continent.

Presently, I was back on good roads, well on my way to the wedding, no longer beset with steering problems or overheating. As night fell, I began to see the glow of the lights of Chicago far on the horizon. I turned east, expecting to bypass the city. To my surprise, I was soon well into the congested metropolis, in the midst of a parade of mostly African-Americans. I rolled down the window and asked a big friendly-looking fellow, "How can I get out of here? I am on my way to Boston." He peered in, looking very surprised, and declared, "My good man, you got to turn that around and go the other way—you're already half-way to Milwaukee!" Apparently upon crossing the road south of Chicago, I had turned north instead of east. I turned around and headed back.

In the middle of the night, I found myself in the midst of a long line of noisy semi-trailers who were travelling uphill and down at about seventy miles per hour. I dared not pass as it would have been foolhardy. Hour after hour, I sailed merrily along like a timid little puppy in the midst of a friendly pack of big dogs. Finally, later in the night, the pack turned off and I continued on my way. Fatigue engulfed me and I became very drowsy. Suddenly, I was jarred awake by flashing lights right behind me. I realized, "Oh no. This must be the long arm of the law." Of course, I pulled over and stopped. A burly state trooper shone his flashlight around the inside of my car and asked a lot of questions. He informed me that I was speeding and immediately commanded, "Follow me!" "Oh boy," I thought, "Here comes a night in jail." You can imagine my utter surprise: I was not given a ticket then and found myself instead being led up a long drive way, stopping in front of what appeared to be a country mansion—tall pillars and an ornate entry. I was ushered into a stately room, where a dignified looking judge, who obviously was wearing his gown over his pyjamas, began a hasty trial. Looking over the top of his glasses, he asked authoritatively, "How do you plead?" Of course, I had to answer, "Guilty, sir," after which I was relieved of a large portion of my gas money in cash before the trooper led me back to the main road.

Now, badly shaken and devastated at having parted with most of my meagre travel resources, but relieved that I was not on my way to jail, I began looking for a place to pull off the road to rest. I reasoned, "That's more than enough for today." As I appeared to be passing an orchard, I deftly guided Lulabelle across the ditch and far from the noisy road. Sleeping in the car was not uncomfortable and I was soon sawing logs. Tree branches guarded my rest until morning dawned bright and fair. I awakened with the early morning sun shining into the windshield. I opened the driver window and plucked a lovely, red apple from a branch and enjoyed it for breakfast.

My admiration for Lulabelle rose with every setback along the way. I suddenly realized that this was the day of the wedding and, as my dad would say, "You better get a move on." I soon wound my way back to the main highway, thinking, "I hope all goes well today." Loss of ready cash had not deterred my driving habit and I was soon flying down the left lane on a two lane divided highway on Route 128, once again singing loudly, "When the roll is called up yonder"—at Gordon College—"I'll be there." Suddenly, a slow-moving car swung into my lane—horrors! The thought jumped into my mind, *"If I brake hard, I will be in real trouble. If I don't, I will not like the result."* The RPMs dropped, but I did not squeal the tires and found our bumpers welded. That was not the kind of wedding I had hoped to attend that day.

The apology of the elderly farmer was profuse, and he said, "I guess I didn't look in my rear view mirror." I replied, "That's okay. If you lift your side of Lulabelle off the bumper as I lift my side, we will see if we can undo this unexpected union." With mission accomplished, we were soon on our way again. He must have thought that I had just appeared out of space. However, my trials for the day were far from over. Not long after, the smell of acrid smoke from burning rubber began to seep into the car. I pulled onto the shoulder to investigate. The sturdy rear left wheel was smoking but the tire had not gone flat. The rim had been spinning inside the tire when it lost pressure due to the collision. Though this six-ply oversize tire still held up its part of the bargain, I had paid a fearful price. I managed to dig out the spare, jack up the car, and loosen the nuts. Gingerly, with a towel wrapped around my hand, I put the still hot victim in the trunk.

Once again, I was on my way, much relieved but not so merrily. My hopes of being on time for the wedding began to fade. As well, the tire would be costly to replace as I would now be required to buy two in its place and to reassign old faithful as a spare. I was disappointed that it now appeared to be impossible to reach my destination of the day—the Bruinsma home—and hence the ability to attend my friend's wedding.

Having turned off the main highway, it became very difficult to find my way to their farm as I had never been there. Despite the fact that I had a map, I became completely lost as I was never able to follow maps even with instructions! Since I had only been able to tell directions with the mountains visible to the west as in Alberta, north, east, south, and west were the jumbled products of my confused imagination. As well, the sights in the countryside along the way distracted me. Being in open farming land, there were no orchards. An old farm truck was coming toward me slowly so I stopped, stood in front of Lulabelle, and waved my arm. In true rural fashion, the farmer stopped right beside me—blocking traffic evidently did not cause him the least concern.

Looking at my dilapidated old car with concern, he asked, "Well, what can I do for you, young man?" Upon informing him of my dilemma, he thoughtfully pulled his chin whiskers then thrust his thumbs under his well-worn bib overalls and solemnly declared, "Well, come to think of it, you can't get to there from here." Of course, what he meant was that I could not get there directly. After pointing in one direction after another and musing, "No, not that way" several times, he laid out a meandering route. I pleaded, "Please don't tell me the direction. Just tell me right or left." He laid out a course, with several observations along the way. With a wry expression, he described the Bruinsma's barn and house so I could recognize the farm when I came to it. He waved a cheery goodbye and once again, I was off without even having to turn around.

After several turns and seeing the sights he told me to watch out for, I came to what appeared to be a dairy farm, as there were several cows in the pasture near the house. Feeling just like I was arriving home, I drove up the rather long lane and stopped near the back door. A huge dog leapt out of the rear end of a rather nice-looking bath-tub Nash automobile that still looked usable. My brother, Don, had one just like it not long ago. I recognized it instantly, and thought, "*This big guy sure has a cozy dog house!*" Since the animal did not bark or growl, I ventured to roll down the cranky window just a little, thinking, "Gee, he might even be friendly," which proved only too true. The dog extended an inquisitive nose. His head was higher than the window and he appeared to expect to be acknowledged so with that I rolled the glass all the way down and scratched his ear. I could have received a sloppy face wash as well had I wanted one. It appeared that no one was around. Since the kitchen window was wide open and a radio was blaring out very brash and loud music, I thought the family must have left in a hurry. Nobody could be home, as how could anyone stand a noise like that! I went to investigate. The dog seemed to want a friendly greeting so I gave the back of his ears a thorough tousling. To my great surprise, two knee-high noisy white dogs ran out the kitchen door as soon as it was open. When they appeared, barking furiously, I darted in and quickly closed the door.

Since I was now in the house and the noisy dogs were out, I thought I should make myself at home and take a much-needed bath. However, my change of clothes was still in the trunk of my car and the two dogs seemed not all that friendly. First, I inspected the bathroom and was met by another surprise—the bathtub was full of coal! The question was, "What to do now?" The yappy dogs took possession of the house again as I left. I got back into the car to ponder my situation. The huge, friendly, Irish Wolfhound simply ignored me. He was quite happy to be protecting his master's property.

I had long since missed the opportunity to attend the wedding and had not recently bathed. Upon turning into the lane, I had seen what appeared to be a small artesian well with a long pipe spilling water into a small stone trough in the middle of the field next to the road. Why not take a bath there! I simply drove back to the road, which did not look as though it was often used, and parked in the ditch, close to the fountain. Since I could not see any gate leading into the pasture, I pushed my change of clothes beneath the barbwire fence and crawled under.

The stream of water gushing into the small stone basin was very cold. Fearing that someone might drive by at any moment, I decided to just splash and dash. As I was attempting to turn the stream into a spray to finish my would be shower, I heard the chug, chug, chug of an old truck slowly approaching. Now it was a mad dash back to Lulabelle. Once again, I rolled under the fence, this time in great haste, and jumped into the car just as a friendly, elderly farmer smiling broadly and waving cheerfully passed by. I quickly returned to the basin for a final splash and dash, gathered my clothes and shoes, and retreated to the car to dress, once again to be greeted by my fierce-looking friend. With the mission accomplished, what was I to do now?

Since the friendly giant had just met me, I hoped that he would remain welcoming. As before, he bounded out of his improvised kennel and appeared to want his ears scratched again. I was much relieved as he was taller than the hood of my old car. Since the pair of barking dogs were safely back in the house, I decided to explore the premises outside. It appeared that there was only one strand of wire which served as a fence to a pasture that looked to be a junkyard. As I took hold of the wire and started to raise my leg, I was greeted with a strong jolt of electricity. Too late, I thought, "Dummy, you should have known." I leapt over instantly. Upon landing safely, I was once again in the company of my new-found friend. How Bowser got there, as if by magic, I never knew. He stayed with me as I investigated a bunch of old cars, car parts, farm machinery, and all kinds of old stuff strewn in every direction. Having satisfied my curiosity, I returned to Lulabelle with the dog close by my side. This time, I held the wire down with a stick and doggie bounded over also. Since I did not relish being with the yappy dogs and I had turned off the radio, the comfort of the car seemed a good place to snooze.

I felt secure as Bowser kept watch over me from his "kennel." I do not know how long I slept as the sun had already set. Sudden exclamations aroused me as Bowser happily bounded out to greet the family when they finally returned home. The owner of the property asked me in great consternation, "How did you ever get in here? With Ripper on guard, we never even lock the door. Nothing has ever been stolen, night or day, since he arrived." I thought then that they had probably befriended him as he had likely been dropped off out in the country when his master no longer wanted to pay the feed bill for such a monster. I had never seen such a friendly giant before or nor have I seen one since.

Someone from the family had evidently waited until the last minute for my arrival before departing for the wedding, and they were doubly surprised to find a complete stranger in their yard, asleep in a beat-up car. I must have looked hungry for they soon brought out a banquet from their car and we enjoyed a good supper.

Because of Ripper's apparent failure as a faithful watchdog, a discussion erupted. When I told them of my exploits with the electric fence, they asked, "Did you ever try to pick up anything when you were looking around?" I replied, "Only a stick to hold down the hot wire upon returning to the car." When I mentioned that Ripper had a mighty fine kennel for which I could imagine a better use, they told me then, "Since Daddy lost his license, it is now Ripper's domain." The family finally concluded that since I had driven right up to the door, Ripper had accepted me as one of their own. They said since the dog had welcomed me, they would do the same—imagine being introduced by a dog. I told them nothing about my earlier hasty shower nor did I tell them of my inspection of the bathroom. I had narrowly missed meeting my friend from Prairie Bible Institute. The bride and groom were long gone.

LAST DASH TO BOSTON–1954

At long last, after surviving many perils along the way, I was just a short jaunt from Boston. I decided to sleep in the car in order to make an early departure the next morning, just as I had when well-hidden in the tasty apple orchard, which now seemed far away and long ago. I asked my hosts if they minded if I spent the night in the car, but they would not hear of it. They said, "No way. Tonight, you will sleep in a bed."

Awakening early the next morning, I detected activity in the kitchen. A hearty farmer's breakfast awaited me, along with their continued amazement that Ripper had even allowed me to get out of my car or that I could also freely walk around the farm as if I was kith and kin! They eventually concluded that since I had acted as family, their famous guard dog could still be relied upon to keep their property safe. As I was anxious to be on my way, I pleaded to be excused. The entire family gathered around the car, along with Ripper, his tail wagging a fond farewell. Once more I gave him a generous rub behind his ears, and expressed a very grateful thank you to the family. Lulabelle, as expected, started instantly and seemed as pleased as I to be on the road again. Ripper escorted us down the driveway before returning to his official duty in the abandoned Nash.

As I discerned that the traffic would soon build up on Route 128, the main road into Boston from the north, I wanted to get to that junction as soon as possible. To my dismay, I saw a flashing red light far ahead with a mile long line of traffic waiting to enter the thoroughfare. Very few succeeded with each light change. I had to wait for what seemed forever.

Without the modern invention of air conditioning, the inside of the car was soon as hot as an oven, even with the windows all the way down. The heat radiated so that you could have fried an egg on the pavement. Few are the merry little breezes in the Boston area during what they call "dog days." Blessedly, I was finally once again on my way. Today, much to my satisfaction, no problems had yet presented themselves. Cruising down the middle lane at about seventy MPH, my usual speed, few cars passed me. The drivers' occasional looks of surprise, humour, or wonder did not dim my sense of satisfaction and gratitude for Lulabelle. They knew nothing of our trials along the way.

With my voice raised in a song of praise for my expected arrival at my final destination, I changed singing from "When The Roll Is Called Up Yonder," to "When The Saints Go Marching In." My gratitude was boundless as we had crossed most of the continent safely. My aim was, "Go east young man in pursuit of all your dreams." The fears of my blacksmith friend had not come true, after all. Sooner than I expected, a horde of vehicles, including mine, descended upon the city where my desires would doubtless be fulfilled in my second attempt to further my education and find the love of my life (as I stated before, the college was often called "Gordon College of Theology and Matrimony" by expectant students). The cars dispersed to their various destinations and I soon found my way to the college.

With Lulabelle parked safely in the alley behind the main building, I went to the registrar's office. She seemed very surprised by my travel-weary appearance. Since I had not informed the college accurately as to the time of my arrival, I assumed that was the reason for what seemed to be a cool reception. Later, I learned that students who left before graduation seldom returned and she probably feared another failure on my part. Such was not the case when I met with Goldie Stocker.

Goldie Stocker was the student advisor who had two years previously rescued me from Aunt Marion's clutches when I fell apart both emotionally and scholastically. Her instant warm and friendly hug was among many that have become the trademark of "The Armless Jim Davis." She sent me to see Dr. Edwin K. Gedney, the Course Advisor. Goldie had suggested a change in course from theology to education.

The new course selection was a welcome experience for me as I no longer had to face the rigours of trying to memorize and translate Greek and Hebrew. However, there was plenty of assigned reading, mostly about the history of teaching methods from the beginning of recorded history to the present; from the peripatetic teachers whose students followed them as they lectured from place to place, to a host of educators too numerous to mention, whose methods from Lancaster, Montessori, and many others have been recorded in detail in numerous volumes. Soon life became a circle of classes, study, work, and some diversion.

Money matters continued to plague me, and I now knew that it would soon be in short supply. My former job at Filene's Bargain Basement was no longer available. What to do was a problem, especially being "armless". With Uncle Stayley's death, I was still hopeful that my former farmer boss would keep his promise and finally send me money at year's end, a hope which proved fruitless. Seven years later upon finding Baldy Larson in the barn milking, I asked him why he did not keep his part of the bargain. He paused briefly, looked up to me and said, "We never seemed to get round to it." I replied, "Why don't you write out a cheque for me now, in the amount that you think my right arm was worth to me?" He went to the house and returned with a cheque for $500. You can imagine how I felt! I just walked away and never saw him again. Sue Larson had told me earlier that I should be grateful that he had saved my life and accused me of blackmail. She said nothing about the real reason he had to save my life nor about his negligence. Such is life. Years later, a friend told me that Baldy was not expected to live much longer, and that I had better go visit him soon if I wanted to see him again. By then, they were living in a nice house in Nanton. When I knocked on their door and it opened, I was met by the icy stare of Mrs. Larson through the screen door. When I asked, "Can I see Baldy?," she replied with a very cold, firm, "No!" She must have thought that I was there to ask for more money.

Since Lulabelle stood in need of an oil change, why not visit the local Studebaker dealership? The manager appeared to be a friendly sort, as are all car salesmen, realtors, and con-men. He offered me a part-time job, with the promise that a fine young fellow such as myself would do very well financially. I was hired to sell cars whenever my schedule allowed. The dealership had two mechanics and a shop foreman who had other assignments as well. My boss loved to play golf and was often away from the dealership. As soon as he left the premises, one of the employees would bring his own or a friend's vehicle and do the repairs on it without a work order. Since they knew I knew and feared that I would report them, they offered a free service on mine. What to do? I said, "You may work on mine, but I will pay the bill. I will not report you—that's your business, not mine!"

Sometimes I had to wait until the boss returned in order for him to approve the sales which I hoped to make. When he arrived, however, he would offer the people a much better deal, of course, at more money, and my hope of a commission died. When I saw my expectations perish, I would remind him that the person to whom he had just sold a car of his choice had actually been my customer. He would apologize profusely and promise to add a token of his appreciation on my next paycheck. As you can well imagine, he was a successful salesman and I was not. Now, since it had become obvious that his generosity was not lavished on his employees, I had a feeling that this was the reason for their "no-work-order" policy with which they made up for lost earnings.

My desire to get Lulabelle going again was encouraged by a very pleasant and unexpected surprise. Upon attending one course called "The Christian Home"—in which almost all students enrolled, even those who had already achieved their "secondary" objective of a happy marriage—I was elated to see that Miss Hazel Miriam Ross was one of the participants. This was the young lady who had informed me in no uncertain terms when I had left college nearly two years earlier that there would be no candle burning in her window awaiting my return. My hopes revived as I wondered why she had chosen this class at this time, while also realizing that the course was required for all students.

Since my father had married a fine Christian lady from out east, I was hopeful that I would have the opportunity to follow his example (like my mother, Miriam hailed from Nova Scotia). My heart had skipped a beat when I first saw Miriam alone in the back seat of the car out front of Aunt Marion's almost two years previously—the day that Aunt Marion had unloaded her acrimony on me when they had invited me to go for a drive with them. Now, however, Miriam did not seem to object when I plunked myself nonchalantly into the seat next to her in the classroom on that most welcomed day, with a cheery, "Hello, Miss Ross."

My job at the Studebaker dealership immediately took on new meaning—now Miriam could possibly be sitting beside me on the front seat of Lulabelle and we could go for a drive all by ourselves. Soon, my first objective was accomplished late one night. Since Miriam worked at the Massachusetts General Hospital as a nurse, her shifts often ended late at night when public transit was unpredictable, so I offered to bring her back to college safely. This happened quite frequently and she soon became my chief joy and delight.

Once upon returning to "Old Faithful," the driver's door was open. I don't think it was ever locked and someone was attempting to hotwire my car. I immediately yelled, "Get out of that car!" A shadowy figure quickly disappeared. Miriam questioned, "Didn't you think that you would get beaten up?" My reply, "It did not even enter my mind." On an occasion when my friend's old Jeep had a flat tire, I was surprised to discover that he did not know what needed to be done, so I changed the flat while our passengers, including Miriam, waited patiently. Later, she observed that it was unusual that the one with only one arm was the man who had managed the task easily and without fuss.

Ever since graduating from PBI in 1952, I had planned to go to Africa as a missionary and help the natives build mud huts while leading them to salvation. Miriam planned to go as a nurse. As we shared the same objective, we often met in the College Chapel to pray accordingly, trusting that I would eventually qualify with CBOMB—the Canadian Baptist Overseas Mission Board—to go to Angola as a missionary-teacher.

I was envious of a couple on campus that were often wrapped around each other very affectionately in the hallways, oblivious of all passers-by. They were engaged but not yet married. Since I had been in Miriam's company for quite some time, as she stood up to leave the chapel one day, optimism and opportunity overcame me and I embraced her fondly, giving her a long lingering kiss. She did not object. My head swam and my insides melted. I had kissed other girls occasionally but none had rang my bell like this. To my great surprise before she turned to leave, she looked me squarely in the eye with a twinkle in hers and asked, "What took you so long?" You can imagine my elation at discovering that although she was a very prim and proper lady, she was not above the occasional kiss.

As my revised course of study did not require as much class time as Theology, there was time available to attempt to sell cars which still did not generate much income. I got along well with my fellow employees and would often keep company with the assistant manager to fetch new cars from the dock to the dealership. He was one wild driver and never seemed a bit concerned if there were any problems with the car, nor the lack of oil, gas, or water. Woe to him who was to purchase one.

Gordon College was across the street from the Isabella Gardner Museum, a familiar landmark on the Fenway. Established in 1903 by Isabella Stewart Gardner (1840–1924), an American art collector, philanthropist, and patron of the arts, the museum was housed in a building designed to emulate a 15th-century Venetian palace, drawing particular inspiration from the Venetian Palazzo Barbaro. This God-given sanctuary often became my "Hiding Place" when either elated or distressed, which were both often my condition in life's ups and downs. This stately, three storey public museum became important to me for two reasons—first as a haven and then as the source for a Fine Arts paper.

In an effort to fulfill my obligations to my Fine Arts professor I chose to base my project on the artist Rembrandt. On the way to the upper floors of the museum, I passed his huge 9 by 12 foot painting, "Peter in the Storm on the Sea of Galilee." Many years later this painting, valued at eight million dollars, was stolen along with several other works of art. To my knowledge, the paintings completely disappeared and have never been recovered. My paper for Dr. Thienemann, my Linguistics Professor, completed my requirements for that subject. Dr. Thienemann commented, "One of the best papers I ever received." This for me was a great honour because of my respect for him. Twice, he escaped Hitler's clutches while fleeing from Europe to the United States of America. My Linguistics paper and Fine Arts project were among the highest grades I achieved in college.

Another notable event happened when our Geology professor, Dr. Harry Leith, spoke of his interest in a glacial erratic which he said, accurately, was near Okotoks, Alberta. Of course, I had often passed it on my way to the church in Black Diamond, where several pretty girls attended along with the generous giver of the oversize rear tires on Lulabelle referred to earlier. Mr. Leith also affirmed that the first chapter of Genesis records nineteen times "after its kind," which is simply contrary to the "law" of evolution, which states that mankind arose from a previous lesser species. What a slur on monkeys! There is simply no valid evidence from archaeology that this ever happened. If it was so, how could there be petrified human and elephant-like footprints found together in ancient layers of sedimentary rock, as confirmed by archaeology?

On one of my car rides around the beautiful New England countryside, alone with Miss Ross, I decided to investigate a lovely, rural church to see if it was locked. It was, but I had a romantic mission in mind. Since Miriam was beside me as I tried the latch, I turned toward her while holding her hand as I knelt on bended knee and imploringly asked, "Miriam, will you marry me?" I do not now remember her reply then, but knowing that her mind ruled her decisions rather than her emotions (unlike me), I was content to wait for her response.

Since the end of my first year back at Gordon was soon to end, final arrangements were made by the Lake George Church in Nova Scotia for me to be their summer pastor. Three college students from Gordon asked for a ride to Nova Scotia as they were going home for the summer break. We arrived just in time at St. John to board the ferry to Digby. My car was one of the last to be swallowed by the big iron whale. Anxiously, I hoped it would not be submerged on the short trip across the Bay of Fundy.

Upon our arrival, my friends departed and I was soon on my way to Lake George where I was to contact Mr. Malcolm Crosby, who would be introducing me to the family that would be providing a place for me to live. Suddenly, I spotted a water well rig drilling a site not far from the main road. Knowing that my Uncle Sid owned Trask Artesian Well Drilling Company, I wondered whether this could be his equipment and decided to investigate. A young man shut down the unit and walked toward me slowly with a puzzled look. To our mutual surprise and amazement, my cousin by the same first name was the operator. He looked a mirror image of me and was about the same age and size. He said, "Oh, I thought you were a bill collector." What an introduction to my mother's side of the family in Nova Scotia! Telling me that he lived at Cambridge Station, he invited me to visit them as soon as possible. He may have wondered if my shabby old jalopy could actually make it that far, having been driven almost all the way across the continent. Lulabelle had just developed a nasty habit of lurching to the left whenever we felt a bump, so our trip had to be a bit more careful.

Upon reaching Port Maitland, I turned inland and finally found a tired-looking farm which seemed to be my destination—the Crosby place. This observation proved to be true. They invited me to stay for supper, after which Mr. Crosby intended to drive me around to see if we could locate a place for me to stay for the summer as he had not been able to arrange one. While supper was being prepared, I excused myself, saying I wanted to tell the Kerfoots of my safe arrival in Nova Scotia as soon as possible. I put my trusty left-handed portable typewriter on one stump and sat on another to complete the task before supper.

Following the meal, we headed out to find accommodations with Malcolm sedately behind the wheel of my treasured old car. Fortunately, our very first stop yielded fruit—the Silver family seemed glad to lodge me. I let Malcolm drive back to his place and then returned immediately for my first night. I seemed to fit into the family schedule nicely. I really enjoyed playing with little Susan, the younger sister of the two children, as I had only one opportunity to play with mine when she was about three or four. The family was probably glad for the little extra income. The home was clean and tidy and the meals excellent. The bedroom-study provided me a quiet and private place to study and prepare my sermons.

As Lulabelle needed repair, Vic Silver suggested that a gentleman of African descent, who repaired heavy duty machinery in the area, might help me. He volunteered and said, "I will take a look." He welded the broken strut and refused my honest offer to pay him. I often stopped on the way by to inspect the huge caterpillar which he was repairing. In all honesty, his nice-looking older daughter may have been an added attraction, or distraction, as the case may be.

Sometime later while zooming around the area near the church, which I considered my extended parish, upon rounding a long curve on a hillside, I faced a car on the wrong side of the road coming right at me, with the occupants looking intently the wrong way completely unaware of me. To try to pass on the wrong side might have ended in disaster so I cranked my trustworthy old car hard right, through the ditch and up the hillside, only to look sideways into a pair of wide eyes and gaping mouths. Fortunately, I dodged holes, rocks and brush, then I was almost instantly back on the road again and gone like a flash. Now, as word spreads quickly in such areas, it was soon told abroad that the "Flying Parson" was driving like a mad man.

However, they did not report the fact that they themselves were on the wrong side of the road.

On a more humorous occasion, having helped my good friend Ernie Robinson chase a milk cow out of the bush just before attending the church prayer meeting, my pants were splashed generously with you know what. When wrinkled noses and puzzled looks alerted me to the fact, I apologized profusely. I do not now recall what evasive action was taken—perhaps early dismissal. Ernie and Hazel Robinson were faithful financial and moral supporters of the church. She was a teacher and he was manager of a government operated fish hatchery. Not many in the area were as fortunate.

Another memory of a different turn of events came about as a surprise for a prairie farm boy. I was invited to a clandestine late night banquet, which was to me of an unknown origin until then. The locals had a way of retrieving undersized or damaged lobsters which had been tossed overboard at the dock to avoid inspection. They returned at night to salvage their catch, and success demanded a party. Hence, the young student pastor was invited as the guest of honour—amid many smiles and chuckles as they thought it was only right, oh yeah, for him also to be a part of their clandestine affair. The officials, whose job it is to inspect their catch on arrival, were rather slack about any further inspection. With much joshing and good humour, they said if they were caught in the act of an illegal party, I, too, would bear the consequences. It was a great evening of fellowship and laughter with them teaching me how to take the ugly things apart.

Bear with me for one more event related to local industry during my first summer at Lake George Church in 1955. One day, I passed an elderly man, who was, as they say, twitching a yoke of oxen along the road. The oxen were pulling a hayrack fully loaded. Of course, I stopped to have a chat with the very obliging fellow. In the conversation, he said, "Gosh dab, I'd like to go down to Port Maitland and get me a mess of herring. They must be landing them about now." I presumed that meant he did not have a car and believed preachers are the ones who help those people in need, and was indirectly asking if I would be willing. It seemed that the next day was suitable for both of us and I took him there accordingly. We went and he got his herring. We became friends and I often stopped by to visit with him. Not much has been said about my activities as a pastor since they very much resembled the time I spent as a student pastor in Okotoks. I shall not expound on that experience, except for one event that happened shortly after my arrival.

Nova Scotians have several nicknames, such as "herring-chockers." "Bluenose" has also been used, since the late 18th century, because of the marks left on the noses of fishermen by their blue mitts; it also gave its name to a very famous Nova Scotian fishing and racing schooner.

One Thelma Allen was the church organist. Now, since Thelma means "willing" in Greek (of which I knew a little), I expected that she would be willing again this year. I was surprised when she emphatically declined my request, saying, "No way. The mice ate the bellows. It's far too hard to pump." Hence, I was faced with a real problem. Asking around for a repairman, I found a man who was prepared to help provided that he had the right material. Fortunately, while visiting a factory in New England that was no longer in operation, I had been given part of a bolt of closely-woven poplin cloth which I had hoped to use to make seat-covers for Lulabelle. The cloth proved to be the answer. After the old pump organ was repaired, Thelma agreed to give it a try. To my utter surprise, her toes barely touched the pedals when her face lit up radiantly. She gladly agreed to do her best. Our services were always accompanied by her lively playing. All I had to do was announce the hymn and the congregation sang like birds.

A day for my final message was chosen along with a roll call and a party that I did not know about. I had asked to visit my uncle near Wolfville on the Saturday before leaving, assuring them I would be able to get back before the service—which did prove to be a challenge as it turned out. Little did I know that the roads early in the morning along the way were full of people going to a different church from ours. Just as I was approaching a little town, Lulabelle's muffler fell off. The car let out a mighty roar. Immediately, just like the Red Sea, there was a parting of the way as people scrambled to the side of the road, and so it was for the rest of the trip. Finally, at five to eleven, this newfound alarm signalled our approach to the church. A mighty cheer arose from a long line of expectant parishioners, who were looking at their watches as we arrived. The service went very well—special music, roll call and all. The roll call was an annual event as many were back from holiday. The potluck dinner was fantastic, but surprisingly did not include lobster. The next morning with the car all packed, I was ready for the return trip to Boston.

GORDON COLLEGE–1955

I don't remember much of my solo return trip to Boston, except that Lulabelle, my amazing old junker with a new muffler, purred along nicely for much of the way on top of a long, gently rolling road built on esker, which our geology professor had told us was left behind when the age-old glacier retreated through melting. Upon arriving, I learned that the college was well underway in their expected move to the 994 acre Princemere estate in Wenham, Massachusetts, northeast of Beverly. With growth beginning to surpass its capacity at Fenway in the late 1940s, James Higginbotham, a student pastor at Gordon Divinity School, approached Fredrick Prince about the College buying his well-endowed property at Beverly, Ipswich, and Wenham. Impressed by Higginbotham, Prince sold to Gordon for a very small sum as well as donating a large amount to reconstruct the Prince Memorial Chapel. The splendid location had been patrolled by men with German Shepherd dogs and had otherwise been long empty. Gordon sold its old facilities to Wentworth Institute of Technology.

The most distinct building on campus is the stone mansion, built in 1911, which had been Prince's residence. Today, it houses the majority of the College's faculty and administrative offices, the Admissions Department, as well as a small number of classrooms. The large residence was similar, I imagined, to an English castle, massive and somewhat mysterious with small stairs hidden in the wide walls leading up to what must have been the servants' quarters. They could be reached also by the central staircase. The room to which I was assigned along with a roommate overlooked a grand scene—the space was big enough for what had once been a huge swimming pool, a grand foyer, and a very large room with a long dining table. The area occupied by the pool became a library and the very large dining room, a study. The property housed several other lesser buildings, a long line of stables which were being converted into students' quarters, and a large, flat area that had been a polo field. The field is now the location of two beautiful buildings, which were still under construction at that time. The once-grand estate, adorned with beautiful trees and a lovely old building that became the chapel, was now the scene of complete chaos.

The Prince Memorial Chapel on the new campus (since razed) was named for Frederick Prince, and Prince's mansion was renamed Frost Hall after Martha Frost. I later won the Massachusetts Bible Society annual Bible Reading Contest in that lovely old chapel. The year-end contest took place during exam time for theology students. The scripture of my choice included the words from Ecclesiastics 12, "Hear the conclusion of the whole matter." When I read, *"Of making many books there is no end, and much study is a weariness of the flesh"* (Ecclesiastes 12:12, KJV) the entire room burst instantly into laughter. This may have relieved some of the seniors' tensions. Then, too, it may be the reason they chose me as "choice of selection suitable for the occasion" was one of their criteria.

In 1962, the school changed its name again to Gordon College and Divinity School. In 1970, the Gordon Divinity School separated from the college and merged with the Conwell School of Theology in Philadelphia, once part of Temple University to form the Gordon-Conwell Theological Seminary in South Hamilton, Massachusetts. Then in 1985, Barrington College of Rhode Island went bankrupt and merged into Gordon College.

Upon arrival, my first assignment along with my studies was to clean the stable which had been used to house the German Shepherd guard dogs, of which there must have been many. There were no kennels. The entire huge room was buried in a thick rotted mass of straw and cabbage leaves. I did not know that dogs would eat cabbage! It took most of my available spare time to transform the sorry scene and render it usable for human habitation.

While trying to sell used Studebakers in Boston and still fitting in time for study, my schedule became a battle which I lost in both areas of time and money. Classes, however, went very well and bonded student and professor in very meaningful relationships. Soon winter arrived with lots of snow. Outside the campus was not so busy, but classes went on as usual. My frustration with time, travel and the shortage of money bothered me greatly. Along with that, my trusty old Studie came to an unfortunate end. While taking a car full of students to attend a lecture in Boston, we were rear-ended suddenly when approaching a green light. The lead car had stopped to wait until there was time to make a u-turn—which was illegal! Crash, crash, crash! We managed to stop when almost touching bumpers. "Oh, no," I thought. "Not another unexpected car-wedding," as a big old Mercury smacked into Lulabelle from behind. Crumple, crumple, crumple! Our grill was smashed and the trunk badly dented, but fortunately, though badly shaken, no one was injured—evidently no whiplash. We were able to limp away from the scene—an even more derelict, two-toned blue disaster. I wonder what the irresponsible driver thought as he observed a long line of damaged cars as he passed by on the other side of the road.

Not long after this incident, a friend borrowed my car. Unfortunately, Lulabelle locked into reverse and had to be towed away. Though the friend apologized profusely and sincerely, I never saw my beloved car again. Such a sad ending! Lulabelle meant a great deal to me: a tired, worn-out old jalopy that had miraculously taken me across most of the continent as well as many other places. She had always met the basic requirements for any vehicle—START, STEER, and STOP. I kept a small piece of the broken grill on top of my dresser for more than fifty years to remind me of God's care for us and Lulabelle's faithfulness. Though some considered her past her usefulness, what a success story she proved to be! The loss of Lulabelle hit me hard. Even though two more followed, neither Studebaker ever provided such satisfaction or lived up to her reliability.

Now, you may be wondering how my hoped-for romance with Miriam Ross was progressing. Being a very optimistic fellow, her somewhat casual greeting did not dim my aspirations. We shared many enjoyable times together. One particular incident occurred before the death of Lulabelle. I splurged and took her to an up-scale restaurant in Boston. Both of us dressed for the occasion. Since we arrived in a downpour, I dropped her off at the door and she was ushered in by a well-dressed doorman. I went to look for a place to park which took some time. It was in a part of the city where three roads met. Having finally found a spot, I used Miriam's umbrella and dashed back arriving somewhat distressed. As you may have guessed, our dinner was both tasty and costly. I suspected that Miriam would be of two minds regarding such extravagance but no mention of such was made. During the meal, she excused herself and returned shortly with an apology. Later, she told me that her pearl necklace had fallen into her brassiere. You can well imagine that this lady was a princess that I anticipated someday making my wife. She herself was a pearl of great price!

Following the meal, I could not remember on which street I had parked the car! Now what? I finally found it—on the last street I searched, of course. Running in the rain with an umbrella firmly clasped in my one remaining hand was not my idea of fun. However, after returning to get Her Majesty, she asked, "What took you so long?" When I told her, she burst out laughing, humour that we were to share on many more occasions.

Not long before Christmas, with the weather being very cold, we were invited to supper with Lynn and Hannah Stairs. They lived on campus in a cozy little house-trailer. We had a lovely maritime meal and enjoyed a very special time of fellowship. Upon leaving, Hannah helped me with my coat and handed me my one glove. With a puzzled look, Hannah said, "And where is your other glove?" I replied, "Hannah, *and* just what would I do with it?," whereupon she burst into laughter. One-armed people do not need two gloves. Had she forgotten so soon, I wondered? Would Miriam have the same regard for me as Hannah, who had introduced Miriam to me two years previously?

With Christmas of 1955 imminent, the junior Stairs invited me to spend Christmas holidays with them at Lynn's parents' farm. I gladly accepted. While there, I was introduced to life in the "Pulp Woods," as they were called in New Brunswick. Helpers gathered and began cutting suitable trees, chopping off the branches. When finished, they whistled for the horse waiting patiently at the pulp yard log pile. The horse would come, dragging a logging chain and stop just in front of the log. When hitched, he would return to the pile, waiting for the next whistle. There was a fire burning near the growing pile to warm bodies and make tea when it was time for a rest. I imagine the horse liked that, too, but he evidently missed out on the tea. When the very black gallon can filled with water boiled vigorously, a handful of tea leaves was added, and then the can was lifted from the fire and set in a snow bank to cool and settle the leaves. Each man had his own tin cup, with more available for those who came to help or just to join in the friendly camaraderie around the fire. Most men sipped away gingerly, as the hot, dark liquid had not sat in the snow long enough to cool. There was no sugar or cream.

Lynn's grandma and grandpa also lived at the farm. One evening, Grandpa Stairs came back to the house during chore time and blurted out, "Maud, Maud, give me the torchlight. I sneezed my teeth into the hog trough." On his return, he stated somewhat glumly, "I guess they're gone," but after chore time the next morning, he announced cheerfully, "They were smiling at me, stuck in the snowdrift on the other side of the hog trough." As Shakespeare would say, "All's well that ends well." All too soon, after a very refreshing holiday, I returned to Gordon. Miriam had fared well in a similar fashion with her parents in Springhill, Nova Scotia. We spent some time reminiscing about our separate holidays.

Too quickly, the demanding schedule of travel, study, and attempted sales came to an end and once again I accepted the opportunity to be the summer pastor at Lake George. "Snorky Grey Dort", a 1950 Studebaker coupe which was pointed in front, replaced Lulabelle. I was alone on my way back to my summer assignment—this time to board with the Porter family who lived nearer the church. A far different atmosphere awaited me. The bedroom in which I slept had been vacated recently by two young boys to make room for me. Evidently, they had been bed-wetters. Enough said, but the problem was soon solved. Their older sister, Shelagh, was about twelve. She was a delight. Her mother, Doreen, was a good cook, but not much at keeping house. I was amazed to see her open the door in the kitchen and sweep the accumulation through the cracks in the hallway floor into the basement.

My pastoral activities were much the same as the previous summer, but several events come to mind. Stopping to call on a faithful parishioner, I discovered that he, too, was using a pair of oxen to pull a load of hay up to the barn, the second time I had seen oxen being used for farm work. He gave the team a rest and came over to the car to visit. He was interested in my sporty-looking Starlight Studebaker and asked how I liked it. I told him that it accelerated like a lead duck. The head mechanic at the dealership had exhausted every way known to him to solve the problem, even so far as installing a so-called "supercharger" on top of the carburetor. The car could not even compare to Lulabelle which had never been described as sporty—

merely economical. Lulabelle had taken me safely from Okotoks, Alberta, all the way to Boston, Massachusetts—a total of 2,594 miles on 128 gallons of gas costing only $44.50.

As a farmer does, he looked at me with a knowing twinkle in his eye as he raised the hood, adjusted the throttle rod, and said, "Now start her up." That is why her name became "Snorky." The car instantly roared to life like it was shot from a gun. What a simple solution! Now, I could still be "The Flying Parson" car-wise, since I had grown used to purring along at about seventy.

Not long after Miriam arrived back home for her recess from college, she informed me that she would like to visit me sometime during the summer. Thelma Allan gladly invited her to stay with them, not far from where I was living. We met in Yarmouth as arranged and celebrated her arrival at a pleasant little restaurant which, of course, featured sea food. The table cloth was decorated in large checkered red and white squares. The meal was a fantastic lobster stew. Upon arriving back in Lake George, I introduced the love of my life to Neil and Thelma and their two children. We all inspected her room as Thelma requested. She had done it up attractively, flowers and all. I do not now remember how long Miriam stayed—not long enough for sure. She was one busy girl and so was I as we shared our company. She returned to Springhill long before my summer assignment was over. After her departure, my expectation of marrying a girl from Nova Scotia soared. Would it really happen? Church work now required renewed and revived attention, though it had not been neglected. Activities of the pastor were soon back to normal.

Another happening during that second summer also had a Shakespearean ending. I was taking a car full of young people home when an on-coming pick-up rounded a blind corner on the wrong side of the road. Horrified, I headed for the ditch, braking hard. Who should it be but the very person I boarded with, Bert Porter. As he turned widely, mouth hanging open, the rear end of his truck smashed into the front left side of my car. Though the light was broken, the fender was hardly dented. Do you believe the old hymn—"Whate'er betide, God will take care of you"? The kids were scared skinny. When I asked Bert, "Why were you on the wrong side of a wet road?" He simply replied, "I was trying to avoid the rocks on the other side." As it turned out, I was soon to appreciate the fact that my passengers overheard what he had said.

There were several Crosbys in the area, at least three associated with our church. Ron, a boy in the car, was also a Crosby and his dad signed my pay check. Unbeknown to me, Bert told Ron's dad that I was on the wrong side of the road. Fortunately, Ron, having overheard what Bert had said, told his dad about the comment Bert had made. Just to confirm the truth of the matter, I took Mr. Crosby to see what had in fact happened. Having stopped so suddenly, there were four tire marks imbedded at the side of the road which were half buried in the ground, along with a few shreds of glass in front still marking the spot.

There already existed a special relationship between myself and Ron as he had recently been told by some so-called "well-meaning" person that he had been adopted. The boy was deeply offended that his dad had never told him. When he shared his feelings with me, I could only say, "Your dad wanted you to know that you were really his son so that you would feel a special bond with him." That suggestion seemed to satisfy him. It is often better to tell an adopted young child that they are special because they were chosen. Years later, my first wife, Betty, and I told our adopted daughter that she was chosen especially to go with her older brother. She reported proudly to everyone, "My mommy chose me special to go with our Bob."

Another interaction with a Crosby family rang a different bell. An ancient gentleman by that same name lived with his two aged sisters. I often visited them as they were church members. Their usual format seemed to be sitting in rocking chairs in the kitchen on the shiny linoleum floor, rocking back and forth at the rate of a slow moving pendulum. Upon arrival one day, the rocking rate had doubled. My alarm bells sounded! I immediately thought, "There must be something wrong here?" Following the usual greeting, the elderly gentleman exploded, "Shameful, shameful, shameful!" He had just donated the land next to the church for the enlargement of the cemetery, perhaps thinking that they all would presently be occupants there. The truck which delivered the fence posts had driven across the resting place of many of the departed and had left deep ruts. This to him was sacrilegious. Telling him that the driver must not have known that the ground was very soft, I promised that I would cut out some sod from the ditch and fill the furrows as soon as possible, assuring him that by fall all traces of the unfortunate incident would have disappeared. He apparently accepted the solution. Once the fence was built and the damaged sod repaired, I returned to tell him that the ruts had already disappeared. He then gave me a new, expensive Strong's concordance which I used for more than fifty years. (It has since been replaced with Crudens which is much smaller and adequate for our present needs.)

This time when my final day arrived, it was vastly different from the previous year's—no last minute roar on a last minute arrival from Lulabelle. Along with most of the congregation, we were already assembled in the church. Once again, we celebrated with Thelma at the organ, special music and speaker (not me), roll call, and the annual splendid pot luck. My farewell remarks and benediction ended the service but not the feast. The congregation's gift of $55 and a card of thanks ended my second year as the Flying Parson of Lake George.

I returned to Boston in my second effort to graduate from Gordon College, but not the seminary. Miriam was now enrolled in a further course in nursing at Boston University. Unknown to me at the time, CBOMB, the organization which would have sent us to Africa as missionaries, had a requirement that one had to be a graduate in Theology in order to go to the mission field. The fear of failure continued to torment me. Being unable to pay for the last year's tuition with no prospect for a job and the new college assignment—"Practicum," which did not allow much time for employment anyway—haunted me as well. Snorky was also in need of critical repair. Everything seemed to be piling up. What to do now?

My starlight coupe had developed a very distressing habit of seeming to lose power when climbing hills. The rear main oil seal was leaking oil into the clutch housing with unwelcome results—the clutch slipped until friction burned off the oil and acrid smoke filled the car. The condition was too costly on my limited budget to repair. Upon returning to college and back at the dealership, they had a big, old touring car which became Studebaker number three, which I named "Her Majesty." This was to be my last involvement with Tom Faye and cars of that make as they ceased production in 1956. Studebakers had become a mish-mash of car parts from other companies. The body parts were designed by Studebaker engineers, but produced by Budd, who manufactured surface rail cars for rapid transit.

As "Practicum" was my first assignment back in college in my quest to become a teacher, I was assigned for a six-week duration to Mrs. Balcomb's grade five class in Topsfield near Boston. This experience was most enjoyable and has become one of my favourite memories of my college "daze." This dear lady was very kind to me. She reminded me of Miss Daley, my grade eight teacher in Nanton. She, too, had a delightful habit of cheering up the class during a dull, rainy day or on any occasion she pleased. One of my favourite memories was when we sang in two-part harmony. The class was divided in half, with our side singing the melody and hers the harmony. We also sang in rounds, row by row. What fun!

Another fond memory involved a classroom trip to the restored site of the 300 year old Saugus Iron works, where bog ore was turned into iron. The whole affair was both ancient and intriguing. The bellows system, for example, was just one: two alternating arms fixed to a shaft at ninety degrees which depressed two huge bellows about five or six feet long. Their sound resembled a giant animal's breathing. It had been restored by US Steel in 1948, at a cost of one and one half million dollars, a fortune at that time. This outing took most of the day.

My next fantastic outing with the Balcombs did not relate to teaching. As they were members of the Boston Symphony Orchestra, they treated me to an evening of classical music. This was the first time I ever rode in a '49 Buick with the newly designed hydramatic transmission, which was very popular at that time. I sat in the back seat between two bass violins while thinking of Miss Miriam Ross. I was wearing the tuxedo which Percy Kerfoot had given me for just such an occasion—what a joyous time! It was as though I had been transported into another world.

My romance with Miriam was progressing encouragingly. Since I was already two years behind her in graduating from Gordon, she took another advanced course in nursing at Boston University. We planned to meet for Christmas at her home in Spring Hill, Nova Scotia, as Miriam would already be there by the time I left. Three fellow students would be riding with me as far as Bangor, Maine. On the day before leaving Boston, the weather threatened to be stormy. That night it began to snow. By morning, ten inches had already accumulated on the ground. Despite my better judgement, the students persuaded me to leave anyway. Thus began the most horrible drive I was ever to experience in my life in my used 1955 four door Ford, newly bought by faith for $600 borrowed from a fellow student.

The car began ingesting snow on the motor, which caused it to misfire badly, then it soon began to backfire. We kept going until forced to stop to dry out the motor in a garage and to get warm—thirteen times in all. The roads were deadly, covered with snow and ice—once all my occupants fell flat while attempting to push me back onto the road. My male passenger actually slid under the car while shoving. He always insisted on sitting in the front by the totally inadequate, paltry heater while the two girls shivered in the back seat. Upon lifting my foot from the gas when we came to a long hill down into Bangor, the car began to rotate slowly as we descended. Three complete turns later, we stopped spinning and were right in the middle of the road as we entered the city.

The girls lived on a farm not far from town. Our challenges were not yet over. The main road was ploughed but the stone walls lining the lane to their house were filled with snow from top-to-top and from one side to the other. I took a deep breath while making a wide turn and put the pedal to the metal. "Black Beauty," as I called my Ford, lunged as the snow hurled past the windshield and over the car. We stopped dead in less than a hundred feet, still more than a mile from our destination. One girl used the door as a battering ram to clear the snow and leapt out only to find herself stuck in very deep snow. Her skirt was filled and she could not even take one step. She fell over and kicked out the snow and began walking. All of us followed in single file, seeking their house and its warmth. It seemed to take forever to make our way there through the three feet of freshly-fallen sticky snow.

What a welcome awaited us! Their parents had been frantic. I don't remember if we were able to phone ahead or not. After twenty-four hours behind the wheel, we had finally arrived. I was absolutely exhausted, both mentally and physically, and was glad for a good farm meal and bed. I slept most of the next day. How it happened, I do not now recall, but my car was by then in their yard and the lane had been ploughed. This storm was a one-time hit in many, many years. Since the day was far-gone and I was still extremely weary, I gladly accepted another night's hospitality. I do not now recollect what became of my other passenger—the fellow who sat by the heater the entire way. At that time, I concluded that this car probably had been made for use in California, but then, too, unknown to me for several years, the car had been in an accident involving the front end and the splash guard had been removed and not replaced.

My anticipation to spend Christmas in Springhill was rising but my troubles were not yet over. As entering the U.S.A. had not caused any problems, I expected no trouble to now arise because I am a Canadian. How wrong I was! Since the car had a U.S. license plate, I was in all likelihood under suspicion of trying to import my car. Since I was only on a visit and would shortly be returning to Boston, I was baffled. I was questioned like a criminal. After many phone calls and a very long boring delay in the guard-house, I was allowed to continue with a very stern warning: on arrival in Springhill, the car was not to be driven in Canada until my return to this very point of entry. You can only imagine my joy at being authorized to proceed. Much relieved, I left immediately and shortly was once again in St. John awaiting the departure of the ferry to Digby, which by now, was familiar territory.

On the way, I stopped at my uncle's place at Cambridge Station which was the home of the Trask Artesian Well Company and then saw my cousin, Jim, whom I had met along the South Shore the previous summer. After an interesting visit, a good meal, a night's sleep, and a tank of gas, I was on my way to my heart's desire. Uncle Sid had told me a great deal about the Trask family—they had lived in Nova Scotia since emigrating from Dorchester, Massachusetts, to be under the protection of the newly captured fort which was taken by the British commander, General Wolf.

Now begins one of my fondest memories of those long ago days—Christmas, 1956. As was once said, "Memories are the comfort of solitude" (and of old age and one's memoirs). The family consisted of three sisters—Christine, Miriam's mother, Lila, and Greta. They had all gathered at the Browns' farm on the hill, not far from town. The hill may have been where Springhill acquired its name (the town was also the birthplace of Anne Murray).

On the morning following my arrival, I had a chat with Clarence, Miriam's dad. Still giddy from her gladsome greeting, I thought protocol demanded that I ask her father's permission since he is the one who answers "I do" when asked who gives this bride away. When I had inquired of Christine as to what I should do, she had responded, "Now might be

a good time. He is downstairs shaking the clinkers out of the furnace."
Like Sir Galahad, I descended the stairs in fear and trepidation. Stiffening
my resolve, I blurted out, "May I have your permission to marry Miriam?"
His immediate response was, "Why don't you ask her? She is old enough."
End of conversation! I probably told Christine, whom I thought expected
a wedding. She was already very dear to me. As for Clarence, that was
another matter. You may remember my dad had married a Nova Scotia
lady and I was more than happy to do the same. Upon proposing marriage
to Miriam, her response was that she would think about it and give me her
answer another time. Since Miriam had requested that I join the family for
Christmas, I concluded there was a possibility that she would accept.

Two days before Christmas Day at the country farm, Miriam had
finished our wash and we were putting it away. As I did not see any "fancy-
pants" in the laundry, I picked up all the cotton undies and was about to put
them in my suitcase when Miriam said with a grin, "Do you think you can
wear mine, too?" Yes, hers were cotton too—no frilly undies for this frugal
and upright lady. A good chuckle was her response.

Since we were going to a wedding of mutual college friends that was
to take place during the summer in Halifax, Miriam had been making her
own dress in a burgundy coloured slinky material. It was already sewn up,
but not yet finished. She appeared with a formal, queenly curtsy, but after
looking at herself in the mirror, she frowned. The dress was on backwards
and she appeared to be rather flat-chested, so she departed to put the
dress on properly. The mirror now reflected the change and she was once
again her shapely self. As the slinky material would fray, she meticulously
bound all the seams. The time-consuming task was finally completed with
"splendid" results (as Percy Kerfoot would say).

On Christmas Day, we returned to the farm for "quite a spread" as one
would say in Kentucky. The house was resplendent with good smells and
the season's decorations. Most of the feast bore testimony to the fruits of
farming in them thar hills: cranberries, blueberry pie, and a table filled
with their garden veggies. Despite Clarence being somewhat distant, I felt
right at home. My main interest lay elsewhere while he was well-occupied
visiting his brothers-in-law, who were also relaxing following the festivities.
The evening passed quickly and all too soon, as far as I was concerned, it
was time to return to town and to bed as it had already grown late. Miriam

and I slept upstairs in a big L-shaped room—she on one leg of the L and me on the other.

During my time in Springhill, my Ford sat in the yard and never turned a wheel. It might have done so as I longed to use it to go about, but Miriam firmly stated, "No, just obey the restriction." With the glorious holiday over, Miriam returned to her studies elsewhere and I was on my way back to Boston. I drove west and south to St. John, thus I did not need to use the ferry from Digby. Upon arriving at the border, other guards were on duty—with only a glance at my notice of entry and required departure noted, I was soon on my way. In no time, I was back at Gordon for the last half of the school year, which began in earnest.

Toward the end of that college year, Miss Miriam Ross finally dashed my hopes. Having met her in 1952 during my first year of failure at Gordon, you may recall that she had said, "Don't expect a candle burning in my window when you return." However, I was overjoyed when I sat next to her on my arrival for the second time in "the Christian Home" course. Could it be possible that we might even join CBOMB together—The Canadian Baptist Overseas Mission Board—and go to Africa as missionaries? Now, I knew I'd be unable to meet the requirements scholastically at the end of round three at Gordon so I still had another year to go.

Miriam informed me that she had decided that she could not marry me and that she and our very dear friends, the Stairs, were all signed up with CBOMB and ready to leave for Africa. Since it was utterly impossible for her to continue a relationship where marriage was not its goal, she cut the string and bowed out of my life. The romance ended and I was utterly and completely crushed. She thanked me sincerely for the wonderful times we had had together and requested that I not contact her or even try. Never had I felt such darkness or despair—the pit opened before me and I feared that it was going to consume me in blackness. Everything had turned to dust. This defeat filled me with anguish for a long time and still has an effect on me to this very day. Simply recalling our parting has brought back a flood of unresolved feelings and the turmoil I suffered over the loss of a soul mate. Miriam had always treated me with respect—never a cross word or a criticism—and we had gotten along so very well.

Even though Miriam would be with them, I wanted to say goodbye to the Stairs. Thus it was that I drove to New York City alone to see them off.

Saying goodbye to Miriam with simply a casual handshake, she boarded the ship with the sisters. I watched the SS Saturnia sail away until it was a mere puff of smoke on the horizon. I returned to Boston and set into motion plans to take two make-up courses at Boston University in order to graduate the next spring. How good God proved to be—even while my heart was breaking!

By attending Boston University Summer School, I was able to complete the two required courses in order to graduate with a Bachelor of Education Degree in Elementary Education. I took mathematics and literature. My much-appreciated left-handed portable typewriter served me well for finishing assignments, but writing with my left hand was very difficult. My literature professor also taught the art of handwriting—which I found impossible. She said, "Don't even try to write, just print. For the letter "E," print 3 backward and the letter "A," as it is written." The problem was solved. I learned to print clearly, but not artistically. Now, years later after suffering several mini-strokes, it is still legible if I stay on the lines. However, the letter "E" is still the hardest to print, and also, by far, the most used vowel in the English language.

TEACHING SPECIAL NEEDS BOYS–1957

At this time, Mr. Gedney, my good friend and advisor, entered the picture. He was the psychologist who tried unsuccessfully to alleviate the phantom pain in my lost arm. He had a plan which helped to ease my troubled heart and financial dilemma. The public school in Wilmington was in immediate need of a Special Education Teacher—a new requirement under Massachusetts law. The third new teacher had suddenly quit. One of his students had pulled a sharpened kitchen knife from his hip pocket and declared, "You touch me and I will cut your guts out." With that conversation, the day ended for the entire class. What a way to get a holiday! As this appeared to be my only solution to my financial dilemma as well as college credit, I willingly agreed that if it could be arranged "I would give it a try," without really thinking about it or being able to discuss it with Miriam. To turn down a dare was never my habit—though this one did not appear to be much of a risk. After all, to threaten a handicapped man would not enhance a pupil's prestige, would it?

Lack of authorization from those in charge could well have ended the opportunity before it even began. There were four hurdles to overcome—first, college approval was required for Practicum; two, acceptance by the harried principal of the school; three, school board authorization; and four, immigration authorization to allow a Canadian to teach full time, rather than the permission I already had to work part time only. As I was not an American citizen, I wondered if this all actually was legally possible. My meeting with the principal of the school was soon arranged. After his evaluation of my ability to meet the challenge, he concluded the interview with these words: "You will need the strength of Sampson, the wisdom of Solomon, and the patience of Job." These requirements sounded humanly impossible for any one person—and so they proved to be for me as well. The principal cleared his throat just as my hand touched the doorknob as I was leaving. He said, as I turned to look, "By the way, don't turn your back on the class and put anything on the board only when the room is empty." Even I understood those suggestions.

The kids did not enjoy a long holiday. I was introduced to the class on the next Monday morning—having had no time to prepare and little time to investigate the resources of the classroom along with no real experience. All seemed in order as we entered the room. I was introduced simply with "Mr. Davis will be your new teacher," coupled with a few other remarks. What did these "scoundrels" think of a timid-looking young man with only one arm, who smiled feebly as he escorted the principal to the door. As for me, I was probably more frightened than Daniel when he bounced off the floor at the bottom of the lions' den. He was fearless and I was not! As I tried to gather my wits, I drew a long breath and re-entered the classroom. The change was explosive—*pandemonium* had erupted. The entire class was playing chicken-out with their combination chair and desk sets in deadly earnest. So, I simply crawled to my desk on all three of my limbs—one hand, two knees—and hid behind it with my nose on the desk while surveying the scene from barely visible eyes. Since some knuckles were likely to get smashed, I raised a rather seemingly silly question, "Who is boss around here anyway?" As you might have guessed, it was the big lad who had wielded the sharpened kitchen knife. It reminded me of another day, not all that long ago, when I had descended the steps to the basement to the vegetable room at Prairie Bible Institute. The same fear and trepidation arose now as I faced a far more daunting task.

Dawn now cracked on Marble-head. "*What do I do now?*" I asked mentally. Out loud, I enquired, "And what is your name?" He said, "Richard White." I then instructed the class to put their desks in place and sit where they liked. A lot of pushing and shoving followed, while I sat deciding, "*What next?*" Later, I came to realize that God had prepared me to some extent, along with His unfailing help, for just such a task. My minor study had been Psychology—that's what determines our feelings and our responses to circumstances. Now, I was given the chance to put it to the test—of reality. The class looked at me strangely. How was I to interpret that look? Did it mean, "Here we go again—we will give this one a hard time, too, and see if he can take it unlike the three others who had quit"? Awareness flooded in that this was only vaguely similar to the time with the vegetable crew.

As there is only one chance to make a first impression, what should I do? It seemed that trying to lay down the law with threats and presumed authority would not be the best way. It had proved to be an ineffective method in my own experience with authority figures during my school days when I was the "bad boy," so why would it work now? So I said, "In our class, it will not be us and them" (meaning the teacher). "It will just be 'we.' I am on your side! We will all work together as one class. I will help you all I can. As you all can see, I only have one arm and I will need your help. Now, what would you like to learn about? That is why I am here." Richard White, without a minute's pause, asked, "What happened to your arm?" Some kids looked surprised, so I simply said, "I had a bad accident on the farm in Alberta when I was 21 years old. When you know me better and I know more about you, and if you are brave enough and have a strong stomach, I will tell you all about it."

I proceeded to take charge. "You will have your first assignment now. You must have learned something along the way. I need your name or what I should call you, your age and your birthday. Don't bother telling me you hate school, but you can tell me what you do not like about school. If you do not like to write, at least be sure I have your name, age, and birthday. I have trouble writing with my left hand so I understand if you do not want to write. Put up your hand and we will all listen, but write or print the information on the space remaining if you want to. Richard, who would you like to pass out the paper?" He promptly chose a shy-looking little boy in the back corner. "You will have enough time to give me your name, age, and birthday. While you work at that, I will put some ideas on the board as to what you might like to do. Remember, this teacher might have eyes in the back of his head. If you need any help, and I don't see your hand, just say 'Teacher' or 'Mr. Davis' and I will come give you a hand, but not the only one I have."

This conversation on my first day in class has been reconstructed both by lessons I learned along the way and by my now-failing memory. Success was not evident immediately, but over time, which included much patience, hard work, and trial and error along with many good days and many hard days, we achieved some success—one which still sticks in my memory is superlative.

As you may imagine, only some of the boys chose to tell something about themselves. The few who tried to write did not do at all well. I was surprised how quickly the morning passed. My evaluation of the students was not encouraging in the least. My last request before lunch was "Who will volunteer to bring a book to class from the library after lunch? I will read it to you all." No book arrived. "So," I said, "after you have had a little time to rest, since some of you look pretty tired, let's go play ball then." No one disagreed.

A new surprise awaited me. Richard gave the ball to a promising-looking lad and left with the bat. Upon arriving, only some of the bases were covered. When the first strike was pitched across the plate, the ball landed far out in the field—no one was there and no one went for the ball. Richard picked up the bat when crossing home plate and chased the next pitcher until he retrieved the ball. Then, the same feat was repeated. Ball did not seem to interest the few who had been part of this fiasco. Having seen enough, we returned to class. As a result of our first attempt to play ball, I took matters into my own hands and suggested to them that we play ball according to my rules and really learn how the game is played. There was general agreement—even "Whitey," as Richard was called, did not disagree.

Fast forwarding to near the end of the school year, it was obvious that their ability had now much improved. Since my kids took a lot of verbal abuse from other classes who considered themselves to be superior, I suggested, "How would you like to challenge the grade sevens to a game of ball?" They were dumbfounded. Whitey asked (in paraphrase), "Do you really think we can beat them?"—he actually used words which were considerably more graphic! I replied, "Richard, we can really take the wind out of their sails." The grade seven regular class readily accepted the challenge. As it turned out, the grade seven teacher, acting as the umpire, asked me to end the game after seven innings as they were already so badly defeated. You can hardly imagine how jubilant our class was—they were just like the winning team who captured the Stanley Cup in hockey or won the "World Serious" (as one of my classmates from long ago in Canada called the World Series). Following this complete humiliation of that grade seven class, most of the students my kids met in the halls stopped harassing them.

To relate all the ups and downs as well as stresses of teaching Special Needs children would be superfluous. However, I will share just one more event as an example. Every class had an intercom connected to the main office. Whenever we heard the tell-tale click of the connection which included all classrooms, we listened carefully to hear from the "voice of God," as it was called by my class, because it often related to general problems in the school. The authoritative voice demanded on one occasion that if anyone knew where the chrome fittings from the boys' bathroom had gone, they should expose the culprits as it had happened more than once and required some expertise. When I asked Richard on the QT what was happening, I was surprised when he told me. After all these years, I have learned a little something about schools, principals, secretaries, and janitors. However, it amazes me what Special Needs children know about authorities and what really goes on in the school system, and that kids don't "squeal" on one another. This is what Richard told me: "Cheese, Mr. Davis, they take 'em off and tro' dem out the winnow. They land on the roof, and then they climb up the fire escape ladder at night and pick 'em up." I "forgot" to tell the authorities as Richard never gave me any names, plus by then we had become friends.

While all this was taking place, the outside world carried on as usual. One event stands out—a very pleasant one. Earlier, I had attended a local church to scout out the possibility of living in Wilmington. To my surprise, when chatting with an older lady following the service and sharing with her why I was there, she said, "Let me talk to my husband and you can come and stay at our house." I could hardly wait until the next Sunday, when she said, "Yes, you can." What a relief as travelling back and forth, especially in the morning, was very difficult, expensive, and time-consuming. I already had more on my plate than I could really manage.

This lady actually became almost like a mother to me. I felt like a spoiled Italian boy who almost never left home. All my physical needs were cared for more than bountifully. Mrs. Woodman provided food, shelter, and laundry along with an abundance of extras. She was especially helpful in giving me an understanding of the home situation and the area in which most of my boys lived. Had it not been for her care, I, too, may have gone the way of the previous teachers of the special needs boys in Wilmington. Later, I learned that my having gained authority to teach bordered on the miraculous! Also, God blessed me in providing a comforter and encourager in my landlady, especially during this time when I needed it most. Being given authority to teach in Wilmington for the entire year fulfilled all my graduation requirements, as I received full credit for the course in Practicum. With that, I finally succeeded in graduating from Gordon, which I left behind with mixed feelings of sadness and relief.

Though my return trip to Boston in my beloved old jalopy Lulabelle remains firmly imprinted on my mind as though written in stone, the memory of my return trip to Alberta has evaporated from the sticky side of my mind like molasses dissolving in hot water. Black Beauty, my trusty '55 Ford, evidently brought me to my home province without any problems, including crossing the border into Canada.

Aunt Alice had moved back to Calgary after the death of her hubby and was living alone in a beautiful old two-storey house at the top of the hill, across from Crescent Heights Baptist Church in Rosedale, a beautiful district north of the Center Street Bridge. After a very heart-warming reunion with my adopted family at Spring Creek Farm in Okotoks, Alberta, Aunt Alice asked me to live with her while I looked for a job teaching in Calgary. Since obtaining a position to teach Special Needs boys in Massachusetts had miraculously come down from heaven in my time of extreme financial stress, little did I know that my chances of another position would be a real problem in Alberta! Number one, my degree from Gordon College was not recognized in Canada. Number two, I was not even a high school graduate in standing with Alberta requirements. Number three, I was not eligible to teach at any school in Alberta consequently. What now? Once again, a solution which seemed impossible but most promising appeared out of the blue, beginning another interesting chapter in the book of my life.

The headmaster of Strathcona School for Boys offered me a position. This school catered to the needs of wealthy families and enjoyed a good reputation in the city. I was hired to teach all subjects in grades seven to nine, which proved to be much more daunting than teaching slow learners in Wilmington. Most of the boys were just spoiled brats who had little respect for a one-armed teacher who was in a trial so far over his head that he could never touch bottom. This school was patterned after the Lancaster School system in England. For example, the school uniform was the required attire. Students were called by their family name, i.e. brothers were known as Ronisch One and Ronisch Two. There were only a few worthy exceptions amid this motley crew. One snooty lad felt it his duty to tell me, "My old man could buy and sell you ten times and still have lots of money in the bank." I was sorely tempted to smack him along-side his head but, of course, did not.

I soon learned that my boss was not all sugar and spice either. When I asked, "May I park my car in the driveway?" he replied, "No, my wife may want to go shopping." When one of his darling millionaire scoundrels hurled a big stone at one of his classmates and smashed my car window, he simply said, "That's one of the perils associated with parking on the street." No compensation from the headmaster, no discipline for the boy, and no request to the parent to pay recompense. All the students knew who threw the rock but no one named the culprit. Another unexpressed clause in my contract required me to supervise their after-school sports activities until five o'clock. The work of travelling across city driving north to south both morning and evening plus getting assignments ready for class the next day was gruelling. However, a more pleasant surprise awaited me before the end of the most horrible of my numerous years of teaching.

Mom and Dad – "Edith and Jasper Davis"

Brother Bill, Dad, Brother Don with Jim in front – 1940

Jim and "Lulabelle" – Mid 1950s

Lucy and Percy Kerfoot

Jim and his wife, Betty – Early 1960s

Jim in the classroom, Northmount School, Calgary

Betty and Jim with children, Beth and Bob
Thompson, Manitoba – August 10, 1967

Jim and Trish's Wedding – 1984

My Workshop – Chair in progress

Camping, 2004 – Jim, Trish, and "Willie"

Son Bob's Wedding – August, 2009
Beth, Michelle, Bob, Trish, and Jim

Sale of House – Jim and Trish – 2010

II

BETTY

COURTSHIP

"For this reason a man shall leave his father and mother and be joined to his wife, and the two shall become one flesh"; so then they are no longer two, but one flesh. (Mark 10:7-8, NKJV)

Shortly after my arrival in Alberta, my wife-to-be entered the picture. Aunt Alice and Emma Bruce lived on the same street. Mrs. Bruce was Aunt Alice's good friend and her weekly bridge partner of many years; their Thursday night sessions were a regular must in the lives of several of Emma's friends, whom she referred to as "the girls."

One stormy winter night, it was Alice's turn to have the girls in for bridge. When I arrived home around 11:00, the ladies were anxiously getting ready to leave. I helped Emma into her beautiful black sable fur coat and offered to take anyone home who did not have a ride. As soon as Emma returned home, she told her daughter, Betty, that she had met the nicest young man at Alice's.

"Why," Emma exclaimed, "he helped us with our coats and even offered to drive us home!"

Emma and Aunt Alice thought this girl and I just might hit it off. Consequently, my aunt suggested that I might like to meet Betty. Arrangements were made for a foursome date on Remembrance Day 1958, agreed upon by all.

During the intervening days, I kept quizzing Aunt Alice about her friend's daughter, and aside from a few general remarks, she reminded me that Friday night would arrive soon enough, and then I could form my own conclusions. At least we were going out to supper. That would get this first date underway early in the evening. Though I didn't have much choice in terms of my wardrobe, I did want to look presentable, so I dressed accordingly.

When Emma phoned to say that they would be along in a few minutes, I wanted to stampede down the stairs and be standing at attention when they arrived. Such was not the modus operandi for Alice, and I knew I should cool my anticipation and let things unravel at their own rate. It seemed an age before we heard Emma's little *toot-toot*, letting us know that they were waiting. As Alice put one last Victorian daub of powder on her nose—she was not to be hurried—I wanted to bound down the stairs, yelling, "I'm coming, I'm coming," but that hardly seemed fitting. I fantasized that with Emma as the chauffer and my aunt getting into the front, no choice would be left for me but to get in beside that gorgeous creature in the back. However, Betty was appropriately seated beside her mother, so I ushered Aunt Alice into the rear seat and walked around to the door on the driver's side. I hoped there would be a different seating arrangement on the way home.

For some reason, I do not remember the meal at Tiffany's on Sixteenth Avenue, but I know that the food must have been delightful. Emma spearheaded the conversation. I realized that she was asking questions for Betty's benefit with either Alice or me quite content to give the answers she already knew. Yes, I had just graduated from Gordon College. Yes, I was teaching at Strathcona School for Boys. Betty had once attended St. Hilda's, the female counterpart.

When the meal was completed, Emma insisted that it was her treat. We stepped out into the chilly November evening with Emma and Alice walking side by side, engrossed in rehashing their most recent bridge encounter, leaving me to escort Betty. *"Should I offer her my arm or should I walk along beside her and let her take her own chances with high heels and cracks in the sidewalk?"* To my surprise and delight, she slipped her dainty, gloved hand into the crook of my arm and looked at me as if to say, "Well, poker face, what do you have to say for yourself?"

Sucking in two deep lungs full of crisp evening air, I searched the contents of my over-stuffed mind for something impressive to say. Just them, a blue 1959 Gullwing Chevy sloshed by and turned into the parking lot. The long, knife-edge on the trunk gleamed in the streetlight. Without thinking, I blurted out, "What do you think of that monstrosity?" Cars were my second passion, so I was sure this would arouse a lengthy and heated discussion. Her casual, "Oh, I guess it is a bit extreme," served to open and close the conversation in one brief sally.

"*Oh, well,*" I silently concluded, "*perhaps cars don't hold the same passion with this gal that they do with me.*"

When we arrived back at the car, Alice and Emma got into the front seat. Opening and closing doors for three gals all at once seemed a bit too demanding. Here we were, side by side in the back seat and that was just fine with me.

The old theatre at the bottom of the Tenth Street hill had been well-known for many years, and that was where we headed on this first evening together. We attended a movie which I still remember well. The film depicted a running gun battle between an Australian cattle rustler and his sons and a law-enforcement agency similar to our Mounties. The conflict raged across a large region of the outback. Early in the movie, one of the officers was killed. Ultimately, all the rustlers died except the youngest son. The colour was fantastic. In one scene, which I recall with delight—after all, memory is "that inward eye which is the bliss of solitude," as the worthy bard Wordsworth has written—a square-rigged, sailing ship bowed gently before a soft breeze, its prow biting through white-capped rollers with its downy sails billowing. I don't remember how the ship got into the story, but it sure left me with a beautiful and cherished memory of that night.

The vast panorama of the desolate outback unrolled before us with its occasional outcrop of barren rocks where one gun battle after another reverberated with the whine of ricocheting rifle bullets. The occasional kangaroo bounded from the sparse brush, fleeing in two-legged wonder across the uneven terrain. I marvelled at the miracle of filming their flight. They were so close that you could see the expression in their eyes. Though they must have been terrified, they retained an expression of detached indifference, which I thought was the prerogative of the camel alone. Perhaps, the kangaroo is a modified Australian dromedary, fitted with a special overdrive. My hand secretly found Betty's in one of those early scenes when blood and bullets mingled with the boulders. At thirty years of age, I wondered, "Is this the end of my yearning to find a mate?" I had graduated from two schools of learning which had a fair batting average in the matrimonial department. Of one it was said, "They took in souls, kicked out heels, and turned out pairs." The other was touted as a school of missions and matrimony. I had regularly played the game of matchmaking for others and had even been asked to sing at some of their weddings, but so far, I remained unhitched.

The failure of my most recent matrimonial effort still brought a dull ache to the pit of my stomach. Sometimes it became a gnawing truth that defied relief. "*Will this friendship bring an end to my longing?*" I silently questioned. Unknown to me at that time, Betty had her own disappointments and frustrations. She, too, had nearly married a Nova Scotian and had just returned from a trip down east which had failed to fulfill her expectations. Though she was her mother's pride and joy, and appreciated her love and attention, Betty longed to live her own life and had found no easy way to liberty. Surely, now I could support a wife. Surely, the loss of my good right arm would not be a serious handicap. Surely, I had done my best to prepare myself to be a contributing part of our society. I wondered what Betty thought of me. I continued to contemplate these facts as the bullets flew and this warm, inviting hand fit so perfectly in mine. "*Will this Betty be the girl of my dreams, or will this be another experience of heartache and sorrow?*"

With the end of the movie and our first parting, which came all too soon, I could not sense any immediate acceptance of me on Betty's part. At least she didn't seem to mind my holding her hand. That was about all a fellow could manage in the semi-darkness of a theatre with a watchful potential mother-in-law and an observant aunt nearby. Emma appeared to never miss a trick and Aunt Alice was no slouch, whether it was bridge, business, or personal relationships.

Alice, my favourite auntie, was the only one of my mother's sisters that I had met before my stint in college. She had been a special friend to me since the death of my mother when I was eight. Since my home in the town of Nanton was poor and plain, Auntie's house in Rosedale was a palace by comparison. When I was eleven and hitch-hiking to where my uncle was working in Cochrane, I had stopped at her house for what I hoped would be a snack and a bit of encouragement. When she opened the front door of her pretty palace, I really wanted to make a good impression. I had tucked in my shirt and slicked down my hair, but when I stepped through the front door in response to her welcome invitation, my feet hit the scatter rug and I skidded under her skirts. Often my attempts to make a good impression ended in disaster. Would meeting Betty be another?

Bouncing Betty Bruce, often a winner in the Rosedale Bowling League, was a very appealing young lady and a pleasing prospect for marriage. Betty's full name was Frances Elizabeth and she had graduated with a diploma in Clothing and Design from the Provincial Institute of Technology and Art (PITA) in Calgary on May 31st, 1955, where she now was a very dedicated and enthusiastic instructor who taught Fashion Accessories, Millinery and Basic Sewing. PITA opened its doors in 1916 and was the first publicly-funded technical institute in Canada. In 1960, PITA was renamed the Southern Alberta Institute of Technology (SAIT) and the art department, although still part of SAIT, became the Alberta College of Art (ACA).

Betty had never attended university and was the only teacher ever hired at PITA/SAIT simply on her ability to sew, without any formal teaching education in that area. Betty had an uncanny ability to match people and patterns, much to their satisfaction. Suggestions like "Shorten the waist of a Butterick pattern, number so-and-so—you will like the dress and it will suit you very well," were typical examples of her guidance. Usually, the student followed her keen directions and was thrilled with the result. Previously, she had been a secretary at the Cathedral Church of the Redeemer in downtown Calgary for several years.

That first evening, we parted with me expressing the hope of seeing Betty soon. However, my wishes in this regard were thoroughly thwarted in the next few days. Always, Emma answered the phone and I was a bit hesitant to be too inquisitive about Betty. More than a week went by before I saw her again. In fact, she was just as anxious to see me as I was to see her. She, too, was wondering if married life was going to pass her by, although it was long afterward before she shared this concern with me. Time to get really acquainted was in short supply since I was kept busy with my teaching duties and Betty taught all week as well as some evenings, but presently on a Saturday, the possibility of living "happily ever after" did become a reality.

The following Sunday, Betty answered the phone when I called, and suggested that I come right over even though the Bruces had company. When Emma introduced me to the Chief of Police for the City of Calgary, my composure nearly collapsed. The habit of driving my '55 black Ford at the comfortable speed of eighty miles an hour often gave me real pangs of guilt, especially if I happened to see a police car in the vicinity. The previous Sunday, I was returning to Calgary from Okotoks after having bragged to Ma and Pa Kerfoot that I had just met a real living, lovely lady by the name of Betty Bruce. "Dear Lord," I fervently prayed as I drove, "You take care of her salvation and I'll take care of her matrimonial status!" I knew that she was a church-going girl even if it was the Anglican denomination, but I did not know if she had experienced saving faith. Black Beauty was moving right along as I approached the city from the south. Just as I topped the rise at the Shell station doing my usual speed, a police car popped up the other side of the hill. I held my breath as I applied the brakes and peered through the rear-view mirror. Though I saw no blinking lights and heard no siren as I proceeded at the legal rate, I worried that they had put out an APB on a black Ford and that it would just be a matter of time before I was apprehended.

Thinking that the Chief of Police might have this information, I was positive that should he look out the window and see the offending vehicle, I would be arrested even though the man was not in uniform—not a good way to start a prospective courtship. Earlier in the week, Lucy Kerfoot had called to tell me that the Okotoks police wanted to ask me a few questions. On the way to Okotoks the previous week, I had given a ride to a hitchhiker who said Okotoks was his destination. Unfortunately, he relieved the till at the local hotel of the daily receipts prior to his departure and the police had been informed that he had arrived in town with a one-armed bandit who was driving a black Ford. Subsequently, these matters were cleared, but in the first few frightening seconds of introduction, all these thoughts flew through my head as I surveyed my record, praying fervently that my past had not caught up with me. Much to my relief, the chief seemed more interested in turning in a good account of his canvassing on behalf of the church and the conversation continued to flow in that direction.

Shortly, however, my attention was arrested by a vision in orange standing in the entrance way. The mirror above the fireplace reflected a beautiful creature in a flowered orange dress with pleated skirt and puffy sleeves. "My, this beautiful gal is one smart dresser, too," I observed. The reflection allowed me the opportunity to have a good look without seeming to stare, but the presence of the austere officer of the law was making me feel uncomfortable. Before long, I excused myself and hoped for a better time to see this desirable lady again. The vision of her beckoned me back with unrelieved intensity during the next few days.

Being Mr. Helpful seemed as good a way as any to impress her so I embarked on such a course. Since Betty taught at SAIT during the evening several days a week, I appointed myself as her personal taxi and was pleased to discover that she found this service quite acceptable, even if I did run out of gas the very first time that I performed in this capacity. Since I had boasted "I never run out of gas," we both had a good laugh on me. When Betty told me that she had been invited to speak to a group of women in Parkland, I happily offered my chauffeuring services. The sky was threatening that winter evening as we left the city, but I was not concerned. *"A little snow makes for lots of togetherness when travelling,"* I mused as we sped south—a trip of well over an hour each way. When we arrived at our destination, a few fluffy flakes were floating down. With the meeting over, we stepped out into a gale and faced a full-fledged blizzard. The feeling of contentment was abruptly replaced with a real concern—ground-drift, about a foot deep, completely obscured the highway. Few cars graced the road and the fences were far apart and not visible in our headlights. A night in the car on our first unchaperoned date did not seem an acceptable solution and finding a place to stop was not a viable option. We agreed that we had little choice but to return to the city, though Black Beauty's tendency to stall when ploughing snow or driving into heavy drifts added to my concerns. The memory of the terrible trip just two years previous from Boston to Bangor, Maine, through one of the worst storms in the history of New England, still haunted me and was an experience I did not wish to repeat.

Snow snakes slithered at us as we crept forward through the storm. At times, the road was completely obliterated. Near midnight, we still had about seventy miles to travel. Miniature white meteors streaked toward the windshield and staring through them was a mesmerizing experience. With both of us straining to visually affirm our position on the road by a glimpse of a white line on the pavement, the miles and the minutes wore away at an agonizing pace. Our conversation consisted of assurance and guidance in our snail-like progress home—not the kind of ride that facilitates cozy conversation, but one that nevertheless affirmed togetherness. It was a relief that I had known the road since childhood and had driven it many times. Our spirits lifted when we had safely passed the half-way mark without the car sputtering, missing or stalling (as had occurred so often during my New England ordeal). As we passed the Amylorne Cabins on the outskirts of the city, I considered asking Betty, "Should we seek refuge for the night?" but I stifled the urge. If I kissed her that night, I do not remember, but my gratitude and relief upon a safe arrival home was heartfelt and profound.

By Christmas of 1958, Betty and I decided to enter what Peter Marshall referred to as "the halls of highest human happiness." As June is the most appropriate month for weddings, we set the date for that month in 1959. On the last day of the year, the time and opportunity arose so we decided that it would be appropriate to visit Betty's mother at her employment to share our good news with her. Our plan was that if we told her when she was at work and she did not like the idea, she would have to keep her composure while she was at the office and would have time to simmer down before she got home. We entered the old CFCN office on 12th Avenue S.E. with all the joy of a couple in love who very much wanted to share their expectations with all the world.

Emma wielded a great deal of authority and influence in an office next to the president, Mr. Love. She had been his secretary and accountant for years and much enjoyed the prestige of her position. We wondered what her reaction would be to our announcement. A visit from both of us at her office in the middle of the day was surely an indication of something out of the ordinary. After clearing her throat several times in a chug-a-rum fashion, Mrs. Bruce looked us both over very carefully with what seemed to be an expression of surprise and satisfaction, ran her fingers down her ever present pencil, turned it over and repeated the performance several times as was her habit when weighty matters needed attention, and then pronounced in a very matter-of-fact manner, "Well, I guess that will be alright," confirming neither surprise nor displeasure. We didn't wait for the rebuttal, but suspected one was already brewing. Later, we learned that she enlivened all departments immediately upon our departure by bursting in on them with the news, "Betty and Jim are going to be married in June!"

For more than a quarter of a century, Emma Bruce had served as confidante, advisor and consultant to a host of employees in matters of matrimony and finances. Gordie Carter, the boss' son-in-law, and Bob Lamb, the chief technician, were very much her boys. She both chided and scolded them as she thought necessary. In return, they teased and admired her. Ever available, wise and sensitive in counsel, she had endeared herself to the hearts of many. Betty's father had died from pneumonia following gallbladder surgery when Betty was only six months old. Bereaved and almost destitute, Emma immediately sought work and found a job as sales clerk at Eaton's at a pitiable wage. Gramma Bruce, not long a widow herself, took over the housekeeping duties and the renovated family carried on in the new mould.

About six months later, Emma answered an ad to be secretary to Mr. Love, manager of the infant radio station, CFCN. Armed with her shorthand and typing skills from her high school days in Mellette, South Dakota, she went for the job interview. To many, Mr. Love appeared to be a very gruff, distant, and demanding employer. Such was far from the truth. Her position at CFCN began a rewarding and loyal relationship between employee and employer which was terminated only by death. Emma never remarried, though I am sure it was not for lack of opportunity. Her work became her life and the family arrangement suited her well. When Granma Bruce died, Betty began to assume the responsibility of running the house. This setup pleased Emma, but it was one from which Betty wished to be delivered. Though Emma was not a domineering person, she had a strong personality. I'm sure that she did not realize that Betty was not only not her little girl any longer, but that she, too, longed for freedom and a niche of her own.

Our backgrounds were very different. Betty grew up in the city on a very short string. She told me that when she was a little girl, she would call to her friends across the street, "Please come and play with me because I can't cross the street." No such restrictions ever barred my liberty. With my mother dead and my father working far from home, I ranged the countryside like a wandering star. This difference in background necessitated a great deal of adjustment when it came to raising our own children. It became known as the battle of the long and short string.

We often went out to the farm to visit Emma's brother George and his wife Etta. George was father-figure to Betty and she was in all probability his favourite niece. When we visited her Uncle George following our engagement, he took her aside and asked, "Do you realize he has only one arm?" What an observation! Though he did not initially welcome me into the family because of my condition, in the course of time, he overcame his reluctance. I was always willing and available to give Uncle George a 'helping hand'—pun intended—and became the first male relative he would call on for handyman services.

For years, Betty and Emma had enjoyed the trip to Lyalta for Sunday dinner. Etta was a cook of cooks. No dinner was complete without at least three kinds of vegetables, two meats, and an assortment of desserts.

George was a little deaf, a factor that stood him in good stead when required. Etta was a good farmwife, his second, and well-acquainted with the neighbourly news. Her opinion as to what-was-what and what should be done here and there was often put forth with conviction. George just became a little harder of hearing when their beliefs did not agree. Debate concerning those who were not present was not his forte.

Once, however, his impairment brought him a split second from death. A rarely-used railroad bisected his land diagonally. Since the crossing on the main road was near the house, he quite often needed to go over the tracks with his John Deere tractor on his way to and from the field. As Uncle George was as deaf as a stone post, he evidently neither saw nor heard the screech of a fast-approaching freight train. Because the recoil on the John Deere seat acted as a catapult, he had fortunately stood up and leaned forward to avoid "the kick in the pants" from hitting a big bump, just as the train roared by, narrowly missing Uncle George but not the fender. The train proceeded to take the rear fender from the tractor, ruining the tire in the process. Fortunately, George did not get a scratch. When I saw the damaged tire by the workshop and asked George how it happened, he said, "Oh, I just had a little accident." The reason for the faraway look in his eye was explained to me later, with the suggestion that the incident was a prohibited topic of conversation.

After losing my good right arm, I was informed by Solomon in Ecclesiastics 9:11 that *time and chance happen to all*" (NIV). If you are in the jaws of the God-ordained laws of physics, the result is inevitable—it cannot be avoided by man but by God only.

George had another little experience shortly following his retirement and his move to Calgary, Since he was still a farmer at heart, Uncle George invested in a new rototiller. The old "poom, poom, poom" of his John Deere was to be replaced with this machine's busy sound. On his first attempt to use the rototiller, just like the Titanic, disaster struck. He still wore his bib overalls most of the time and the pant cuffs were a little frayed. George was just getting the hang of turning the little monster when one of the diggers grabbed his tattered cuff. Try as he may, George could not get away from the churning, whirling teeth of that half-pint machine. In his haste to escape the snarling beast, he didn't think to shut it off. Falling over, he and the machine began rolling in mortal combat. He was much too occupied with his fast-disappearing overalls to grab the spark plug wire. By the end of the ordeal, the rototiller was still chewing away on his clothes and Uncle George was standing in his BVDs. This time, however, he bore a few bruises. Though the topic was once again rated taboo, he was certainly teased by his friends afterwards. "You sure are no city farmer either!"

Betty had fallen heir to the Bruce house on Seventh Avenue NW and we were anticipating living there as soon as we were married. I often teased Betty, "You have a house, a fur coat, and a fur jacket. What man could turn down a bargain like that?" When February rolled around, Betty told the tenants that we would like to have the house in June, thinking that it was thoughtful to let them know of our intentions early so that they would have time to look for another place to live. She also requested they stay until the end of May. Two weeks would be enough time for us to tidy the place before moving in. To our surprise, the tenants found a house immediately and moved out at the end of February, explaining, "Well, we found another house that we like, and you know how it is trying to find suitable accommodation in Calgary." The loss of revenue for three months and an empty house did not seem to concern the Bruce women.

Damage deposits were not customary then. Upon inspecting the house, we discovered many things which needed work. The floors in the bedroom were fir, and nicely varnished once upon a time. When I asked what the round white marks on the floor were, the lady of the house casually explained that I would understand it better when I had kids of my own—I didn't! When we asked what had happened to the briquettes in the gas stove in the fireplace, she responded, "Well, the kids like to ride their trikes in the house." About the crayon marks on the walls, we did not bother to enquire.

When we returned to the car, I expected the tenants to get a real tongue-lashing in absentia, but Betty merely said, "Good, I always wanted to renovate that house anyway. Gramma Bruce used to let the cats do their business in the sink and the thought of washing dishes in it sickens me. I hate that old tub in the bathroom, and those old floors need to be replaced anyway. We'll soon fix those white patches in the bedroom."

This woman's matter-of-fact way of handling problems never ceased to amaze me. We discussed what we would like to do and I found it easy to agree with her suggestions: I usually liked what she liked, she was paying the bill, and I found it quite hard to change her mind when she had the bit in her teeth. Before we had turned the corner, Betty had the whole job completed in her mind. She knew instantly who was the best person to call for each job and exactly what she wanted done. Though much of the work on the house was hired out, a great deal of it was left for us to do and we went at the tasks with delight and enthusiasm. We repainted most of the house ourselves and Betty chose to make the drapes. Being in love, nothing appeared to be daunting and working together proved to be a pleasure.

The main tasks fell to the plumber and the flooring man. Both had been in business in Calgary since year one. To save a few dollars, I tore up the old fir floor and flung the tattered boards out the window. The little old plumber was so bow-legged that you could run a wheelbarrow between his legs without touching them, but he knew his job well. The elderly gentleman who did such a beautiful job on our bedroom floors had laid flooring for so long that he could hardly walk. The sides of his old boots were so worn that his socks were sticking out. When these two ancient craftsmen finished their job, I acknowledged that Betty knew a thing or two about subcontracting.

Meanwhile, we were shopping for bargains in furniture. Upon going down to Neilson's during a sale, we found a beautiful chocolate brown chesterfield and chair that had been returned to the warehouse because of non-payment. Betty had a nose for deals. "That's good," she evaluated quickly, "Those wide flat arms are just right for sitting a cup of coffee on. The back is not as high as it should be, but that's okay." She asked them to deliver it the first week of June. On the way to the service elevator, Betty spied an old oak dining room suite gathering dust and looking most forlorn. The glint of the sadly streaked mirror caught her eye. The beautiful, leaded glass in the buffet doors was pushed in, and the pedestal leg of the round table was split in two. "Jim," she cried in ecstasy, "Could you restore this old suite?"

Upon examining the suite, I was surprised to see that it suffered more from neglect than real damage, although there were cigarette burns on the table top, the webbing on the chairs was broken, and the seats were tattered. As our eyes met, we gloated over this discovery, but we dared not transmit our eagerness to the somewhat bored salesman who had had quite enough of two starry-eyed bargain hunters. It did not appear to sit well with him that the chesterfield suite had to be stored until June. "How much for the dining room suite?" Betty inquired, holding her breath. "Forty dollars," he resolutely responded, "if you take it today!" That was exactly what we had allowed for it. We could have danced for joy, but by the time it graced our dining room in its restored splendour, we had a much greater appreciation of what that transformation required. Neilson's delivered the wreck to 134 – 7th Avenue N.W. the following afternoon, and I was there at four o'clock to let them in. They dumped the trashy-looking assortment of dusty pieces on the dining room floor with an air of relief, and departed with my signature on the bill.

Time was moving on and we wondered if we would have our dream house ready for occupancy by June 20, with Betty teaching and me committed to the Strathcona School for Boys. The responsibility of supervising sports after the regular school day added to the problem. It was often 5:00 before I began to push Black Beauty back to Auntie's through the rush hour traffic. After supper, I pored over lesson preparation to meet the requirements of a demanding headmaster and fretted over math problems that I did not understand. As well, being very much in love, it was nice to smooch from time to time, especially when Emma was off to bridge, but the slow progress of renewing our home and the added task of restoring the dining room suite gnawed away at our composure. Perhaps we had been too ambitious with our renovation plans.

Covering the dining room floor with newspaper, I began the difficult task of bathing the various pieces of the suite in Three-Star paint and varnish remover. Using a toothbrush, rags, and steel wool, I worked away at the reluctant finish. The old varnish did not want to part company with the wood. Since the brass handles were also covered with varnish, I concluded that someone had attempted a restoration earlier without removing the previous finish. We sent the mirror to Edmonton to be re-silvered and replaced the broken leaded glass with plain glass, since sections of the original windows were broken and missing. As usual, Betty responded with cheerful resolution, "That's all the better. Now we will be able to see all the beautiful china that we have when it's in the buffet." I had so little to share with this beautiful woman—how could she say so positively, "We have, we will be able, and it's ours?" All that she possessed was suddenly ours and we were not even married yet.

When it came time to work on the table, I quickly realized that it would be impossible to sand the table top and the spreaders by hand. I worked hours on the cigarette burns and they still loomed long, black, and reluctant to disappear. When I finally quit sanding, the marks still glared at me and along with the burns, I had created an even more noticeable depression in the surface. As I looked at the calendar each day and matched my progress with it, I worried about the varnishing yet to be done. I began to despair, "Our home will not be ready before our wedding." "Yes, it will," affirmed Betty, "we will just keep at it and we will get it finished." In desperation, I took the top and the spreaders to a friend who had a belt sander and he very graciously finished the job for me.

We faced the task of painting the house and finishing the dining room suite at the same time. The thought of dripping wall paint on the dining room suite haunted me and working at both jobs became quite a drag. The daily round became a daily grind. One of Betty's classes asked if they could help with the living room drapes, so Betty provided the material and the class made a beautiful set of drapes. If I remember correctly, they had big flowers on them and the colours were orange, tan, and brown. We matched the off-white background of the drapes and painted the living room and dining room to match.

A walnut rubbing stain and fill for the dining room suite to accent the brown tone of the oak was chosen and I began the task of rubbing and wiping until the colour was pleasing. The staining went well and was done quickly. The pedestal had been glued back together and held in place with rags twisted firm with sticks and screwdrivers. Fortunately, all the chairs were sound except for the webbing. Now, the table could be reassembled and a finish chosen to complete the work. Old types of varnish were no longer available and urethane was my only choice. I sighed with relief as I dipped the brush into the can for the first time. Immediately, the colour brightened as the brush glided back and forth.

As we had finished painting the house and the damaged dusty flooring was long since gone, I doubted that dust would be a problem, but my heart sank as I examined the table top the next evening before starting the time-consuming preparation for the next day's lessons, running my hand over my hours of labour and finding a bunch of prickly little bumps. What does one do with a prickly urethane finish? The next evening, instead of forging ahead with brush and urethane, I timidly rubbed all of the tiny sharp protuberances with wet and dry sandpaper and gave the whole top a good wipe with a damp cloth. Now, a little oval ring appeared in the place of each dust bump. It looked as though all my efforts would go down the drain and we would be left with a pockmarked finish despite hours and hours of labour. "Not to worry!" were the words I heard from my good friend and counsellor, Jim Burrows, who had been so kind lending me tools and giving me free advice, "those marks will disappear when the next coat is dry. Just be sure to brush the urethane on thin for the next coat or two." When the job was finally finished—not long before our wedding day at that—others admired the splendid job of restoration, but I still fretted over the mottled finish. Once again, Betty restored my courage. She covered the dining room table with her grandmother's lace tablecloth, kept for just such a purpose. It would also hide the cigarette burns and the imperfections in the finish as well as provide protection to the tabletop if some offending article should be placed on it.

The webbing in the chair seats was replaced with new Naugahyde. Betty assured me she planned to make needlepoint seat covers to replace the imitation leather. Sadly, this was a project which she later had to abandon. The restored mirror was put in place and the new glass was secured in the buffet doors. All was in readiness for the vast collection of china that Betty had acquired through several generations. As well, each of her sewing classes seemed to vie for the special honour of giving her the most beautiful cup and saucer that she ever received. At the moment, they graced her mother's home, but her anticipation of having her own home was keen. She also had treasures handed down to her from the Bruce family—one member had been the proprietor of a jewellery store in New York in years gone by.

The drapes were hung, the chesterfield arrived, the new bathroom fixtures, countertop and vinyl flooring were all in place, and our oak bedroom floors gleamed in their new splendour. Our house was beautiful and we experienced a great deal of satisfaction and pride as we surveyed the results of our efforts. When we had our first open house, it was a thrill to be asked, "And who was your interior decorator?" Our wedding was near and our house was in complete readiness for us to enter the "halls of highest human happiness." All we would need to do was bring in our suitcases following the wedding and we would be in business. During these months of renovation, Betty and Emma had not been idle concerning arrangements for the wedding. Emma launched into the affair with keen delight. She aspired to give us a wedding that we would remember for the rest of our lives.

We attended premarital counselling sessions with Dean Noel, Rector of the Cathedral Church of the Redeemer. Betty had been secretary there for three years prior to teaching at SAIT. She and the dean were good friends, and Betty and Emma naturally chose the cathedral for the wedding. Before this Baptist boy came alone, Emma and Betty were regular in their attendance. We often strayed from the topic of marriage counselling—the Dean admonished me to become an Anglican or at least intimated that I had the makings of an Anglican minister, while I tormented him with all the good points about being a Baptist. My challenge that he would make a far better Baptist than an Anglican went unheeded, as did his rejoinder. When I questioned him about the meaning of the word cathedral rather than church, he told me that the word meant "the place of the chair," hence the church where the bishop met for official functions. When the bishop speaks "from the chair," it is the official word of the church. That was a hard concept for a Baptist to accept, but it did explain why some are churches and some are cathedrals. I did not remember much about the course in pre-marital counselling, but we sure had a good time together—it was a good ecumenical convention even if the numbers were few. I admired and respected the dean tremendously.

Several teas and showers preceded the wedding. One in particular is forever etched in my memory. Norma Trussler, an administrator and fellow instructor at SAIT, gave me instructions to bring Betty to her house on such and such a night on whatever pretext I could manufacture. I soon learned that surprises were not the order of the day for Betty Bruce (nor for Betty Davis). When we arrived there, Betty was annoyed with me for not having a good reason for wanting to stop in at the Trusslers'. She was still giving me the third degree as we entered the house. Only Norma appeared to be there until the quietness was dispelled by a bevy of ladies bursting forth from the bedrooms, proclaiming, "Surprise, surprise!" What followed was a surprise for me, too. Betty turned on me with flashing eyes and accused me emphatically, "You, you, you knew about this all the time and you didn't tell me!" What can a prospective husband say in circumstances like that, with a bunch of women looking at me like I had just committed the unpardonable sin? I beat a hasty retreat, hoping that she would cool down before I came back for her. She was still tart when I returned and I resolved that there would be no more surprises for Betty after we were married.

Betty had taken a driver's education course once and had flunked the parking test on the first try. Her mother was an excellent driver and had driven the family Model T to Banff when the road was just a pair of muddy ruts. She often reminded me that things were not like they used to be and that holding the Ford in low gear all the way back from Banff was a gruelling experience. In any case, Betty did not go back for her license. When I arrived on the scene, I assured her that I would be happy to be her chauffer anytime, anywhere—a promise that I kept faithfully. Even though I encouraged her to go for her license again and again, she never bothered.

June was bursting out all over with flowers of many varieties. Lilacs must have been the landscaping specialty when Rosedale was developed. Almost every yard boasted a hedge or a bush of white or lavender lilacs, the latter being one of Betty's favourites. On one occasion when I whipped into the house to take Betty to one of the many premarital functions, I scooted into the bathroom to be greeted by a bathtub full of lilacs. They were just freshening up, Emma assured me in order to be ready for the tea that was to be held there the next day. *"Boy, this business of getting married in the Bruce household has more kinks than a coronation,"* I sputtered to myself as I hurried to take this gorgeous creature to another whing-ding. Once again, Betty was standing by the mirror over the mantelpiece. This time she was arrayed in a deep blue velvet suit which made her sparkling blue eyes more intense.

Betty never seemed to wear her gloves, but when she appeared with hat on and gloves in hand, you could be sure that she was off to an affair that she considered as important as the Ascot Races.

I always felt a little reluctant to kiss Betty when Emma was around, though with this dizzy round of parties and all the work that needed to be done at the house, there was not much time for billing and cooing. Then, too, with the headmaster at the school supervising my teaching with a cool and distant stare, I was very stressed and about to come apart at the seams. Throughout my courtship with Betty and renovation of our new home, I continued to teach at Strathcona School for Boys. As well as attempting to keep order in the class and to cover all the courses, teaching grade nine math was turning out to be a disaster both for me and the class. In the midst of this tornado of activity, the headmaster of the school came to my rescue. He stated, "At this rate the grade nine students will never pass math." That decision removed most of my teaching problems with the class and "himself" held forth in the front porch where he taught them math.

As a consequence, "Mr. High and Mighty," Knight of the Lancastrian School System, informed me that he would be docking $600 from my salary. The adjustment left me with almost no pay for the last three months of the school year. I did not choose to seek recourse through the ATA because I was teaching at a private school and I was afraid that he could replace me on short notice. Then, too, I was determined to keep my part of the bargain despite the headmaster not keeping his. When my paycheque did not arrive, the headmaster informed me he had deposited the pittance in the main postal box downtown. Three weeks later, I was informed by the Post Office that it had been retrieved from the bottom of the box with the explanation, "We don't always empty the box every day."

The calendar informed me that my first year of teaching in Canada was coming to an end and so was the so-called "bliss of singlehood," which had been my unwelcome condition for so many years. School was to end on Friday, the 19th, and Betty and I were to be married the next day. I attended my very last function at Strathcona and the school presented me with a wedding gift which I very much appreciated. My contract at the school was not renewed and I would not be returning in the fall. The finale of this whole doomed teaching year occurred on my last day of school. Leaving with my small spirit duplicator under my arm for which I had paid $70.00 with hard-earned money, the headmaster took it from me and nonchalantly stated, "Objects purchased for the school become the property of the school."

Betty and I had hoped that the weather would be nice on our wedding day, however we awoke to an overcast sky. Since the friend of longstanding that I had considered for best man was sporting a black beard, I felt that I could not ask him to do the honour of standing up for me as somewhere along the way I had heard Emma's opinion on beards. I did not want to introduce anything into that wedding that would upset my soon-to-be mother-in-law. Consequently, I considered a newfound friend who seemed to be just as much a character as me. He was indeed! And therein lay the seeds of disaster as far as etiquette was concerned.

Since our house was ready for occupancy, Brent, my best man, was given a key and told that he could have the honour of being the first one to sleep in the guest room. The night before the wedding all was in readiness. I was still staying with Alice because Betty and I wanted to move into our beautiful, restored home together as soon as we were married. The fact that we should have a guest before we lived there ourselves was considered a good indication of things to come—hospitality would be a hallmark of our marriage.

Auntie Alice suggested that I could use her beautiful bronze Chevy which was nearly new if I so chose. She knew that my car, according to plan, would be hidden several days prior to the wedding. I resolved that no one was going to mess around with my vehicle on our wedding day. In any case, I assured her that my best man would supply my transportation needs and that all was cared for in that regard—a decision I soon regretted. Part of my best man's responsibilities was to deliver flowers to Emma and Alice prior to the wedding and pick up Auntie Alice and myself on his way to the church. A then-popular song that had little meaning until my wedding day, but which still fills me with dread as a reminder of near disaster, was "Get Me to the Church on Time" from *My Fair Lady*.

My new suit was hanging in the closet in anticipation of the great day and everything was in readiness for the wedding. My best man was to pick me up in good time in the morning and take me to the tailor shop where I could have the trousers shortened. In honour of the occasion, Alec Kerfoot was to have his first store-bought suit. Three suits for one wedding was not a bad deal for the tailor, who gave us a bargain accordingly. As per plan, Brent came for me around 10:00 in the morning, taking me, and Alec's trousers, to the tailor. He was to return to the tailors' for me long before the wedding so that I would have time to dress and "get to the church on time." I'd often thought of Brent as beady-eyed, eager, and perhaps a bit rattled, but surely a dependable fellow on one's wedding day. (My auntie gently reminded me long after the wedding that his car was not very clean and that it smelled like a horse barn—actually I quite liked the smell, an aesthetic appreciation evidently not shared by elite society.) I cheerfully waved the trousers at Brent as I pushed the door shut with my foot and parted with an optimistic, "See you in a while."

Unfortunately as it turned out, Brent was not familiar with the new districts in Calgary, nor was he aware of the length of time that it took to transverse the city. He went off merrily on errands of his own, promptly forgetting about the clock. He thought it was a good time to take advantage of the shoe sale he saw advertised that was near his brother's place, and since it was Saturday and his brother was home, he could just stop for a little visit. Alec's trousers were soon shortened and paid for. The shop was lower than the sidewalk, and I stood by the window looking through the security bars and cobwebs at all the trousered legs walking by. By this time, trouser legs and best men were a sore point with me. "Surely," I fussed, "he will be coming any minute." As my daddy used to say, "Hindsight is better than foresight." I could have phoned a taxi or had Aunt Alice come to get me, or a host of other wise and wonderful things, but I did not. Instead, I did nothing and fretted and fretted and waited and waited. This just could not be happening on my wedding day! There was no point in sharing my woe with Betty and upsetting her.

Twenty minutes before the bells were to toll, old "beady-eyed and eager" tooted on the horn and I bounded up the stairs like a deer. Brent was muttering something about corsages. I tried to ask nonchalantly, "Wherever have you been?" as he pulled away from the curb like a rabbit. *"Why hurry now? The damage is done!"* I fumed silently. *"Phew, just twenty minutes in which to shower, shave and dress and get to the church on time,"* I groaned. *"Whatever will Alice think of this fiasco? My, my, my, what a thing to have happen on my wedding day. Besides, it looks like rain."* To add to my dismay and horror, Brent's complete car care in preparation for taking my auntie to the wedding in fine style consisted of throwing a smelly old saddle and a bag of oats out of the back seat. I began to feel like the prophet of old, *"Woe is me! for I am undone"* (Isaiah 6:5, KJV). When we arrived at my aunt's, I hurried up the stairs, unbuttoning as I went. What could I say to my charming, socially meticulous aunt? I had phoned her several times, groaning, "I don't know what's happened to Brent. We'll be there when we get there."

Thankfully, my beautiful new clothes were all lying in order on the bed. After a thirty-second shave, I jumped into them as quickly as I could. I suppose that Brent took the corsages over to Betty, but he was soon back and came bounding up the stairs with the corsages for this household. Auntie was not usually one to scurry down the stairs but today was an exception. I hardly knew if my pants were on frontwards or backwards, but I did not miss the slightly arched eyebrow as I held open the front door to the old, grey Volkswagen that had not had a bath in a very long time.

I had expected to be chewing the fat with Dean Noel and admiring Alec in his new trousers long before Betty arrived at the church, but such was not to be the case. As we came careening around the corner in the old grey wonder, Betty was just getting out of the back seat of her mother's pretty blue '56 Ford Victoria, which glistened in the sun that peeked out from behind the clouds for just a few, fleeting seconds. We turned into the alley, stopping rather unceremoniously at the curb to let Alice out. While Brent parked the car, I ran in the back door with Alec's new trousers flapping over my arm. By the time Alec had donned his new trousers and I had puffed out my apologies, "beady-eyed and eager" had joined the boys in the back room, and we were ready to enter the sanctuary. The bride in her mile-long gown was waiting peacefully at the back of the church. She was just as much at home in that church as she was in her mother's house on 5th Avenue.

The lump in my throat refused to go down, no matter how many times I swallowed. There we were at the front of the church, facing the chancel. The dean stood facing the congregation as the strains of that beautiful organ began to peal out the familiar "Here Comes the Bride." I was in such a state that they may just as well have played "The Last Post." The long red runner that the church used to protect the gowns of dignitaries as they marched down the aisle in solemn procession had been loaned to another church and was not available to grace our wedding day. "No problem," said Betty, when the good ladies of the church informed her of this problem the day before her wedding, "There is a big roll of white paper in the storeroom in the basement that is used to cover the tables at the annual church dinner. Just cut off a strip and it will do fine."

Consequently, the bride's aisle was adorned with a long, white sheet of table-top paper. I knew that Uncle George would be escorting her down the aisle and that he would be on his best behaviour. After the earlier sceptical reception, we had become good friends. All went well, the music stopped, and the dean, in his best booming cathedral voice, asked, "Who giveth this woman to this man?" A rather timid and squeaky voice was heard in reply, "I do!" followed by the sound of scrunching paper and stomping feet. George's best shoes, shined to perfection, had caught in "that confounded paper," as he called it ever after. Try as he might, he could not free himself from the crunching mass, even while stomping out an informal jig. A few titters and the odd chuckle followed his embarrassed journey to the seat of honour beside Etta, whose eyebrows, one may assume, would have been halfway to her hairline. Such minor disturbances were not to ruffle the dean one little bit, but I am sure that he had a hard time controlling his own laughter. This unexpected event did not diminish my unstrung state in the least.

Hearing the majestic, unruffled voice of the dean as he began the official part of the ceremony somewhat eased my distress. We had agreed that we would follow the time-honoured traditional marriage vows, but in my frazzled condition, I proclaimed, "Thereby do I plight thee my *trough*" (which is a long narrow container for holding food or water for animals, rather than the actual "troth"). Yes, sir, this Baptist boy was in way over his head in this august company. I noticed the Dean's eyebrow arch just a little as the farm invaded that sublime sanctuary. Thereafter, he spoke even more slowly and deliberately, but I even managed to change the order of the words when it came to that final "Until death do us part." Betty, on the other hand, performed perfectly as she repeated her vows. The ring part of the ceremony went well as both hers and mine fit perfectly.

Nearly fifty years later, I still remember a most unusual part of the hitching party. The long white stole or silk scarf around the dean's neck was adorned with the indications of the wearer's status as a clergyman; since he was dean of this cathedral, his was very ornate. While Betty held my hand, the dean ceremoniously wrapped the stole around our hands, tied a single knot, and gave it three firm tugs, solemnly proclaiming, "In the name of the Father, the Son, and the Holy Ghost, I now pronounce you man and wife."

He then indicated that we should kneel while he pronounced a stately blessing and benediction. After this, we followed Dean Noel up the chancel steps to the altar rail, where he announced that we had had our first little walk together as man and wife. What followed was a rather long discourse on the responsibilities of a man and his wife—basically, the man should love and the wife should obey. Thus, this part of the wedding ceremony ended.

While the organ played, we retired to the vestry to sign and witness the marriage certificate which took quite some time. Following this official task, pictures were taken and then Betty's neighbour whisked us to our reception which was catered by the appropriate department of the soon-to-be Southern Alberta School of Technology. Making good use of their opportunity to demonstrate their expertise, the staff and students had excelled in their preparations. One delicacy which was part of the hors d'oeuvres aroused smiles, frowns, and strange looks. Apparently, some of the guests had not previously encountered the so-called upper-crust dish of consommé—a cold, jelly-like beef broth. Since Alberta is the home of A-1 beef, the main course was superb, and what is beef without horseradish, whipped potatoes and thick brown gravy accompanied by tiny green peas which can always be corralled in the spuds? Of the desserts, which must have been of equally lip-smacking status, I remember nothing except that I was hoping to depart without too much delay.

Since our well-wishers assumed that our car was hidden on campus, we were watched and followed by some would-be pranksters. Our chauffer immediately departed and the city-wide chase began. Betty's mother had a good friend, who resided in a duplex under which was an empty garage where I had hidden our Ford. The supposed clandestine chariot was to be our means of escape but the posse simply waited in hiding until we were flushed out. I was not called the "Flying Parson" during my student minister days in Nova Scotia without reason and "Black Beauty" did not let me down now. The chase was once again on. I was not about to be bested by these insistent tormentors who intended to pursue their prey to its destination. Unlike some who were very eager to obtain their objective, I actually stayed within the law while attempting to lose them within the city limits. Since our newly-renovated house was doubtless under surveillance, deciding what to do became a frantic preoccupation.

Finally, we stopped at a motel on Macleod Trail, explained our predicament to the clerk, paid the bill, and hoped for safety and sleep. However, such was not to be. The night proved to be hot and stuffy with no air conditioning, and the company very aggressive—a million starving mosquitoes and no fly swatter. With my underwear being the only available weapon, Sir Galahad to the rescue. It was a failing attempt but I gave it my best effort while Betty hid under the covers, occasionally spotting the enemy. Ultimately, I gave up in despair—the day was at long last done and so was I. Trusting that we could safely return to our new home in the morning, we must have met our objective and slept some.

What a surprise awaited us the next day! Trustingly, I had given my "best" man a key to our new abode so that he would have a place to sleep the night before the wedding. Unbeknownst to me, he had made a copy of the key and had let our tormentors in. Confetti, which had not been tossed after our wedding, now infested our spotless home with only the bed being spared. Evidently, my best man had told them that we anticipated coming there following the reception and the pranksters had departed in haste. Trying to rescue our house from the confetti invasion required considerable effort. Even a year later, we kept finding pockets of the artificial flower petal.

We had reserved one night in Banff by way of a mini-honeymoon before going to Edmonton to upgrade my education at the University of Alberta— the only university in the province at the time—in order to qualify to teach under the requirements of the ATA—the Alberta Teachers' Association. One memory of our very short honeymoon will never be forgotten as indigestion—now known as acid reflux—deprived me of another night's sleep. To my later dismay, I had requested a much-overdone slice of roast beef and, since I had no medication to offset the result, I hardly slept. We were all too soon back in Calgary, getting ready to set up in Edmonton and enroll in the required courses.

MARRIAGE

After a year of teaching at a school where I did not require an Alberta teacher's certificate, I was immediately required to improve my qualifications in order to teach in a public school in the province. I might just as well have been a foreign immigrant in spite of having graduated from college in the United States. To me, it all seemed so ridiculous since I had been accepted to teach a Special Needs class in Massachusetts without even being a graduate or having had any formal training for the task. Now, it was necessary that two summer school courses at the University of Alberta in Edmonton be completed. My post-secondary experience proved to be somewhat of a joke and it could not end soon enough in my opinion. Betty and I were able to rent a lovely house near the university as the owner, a teacher, was on holiday. Thus began a long, tedious journey toward certification to teach in Alberta and a position that would hopefully be better than teaching at Strathcona School for Boys. Much later in life after the school had been long amalgamated with the girls' edition of a similar private school—St. Hilda's/Tweedsmuir School—and became known as Strathcona-Tweedsmuir School, I discovered I had been elevated to the status of alumni.

Attending Gordon College was very different from attending the University of Alberta. A requirement had been to prepare a paper on education prior to admittance, which I handed in late—using my recent marriage as either a reason or an excuse. My professor accepted the paper and gave me a very good grade. I was elated, but soon found that his class decorum was meaningless. He simply sat comfortably behind his desk and told endless stories about Alpha schools and Beta schools (I doubted that he even knew any Greek). Anyway, each class ended with long reading assignments from a costly pile of books, which were only partly read by me. Seldom was the material discussed in class. Alarmingly, the final exam asked very specific questions—and guess what?—yes, only on the assigned reading. My course on my Introduction to Administration in Alberta Schools ended with barely a pass, despite my excellent paper which compared education to the Hippocratic Oath—"If you do no good, be sure to do no harm," which violated his method of teaching, though it was my strong belief.

My other professor was even worse. He was a very conceited, bombastic, and even rude man, but there was some discussion during his class. When a student made a comment, he often declared, "Not substantiated by research," which was repeated for emphasis, or simply, "unfounded opinion." His manners were sadly lacking. One day as I carefully balanced on the improvised walk to the building where he taught, trying to avoid the deep, newly-laid soil on each side which had been soaked by the previous night's rain, this man simply charged past me like an angry bull and stomped his muddy feet down the freshly-polished hall. "My, my," I thought, "is this an example of what Alberta education produces?" One day in class, following his rude remarks, a classmate leaned over and said, "If that oaf makes another comment like that, I will get up and leave." Only blackmail kept him in his seat—simply, if you don't pass, you don't teach in Alberta. I felt much the same and again I barely passed.

Since all my post-secondary education had been in non-accredited schools and I had not graduated from high school, it took much wrangling to obtain Alberta Teacher Certification, which was finally awarded years later. In order to be certified in Alberta, a person had to have standing in six grade twelve subjects—I only had five. Though I started taking Math 30 in night school eight times, the subject continued to elude me. On one occasion, when I asked what to me was an utterly confusing question, the highly qualified teacher appeared to develop apoplexy, turned red and emphatically proclaimed, " Well, my dear man, if you don't know the answer to that, you don't belong in this class!" I could not have agreed with him more.

Upon surviving the educational fiasco in Edmonton, Betty and I were relieved to return to our newly-renovated house in Calgary. During this time, we attended Crescent Heights Baptist Church. We especially loved teaching the senior Bible class. The class presented me with a beautiful Thompson Chain Bible, which gave me a helpful source of preacher preparation for years and which, I am proud to say, I still have. It was at that time that I began taking the elderly to church regularly. One couple rode in the back seat and continuously argued vehemently with each other to and from church. I vowed never to let that happen in our marriage, which was "easier said than done" as my daddy would say.

When Betty became pregnant, she said, "I do not want to bring up a child in this area." Just why, I do not remember, but after searching, we found a new house in northwest Calgary which Betty immediately and enthusiastically desired. She especially loved the large kitchen. Though this house was the pride and joy of its builder, it had been on the market for a long time. He extolled its merits—cathedral windows, drive-under garage, sunken living room and dining room, and other virtues. However, there was no back door from the kitchen so just to take the garbage out, one went downstairs, through the carpeted living room, downstairs again to the hall leading to the backdoor, upstairs to the walk, and out to the alley. To reach the bathroom from the master bedroom, which faced the open living room from an elevated hall, one had to sprint the length of the house. The driveway to the garage filled with snow in the winter and the oily car-smell sneaked into the entire house. This was not my idea of convenience, but Betty loved the house so we sold ours and added a hefty mortgage to our budget for the purchase of 21 Chisholm Crescent. With that, we bid ado to the home we had so lovingly renovated.

Soon after moving in, another disadvantage of a more dire nature was discovered with the house. The downdraft from a strong west wind would blow out the pilot light on the kitchen stove. Occasionally, we returned home to discover a house full of natural gas. Had there been a spark, I am sure it would have been blown sky-high. Betty was working at CFCN Broadcasting at this time—fortunately, the station upgraded their kitchen stove and Betty's mother gave us the old electric one.

It was a relief when I learned that Betty's boss did not mind a pregnant lady working at CFCN. When Betty asked him about it, he simply said,

"No problem! I will gladly take you to the hospital when the time comes, if necessary."

By now, I had my first artificial arm, which I was just beginning to use. The driveway to the garage had filled with snow so I decided to try the new device out by shovelling. Almost immediately, a huge shovel full of heavy, wet snow stuck to the shovel and pulled off my artificial arm. I fell head first into the snowdrift. Getting up, I stood on the shovel handle and tugged until all the straps came undone and then I kicked the contraption into the snow in disgust. Betty watched from her kitchen window and laughed. That was the end of artificial arm #1—simply a hollow leather sleeve held in place by straps with a claw on the end. My second attempt also ended in failure. I had taken Emma, my mother-in-law, to the airport and while carrying her suitcase on the concourse, the arm rotated and the suitcase went between my legs, causing me to stumble. My stump was too short to provide good leverage. As there was little flesh across the end of the bone, it was also very painful—no more artificial arm for me!

Around 3:00 one morning in 1962, Betty woke me and said, "I think you had better take me to the hospital right now." During the long ride across town, I thought, *Go carefully or she might start to have the baby in the car.* She later asked me, "Why did you drive so slowly?" I asked to be with her during the birth but was told, "Just wait here. We are very busy tonight." I certainly had not needed to hurry, as it was only much later that I was told, "You have a lovely baby boy." I do not remember my first look at Robert (Bob) Bruce Davis—to me there is sameness in all newborn babies—but I remember telling Betty, "He has a Jimmie Durante nose and a Mitch Miller chin." Only the joy and relief of his safe arrival carried me through another day of my first teaching opportunity with "Slow Learners" in Calgary, as such classes were then called. By now, Betty no longer worked at CFCN, of course, and Mr. Love had not been required to drive her to the hospital after all.

Since Bob was bottle fed, Betty was once again hired by SAIT to teach a new course, the "Bishop Method of Sewing." She enjoyed working alongside Norma Trussler, her boss, who also became a very close friend. The BMS style of sewing, which was more simple and faster than older methods, required the use of a point presser, a pounding block and a table-sized ironing board—all made from wood. Betty brought home a set and enquired whether I could make them as they were costly, having to be ordered from the USA. This project renewed my love of working with wood and promised a supplementary income. Though woodworking provided me with an enjoyable, relaxing hobby, it did not prove to be very profitable as I always wanted more tools and supplies, greatly cutting into any revenue.

LONG YEARS OF
BETTY'S ILLNESS

When our growing boy turned two, Betty, who was always healthy and active, suddenly became very ill. She had developed a case of acute rheumatoid arthritis. What a devastating blow! Her mother had always said that Betty could organize a Roman army, but not anymore—she was very soon almost unable to care for herself. We began a fourteen-year battle in which there was no surrender or victory.

Betty's doctor advised us not to have any more children. Betty said, "Should we apply for adoption? I don't want a child of mine to grow up alone." We applied to Social Services almost immediately, but our caseworker cautioned, "I don't think you will be successful because of Mrs. Davis' health." However, she asked us to tell her about our expectations. I said, "If you make them up to specifications, here are ours: a beautiful, blue-eyed girl with dark hair." This resembled the last memory of my baby sister. In 1964, shortly after we returned from a trip to the Mayo Clinic, our case worker called to tell us that a baby had just become available. Would we like to see if we wanted her? On arrival, she showed us a lovely little girl. After conferring, we delivered a jubilant "Yes." The worker then informed us there was a waiting period of five weeks in case the mother wished to change her mind. We left very happy that our baby had arrived, but saddened by the wait to take her home.

When Edith (Beth) Elizabeth Davis finally came home, Betty contacted a paediatrician for an appointment. After his examination, we were told,

"You have a healthy baby here. Just dust her bottom with cornstarch when you change her and give her all the two percent milk she will drink." Beth at first was very inactive. She held her hands tightly across her little chest. If an elderly grey-haired lady bent over her buggy to admire her, she became very upset. It wasn't long, however, until she kicked vigorously and flung her arms into the air as soon as she heard my voice upon my return from school.

When Beth grew older, it was almost impossible to keep her in her crib at night. I attempted to make her escape impossible without any success, and it became an ongoing contest for quite some time. One night, she came crawling along the hall in her Swee'Pea sleeping bag and announced, "I'm wone-wee." Another time, I was awakened late at night to hear a strange sound from the bathroom. Investigation revealed a miniature warrior with a painted face, who peered at me from under the counter while attempting to rid her fingers of her mother's makeup by rubbing them on the air vent. I was both relieved and annoyed. After attempting a hasty repair, I tucked her back into her crib. Beth was a delight, just the same. Bob and Beth became close friends. Imagine this: if we were in a mall or a public meeting place, we allowed them to investigate their surroundings with never a care for their safety. Would that be done today?

Since it had become a real challenge to get Betty in and out of our house, I considered moving—hopefully in the same area as Northmount Baptist Church, which we now attended. When Betty had to be hospitalized, I set out to find a more suitable home and discovered a beautiful bungalow located nearby which had been built by the same developer. It, too, had been on the market for quite some time. The house really attracted me and was much more accessible and convenient than ours. Taking Betty from the house to the car by wheelchair, and then putting the chair into the trunk, was a real challenge for a one-armed man. Since this house was also well-constructed, it seemed like the solution to our problem. However, when I told Betty about it, she was not interested in the least. She simply said, "If we must move, I don't care where or what house we live in." Selling our house seemed an impossible task—many people looked but none would even give us an offer until a hoped-for-purchaser entered the living room, glanced around, and said, "This house is just perfect for my sound system." He was finally able to buy it when I agreed to a small second mortgage. Betty did not share my enthusiasm for the new house, but we lived there for several years.

Coming home one day, I saw Bob tramping soggy soil around a newly-planted tree in the park near our house, imitating the city workers he had watched earlier (although the workers tramped only dry soil). I was horrified as we had just purchased him a new pair of expensive orthotic shoes, which he had thoughtfully taken off. His riding toy was parked nearby (my slow learners at school had made it and many more). I tied his shoes and said, "I will race you home."

Bob had been told, "You must never try to cross Northmount Drive." I had often seen him use his feet as brakes when riding on his toy when he came flying down the street from home, stopping just inches from the curb and traffic. No wonder his shoes wore out so quickly! On another occasion upon arriving home, Bob was not to be found anywhere. Betty was very distraught. "*Ah, yes,*" I thought. "*What about my orders 'Do not cross Northmount'?*" Sure enough, I saw two small boys in the distance, one on a tricycle and the other on his favourite riding toy. Bob and the neighbour boy had decided to explore the forbidden land. Of course, it was all the neighbour boy's fault—oh, the joys of parenting!

Beth was also a very active child. Fortunately, I was home when I heard Beth crying in the back yard. Her instinct not to be confined had caught up to her and she was hanging upside down from the fence—her feet caught between the two top boards. Enter dad to the rescue. After she was firmly back on the ground, Beth didn't even seem to be upset.

My job teaching slow learners with the Calgary School Board was not one that was held high on the ladder of esteem in the teaching profession, but it suited me perfectly. I began teaching at Northmount Elementary School, not far from our home. Such classes were not often welcomed by the other students or teachers. Johnnie Suiter, the Principal, was a real gem and a veteran. We became very good friends. On my first day as he, the other teacher, and a student approached my classroom, the boy said, "We are going to have another 'slow learner' class!" Mr. Suiter was dumbfounded and he promptly phoned administration and complained, "How come a slow learner informs me that I am having another Special Class?" Carl Safran, a good Jewish lad, simply said, "Oh, Johnnie, didn't I tell you?" He was Chief Superintendent then and later became Special Education Superintendent. Cecil Sangster followed him at a later date. They were both fine men and their annual inspection was simply a friendly visit and a chat in the hall with the usual, "How are things going? Do you need anything?" I subsequently learned that that was not necessarily the case with other inspections.

While teaching at Northmount, Canada had a peace-keeping mission in Cyprus, which was often in the news. The school held a Christmas program to which parents were invited. For our part, my class wrote and directed a skit called "Check Point Charley" which depicted a scene on the island. What fun we had! Mr. Suiter, a real packrat, had World War II uniforms, which he stored in his bedroom at home and allowed us to use. The class had a great time wadding newspaper into balls to fill several gunnysacks in order to make the inspection station. I made a wooden mock-up of a machine gun on a tripod and we dressed up several boys in supposedly Cypriot attire and wrote the dialog. I phoned the Calgary Herald and told them about our project and asked if their peace-keeping correspondent could possibly visit the school and critique our skit. I was elated when they agreed to ask the correspondent and get back to me. To our surprise, he did visit us on the appointed day as arranged. He was dressed in typical correspondent garb and the kids were thrilled. He said our script accurately depicted the real checkpoint. After wishing us well, he went on his way. The students' efforts were well received and got loud applause—a real boost for the kids' morale.

When spring came, permission was granted to wash, wax, and vacuum teachers' cars. All went well except that one of the regular class teachers saw a boy supposedly fiddling with her radio and told me she did not want one of "those kids" messing around with her car. The boy was merely being inquisitive.

As there was a public swimming pool not far away, I obtained authorization to take the class to it by city bus. While there, the students jumped off the low diving board and challenged me to dive off the high one. After a demonstration of pseudo fear, I jumped. Meanwhile, one lad who had chosen not to swim simply sat beside the pool, watching. I was horrified when he shouted, "Someone is lying on the bottom!" Having never been informed that Glen Sherwin was epileptic, I was unaware of the possibility that he might have an attack. The guard quickly pulled him out and laid him beside the pool. In a few seconds, he opened his eyes as if to enquire, "What is all this fuss about?" Glen was the only son of a single mother and the most promising and able boy in my class. The guard was very upset, but you can well imagine the relief we both felt at the positive outcome.

I really enjoyed my two years of teaching at Northmount. The school was cement on the inside with brick on the outside, which did not always make for quiet classrooms. Fortunately, silence was not my objective and the room was often filled with laughter. Sometimes, I returned home with my head still ringing. The second year, the children did a skit called "Clampett's Christmas," a take-off of the popular program, The Beverly Hillbillies. Jed had cut down a lovely tree in what we called Central Park. The very irate Park Superintendent came looking for the culprit and said, "That's not yonder forest—that's my prize spruce tree!" Colin often said during practice, "That's my prize juice tree!" Of course, laughter followed, without Colin probably being even aware of what they were laughing at.

In my third year, the Haultain School, located right downtown, needed a teacher and the school board appointed me. This time all classes were Special Education. I always tried to arrive early because the staff room was a merry place. In spite of the fact that our school was his first assignment in the top position, Reg Houghton was a fantastic principal. My class consisted mostly of boys from the Emerald Children's Home, which was under the Child Welfare Program. This proved to be a real challenge but a very rewarding one. One lad, Calvin Tyson, had run away instead of going to school on day one, and was brought back by two men in white gowns. Calvin was very cross-eyed and most likely had been badly teased. School must not have been a total loss for him because he never ran away again. As I was able to make arrangements to have his eye problem corrected, he soon became a different boy and grew quite attached to me.

When I was employed as a teacher in what was then called "Special Ed," it was my experience that by the time senior boys arrived in my class, they hated school with a passion. On the first day of class, I would catch their attention by crawling on my hands and knees to the teacher's desk, climbing laboriously into my chair, and surveying them cautiously. Finally getting their attention, I asked them to hear me out and would declare firmly: "School is fun! You will learn and we will have a good time together." You cannot imagine their groans. My only instruction from administration was, "Keep them out of the principal's office!," which I thought was a good plan.

This was accomplished very simply. Since I had almost no course of studies, I decided "School work in the morning—Arts and Crafts, after lunch. You keep me happy in the morning and I'll keep you happy in the afternoon."

Because the students had little interest in learning, I attempted to discern what might keep their attention. For example, one course was titled, "The History and Development of Modern Small-Bore Firearms." Did you know that Daniel Boone was one of the first defenders of America to own a gun with a "rifled barrel"? He could put a slug between the eyes of an enemy with his gun at a far greater distance than any other musket ever could—small wonder that he cherished "Brown Bess." As to motivation, I requested, "Behave yourself in the morning and get your work done, and we will have fun after lunch. Give me a hard time in the morning, and you will be sitting in your desks all afternoon." It worked very well.

There was no "us and them" in my class—just "us." In my many years of teacher education, no one suggested such an MO. This method of teaching, in principle, could keep more boys interested in high school and help them become successful learners: academics in the morning only and vocation in the afternoon, using teachers borrowed from industry. Follow Lancaster's method in the morning—that is, use promising students in grade eleven and twelve to help younger primary students in the morning in partnership with elementary and primary teachers for later university credit.

In the afternoon, upon returning from lunch, I insisted on at least twenty minutes rest: "Read or relax, just be quiet: it's my turn to read." This time was also used to prepare my lessons for the next day. I found that since Special Ed students were bussed to schools with small enrolments, we could use an empty classroom as an Arts and Crafts Center. In larger schools, we could use the shop. Weather permitting, we could wash teachers' cars for free, or play ball. However, we also made a lot of items: totem pole lamps, glass bottle lamps, cactus lamps, ride 'em toys and even an eight-foot punt (boat). As far as I know, the punt was used for years.

At Haultain, a room at the school was our morning room and another became our afternoon room—a so-called Industrial Arts Centre. One of my students, Don Cordic, asked, "Mr. Davis, can we make a punt?" "Well", I replied, "that is a tall order but we will give it a try. Just remember, punts are hard to paddle." I will not explain all the problems or solutions, but we made a punt. He tried it out and complained, "Mr. Davis, it's too hard to paddle!" "No problem, Don, just bring it back to school and we will put a point on the front of it and use it as a water-tight compartment." We added a two-by-four prow on two sides and a lid. Now he had a watertight compartment and he was happy as it was also easier to handle. Previously, I had sent this particular student to the little storeroom under the stairs for misbehaving and said, "Stay in there until I let you out." After school, the janitor heard him grumbling and released him. Don said, "Mr. Davis told me to stay here until he let me out." The janitor replied, "That's okay, Mr. Davis said to let you out. You can go home now." I spied him on the way to his bus and he vigorously shook his fists at me—little wonder! Of course, I really apologized and that may have been why I agreed to help him build his punt.

We spent a great deal of time in the gym playing volleyball. Alfie Beauregard was short and fat, but he could slide under a spiked ball and almost always put it in the right spot for Albert Jackart to smash suddenly and forcefully to any open spot on the opposite court. With his ability, against huge odds the kids won the City of Calgary championship for our zone. They were then scheduled to meet Mount Royal, the champs in their area. Alfie had a paper route right after school so this presented a problem. What to do? Reg, the principal, came to the rescue, saying, "Why don't you take Albert and Alfred after lunch and do his paper route and be back at the school as soon as you can? I will look after your class." He wanted us to be at Mount Royal School in time for the game just as much as we did. I had told the boys, "If the ball comes right at you, return the serve. But if you see Alfred going for it, just get out of his way and we will win again."

The Mount Royal class was ready and waiting. They looked confident and splendid in neat matching outfits. My boys came straggling in looking stunned and very raggedly attired—some with their toes sticking out of worn out runners—and were met with stares of apparent contempt. At the beginning of the game, Mount Royal did very well, but soon Alfie and Alfred got their rhythm—set, spike, set, spike—bam, bam, bam. Not surprisingly, Mount Royal's pride and confidence evaporated. In a way, I felt sorry for them as they were squirming on the floor like worms on ice. We won decisively, but I had no idea of the storm we had caused. The astonished principal called the city-wide Physical Education Director and complained bitterly, "What do you mean, allowing fourteen- and fifteen-year-olds to play against twelve-year-olds?" The fat was in the fire. However, the city-wide Physical Education Director was Reg Houghton's dad. Unknown to us, Mount Royal's principal's complaint led to a complete revision in the system which corrected the problem—age correlation became the rule, not the grade level of school attended. The fire was extinguished but our win was not overruled. Reg was elated. His school had been honoured and so was he as its principal.

The following year, Glen Milne became our principal, as Reg was busy climbing the ladder of administrative success. My care for Betty was becoming very time-consuming. One day, I crawled into the staffroom on hands and knees only to be helped to my feet by two sympathetic fellow teachers, who promptly assisted me to the sink and pushed my head under the cold water tap. I was doused before I knew what was happening—was this truly thoughtful of them? Fortunately, the principal was not present at the time. Glen was also very understanding of the needs of Special Education students and their teachers.

That year my class decided—with a little persuasion—to honour Queen Victoria, whose memory was very much in the news. The Glenbow Museum graciously loaned us loads of memorabilia including one of her black dresses—she only wore black after her hubby died—displayed on a wire frame. It was quite impressive as she had a 52-inch waist. (Fortunately, we were not yet afflicted by the metric system.) Parents were invited to see the display and it was very successful. Somehow, I doubt very much if any museum would lend out artifacts in this day and age. That was a very different, more trusting time.

At Haultain School when you came in the door, there was an antique chesterfield next to the principal's office; I often teased Glen by asking, "Can I buy that old thing?" It reminded me of one which might have been used by Antony and Cleopatra, as it only had one raised end and was more like a recliner. Years later, Haultain School burned, though fortunately at that time it was only used for storage. The cause of the fire was arson. How sad—I should have been more insistent about the couch, not that it makes any difference now.

Another place where I taught was Victoria Elementary School, not far from Haultain. It roused emotions within me that I would be teaching where my mother had taught Domestic Science forty years earlier—who would have ever dreamed of such a possibility? Principals come in various guises and I will not tell you the name of this one. On many occasions after school, he invited me into his office and, like the Spanish Inquisition, quizzed me about how I taught Special Ed, often interrupting me. Besides that, he had other characteristics which annoyed me. Since he knew I appreciated quality tools, he bragged about buying an expensive skill saw for which he paid much less than the man asked because the man was out of work. I was not surprised to learn that he later became Special Education Supervisor in Vancouver. My only satisfaction at Victoria School, besides the teaching itself, was that I had been able to teach at the same school as my mother.

In order to augment my income, Betty and I had invited a young teacher to live with us in our newly developed basement. Beth loved Miss Smith, who was so small that I said, "You might like teaching primary children." Miss Smith, who had also been born in Nanton, simply loved teaching and taught junior high in a school in our area. Glen Milne was her principal by then and she also really appreciated him as boss.

A new storm arose on the sea of life. As her father had died when she was just a baby and she was an only child, Betty and her mother had always been very close. Emma was more than generous to us but tension erupted when Betty absolutely refused to answer the phone. Emma, being very concerned at the rate of Betty's worsening arthritis, called every morning and at supper time. My sympathy was with my mother-in-law, as it is very trying to watch someone you dearly love fade away. Betty regarded her mother's concern much as I had the Spanish Inquisition from the principal at Victoria Elementary School. At times, Betty simply cried and cried, pleading with me, "Just put me in a home. Marry someone else and make a life for yourself." I simply replied, "That was not included in our marriage vows. You are needed here. Your brain and memory are essential as is your love for our children."

My relationship with Mrs. Bruce was very interesting. Emma had always taken great delight in Betty's accomplishments, regarding her still as her little girl. I, on the other hand, was accepted as an independent adult and found myself in the position of referee between the pair. A casual comment from Emma's friend and neighbour now became meaningful to me. "Remember," she said, "that when you marry Betty, you also marry her mother." I had replied, "I get along with Emma very well." Later, I jokingly told Betty, "If you are not nice to me, I will go home to your mother." It surprised me that I became friend and counsellor of sorts to Emma. As the man of the family now, I became the maintenance advisor and was more than happy to be Emma's odd-job man. She was a wonderful mother-in-law and I have never understood why there are so many jokes about them.

Since I had no close family ties, I was content to have Betty's family become mine. The Bruce twosome became a threesome even before we were married, an arrangement that I thought was working very well. However, gradually Mrs. Bruce's oft repeated remark, "It's none of my business, but..." became very abrasive even to me. One day, with my heart in my mouth and in defence of our own little family unit, I firmly responded, "Emma, dear, it is none of your business—period!" As kind, impartial and honest as her advice and counsel was, it became salt in an open wound no matter how strongly we reasoned with ourselves.

We had regular medical appointments with our arthritic specialist. On one such visit, he told us, "Mrs. Bruce needs to make a life of her own." What happened next was a real challenge. Since I really enjoyed preaching and being a pastor, I contacted Mr. Trites, the Home Mission Director for our denomination. I was on the committee which had just started a church in Bowness. When I explained our situation and my background, he said, "You probably have more education than most of our Home Mission Pastors. There is a need for someone to take the church in Thompson, Manitoba, right now."

Having finished teaching at Victoria Elementary School, it was still too early to find out where I might be placed. I had learned that the principal made a very real difference in the attitude that was held toward Special Education classes, and I did not want to teach at Victoria Elementary again. Now, the pieces of the puzzle seemed to be falling into place. The church must have been desperate as I did not have to give a trial sermon first as usually required. I would not have wanted to be away from home in any case. So, at the end of the school year in 1967, we pulled up roots and planned a fresh beginning in a different province. Yes, we would be on our way to Thompson and be well-established before Christmas—all being well.

MANITOBA

When we informed Emma of our plans, she was devastated—in her eyes, we were turning our backs on her and she wondered why. However, Betty was very thankful to be moving. Arrangements for the move were soon completed to our satisfaction. We thought all was well, but a huge surprise awaited us upon our arrival in Thompson. The parsonage was empty. Our furniture and belongings had not arrived, although they left Calgary before we did. The chairman of the church board was also surprised, but immediately invited us into his home, even insisting that we have the master bedroom.

Upon calling the company in Calgary, I was told to phone Winnipeg as it was not their responsibility. When I phoned Winnipeg, I was told to phone Calgary. After pleading with Winnipeg, they finally informed us that our belongings had been found in their warehouse and that they would send them to us as soon as possible. It must not have been "possible," because we waited and waited. Finally, some things arrived. We did not even have a record of our belongings but we knew for sure that two lovely British India rugs were missing. My call regarding the rest of our belongings was quite testy. Again, we waited and waited. When I called again, I asked, "Would a lawsuit help your memory? The rugs are valuable." When we were able to finally move back into the parsonage—a residence above with the church below—we still had to borrow cooking pots and dishes. Betty had stood up well to travelling and all the confusion but we were relieved to be by ourselves again, along with our children who seemed to take it all in stride, even as young as they were at the time.

I really enjoyed being a pastor again. I was soon asked to give a short devotional talk on the local television on a weekly basis, which was well received. Because the church needed more space for Sunday school, we moved into a huge four-level apartment which was constructed on piles due to the permafrost. There was an arena close by, and even though Beth was only three, she walked over there with her skates and sawed-off hockey stick. Girls at the arena put on her skates and Beth banged the puck back and forth until noon when she came home for lunch. Thus began her many years of playing hockey, ball, and soccer.

The space below the bottom floor of our apartment building allowed access for service. One night we heard voices which seemed to be coming from down under. Since we were near the entry, I put on my dressing gown, opened the trap door, and commanded sternly, "Come out whoever you are!" Two young First Nations children emerged. It appeared that their parents had left them in a cold car and they had discovered a warmer haven. I do not now remember where they went, but they ran out the door quickly.

The church was going very well—or so I thought—into the second year but then the overly-friendly chairman of the board, Guenther Neff, suddenly called for an unexpected vote of confidence. It went sixty/forty in my favour. I notified him just the same I would resign as the support was just not good enough. When we needed permafrost testing to build the upcoming new church, Guenther informed me that as a builder, he alone could make the arrangements with the town. Upon checking with the town office, I was told that they would do it the day after tomorrow, but I wondered at the time, why the unusual look? Guenther had also requested a local company to draw up a set of preliminary plans for him. They were much too elaborate for a small church and were promptly rejected by the Home Mission board. For years, the Thompson church board had been previously well served by a Christian builder and he was asked to review the plans. He could not have met a more accommodating person than Guenther Neff and the builder immediately agreed with the new plans.

We arranged to buy a house in Thompson and two Mennonite lads, Len Peters and Ben Borne, who attended our church, developed the basement as a place to board with us as they were unhappy with their present accommodation. Now, while helping us move, a fine Scottish fellow whose wife attended our church told me, "Aye, lad, you may as well know it, the man has a knife in your back." He was quite correct. I later learned that Guenther offered a friend in Winnipeg my church, saying, "I can get a church for you in Thompson, Manitoba, if you like." I sent my resignation to Mr. Trites. In response, Dr. Harry Renfree, the General Secretary of our denomination, came out to see if the rift could be mended. Upon investigation, he told me, "Mr. Davis, you have handled the situation very well. I will recommend you highly when another church becomes available," which did not happen.

By this time, I had already been hired at a school in Thompson by Superintendent Henry Letkeman to teach Special Education, which was apparently needed badly. To the great dismay and sorrow of everyone, he drowned while fishing with family and friends in the Burnt Wood River. Unfortunately, his replacement, Mrs. Engals, had a very different vision.

We now went to the Mennonite Church which Letkeman had attended. There, we received a very friendly welcome. Once, at a pancake breakfast at our new church, the fellowship committee served crepes. I asked Betty, "Should we show them how to make pancakes? These are as thin as paper." She laughed and said, "You better not. They are crepes which are a real specialty."

One day, George Nelner, the pastor who had replaced me, asked, "There is something going on at our church and no one will tell me what it is. Mr. Neff says we have a bill from a contractor which we do not have to pay." I responded, "Probably you should pay it if you want a good reputation in the community. That company had been asked to prepare a prospective plan for the church. Their plan was much too grandiose for a small place and it was rejected." The rest of the story is quite interesting. The RCMP investigated the case of an abandoned snowmobile, which was found beside the Burnt Wood River near town. When George Nelner was asked if he knew the whereabouts of Guenther Neff, he simply replied, "I think you should look in Germany." He and a lady from another church were both missing. No doubt, Pastor Nelner had a much more successful and pleasant ministry than I enjoyed at that church.

Parker Collegiate was a fast-growing school with teachers who were hired from far and wide, with yours truly as one of the new ones. When

Mrs. Engals, the new superintendent, interviewed me for the position, I simply told her that Henry Letkeman had said that I would be teaching slow learners, which was a class he felt was needed in Thompson. Her tart remark, "Well, that's not what I have in mind for you," caused me to think, "*Too bad that he drowned.*" My assignment was to teach grade 9F. Mrs. Engals followed the silly policy of Homogeneous Grouping, 9a being College prospects. I did not know until later that her son was developmentally disabled. In consequence, another challenging chapter in my book of life began.

The young First Nations students lived on a nearby reservation on weekends and holidays. During the school week, they were boarded in town at the taxpayers' expense. I'm afraid that money rather than loving care was the reason many took these children in. The question arose as to just how I was to teach them. As usual, I began with the same method that I had with slow learners—academic activities in the morning and vocational in the afternoon. In other words, school in the AM and fun in the PM. I did not use my usual greeting, "School is fun," but thought, "*here we go again.*" I had accumulated a milk carton full of classic comic books. The library books in the school were of no use to us and suitable films were not available. My morning class generally followed this pattern—we relocated to a social room which had upholstered furniture. Either each student chose his/her story to read or I read one aloud to them, teaching the history behind the title. Discipline was never an issue.

Following lunch, school was a different kettle of fish. Betty had plenty of yarn which she now knew she would never be able to use. It filled a huge cardboard box and I took it to school. There were many colours in both small and large balls. She said, "Buy some plain gunny sack material and make pictures of animals or scenery and draw them on the sacking with coloured felt pens. Use a bodkin with a running stitch or a cross stitch." So we did. One girl really took to the project but not so the boys. What all I did with them, I do not now remember, but I know we did have fun.

I tried to get my head around the First Nations way of thinking by trying to learn something of their lives, beliefs, and history. Norman Linklater told me the tale of how the ducks got webbed feet. As I remember it, he said, "Once there was a big fire in the grass and a flock of ducks landed and stomped out the flames." Of course, there was much more to the story but that is the gist of it.

During this time, I did teach one delightful class of regular students. Our English assignment was based on the book *Mutiny on the Bounty*. Captain Bligh was a heartless, aristocratic British captain, who showed no mercy to his crew, resulting in mutiny. Of course, quite often we took turns reading in class. To increase interest, we made a mock-up of a Tahitian Island hut. I made it at home in sections and we set it up at the back of the class. The light frame, six feet by eight feet, was first covered with cardboard and then with white paper. The artistic students among our class painted a hula princess on each side of the front door and added an islander asleep under the side window. A chair, a table, and a display shelf adorned the inside as furnishings. Since many in this class had visited the South Pacific, they brought in many items from their travels. One lad brought a red lantern which we hung above the door and another made a wooden copy of the two stone tablets with five of the ten commandments printed on each side.

Our project was popular with student and teachers, and both groups made good use of it. The bench at the back seated about six people. Students could take turns to use it as a study. During staff meetings or parties that convened there occasionally, members argued as to who would occupy our hut. Once during a volleyball tournament which students from Churchill were attending, several families who provided hospitality for visitors suddenly became ill. Two girls, who had stayed up all night to arrange alternate accommodation, were so exhausted in class the next day that I let them snooze in the hut—one on the floor and one on the bench.

On another occasion, something quite unpleasant took place. I had borrowed a book from the teacher in the next classroom and had forgotten several times to return it. Our school was very modern and boasted open air classrooms. While the hall was being finished, students reached Mr. White's classroom next door by going through mine. When late for class, he would swear angrily at them. On the day I handed his book back to him in the hall, I foolishly said, "And you know what you can do with it!" He grabbed my tie and began yanking it. I clenched my fist, thinking, "*I will smack you under the chin so hard, it will stop this nonsense immediately.*" Unknown to me, a fellow from administration reported to the principal that Mr. Davis was fighting upstairs in the hall. No mention was made evidently of Mr. White. When I checked my box next morning, I received a note which said, "Do not go to your class. You are suspended. Come to my office immediately." I did as instructed and found our conversation very unusual. The principal was a fellow Christian and we attended the same church. He underlined how disappointed he was with my conduct. I simply said, "Henry, if I am a teacher, he isn't." I was immediately summoned to her majesty, Mrs. Engals, and told, "If that ever happens again, Mr. Davis, your contract will be terminated immediately."

And as Paul Harvey would say, "Now, here's the rest of the story." Mr. White was also a coach. He later erupted at a basketball game, which was being attended by another school. It took three men to stop the fight which he started. He was immediately terminated and sent off for psychiatric help at full salary. At the following staff meeting, Mrs. Engals solemnly proclaimed, "We had no idea that Mr. White had any emotional problems." His résumé was appended with a clear message that he was not allowed to have a coaching position. It made me wonder why I was designated a pugilist. Nothing was ever said to me by way of apology by either the principal or the superintendent.

During my time at the school, suggestions that might really help the First Nations students were rejected. One such was to allow the boys to assist the local pilots from Lamb Air in helping them to load and unload planes and to act as interpreters as needed during spring break. The idea was vetoed with the excuse that the students would miss Easter exams. A firm "no" was also given for another suggestion which would have allowed the boys to help the local company that sold and repaired snowmobiles where the students could have learned both to use and repair the machines. I was firmly told by administration, "That is impossible. How could the School Board cover their insurance?" Both companies had agreed with my idea and they felt it would be very favourable, both to them and to the boys. When I asked one promising lad, Norman Linklater, why he had no interest in learning, his reply was, "Why should I try? As an Indian, I don't have a chance." If this was the case, why not equip them with something that would benefit them! In the educational system, the best instructions seem to be "Don't rock the boat; yours is not to reason why: yours is but to do and die."

About the time of the fiasco with Mr. White, Emma visited. She was glad to be in her only daughter's presence, but very distressed to see that her physical condition had deteriorated. Emma herself was not feeling well. As we had great confidence in our family doctor, we arranged for her to see him. When the doctor asked about the pills she was taking, he was shocked. He immediately asked her to stop all medications and he prescribed a new, smaller list which he felt would be adequate. To our sorrow, Emma died not too long after returning to Calgary. Sorrow upon sorrow!—we could not attend her funeral as it would have been too much for Betty. We had to arrange for Emma's nephew to make all the burial arrangements and rent out her house. In spite of trying not to add further stress to my wife, we soon had to make a trip anyway as our doctor arranged for Betty to be placed under the care of an arthritis specialist in Winnipeg. Once again, we were faced with another unexpected detour on the roadmap of life.

Easter was coming. I put a plan in motion, which necessitated a dreaded appointment with Mrs. Engals—one I did not look forward to because of all the changes that were required. To my amazement, she was very accommodating. Perhaps she was glad to see me leave. My contract with the board was terminated and I was given the opportunity to apply for a job in St. Boniface teaching eight-year-old children who had failed in school twice and were now classified as trainable rather than educable. Their previous teacher would be going on maternity leave right after Easter. Len Peters arranged for his parents to care for our children until we were settled in Winnipeg. We were amazed to learn that a couple who lived in Thompson, and were good friends of ours, had just received notice that their mortgage payments on their property in Dugald, Manitoba, had not been paid for five months and foreclosure was imminent. As it was imperative that the house be rented right away, we became their tenants, solving a problem for both parties—the timing could not have been better. Even in all this, it seemed that God would take care of us. I was given time off to go to Winnipeg to finalize arrangements. Dugald is 22 kilometres east of Winnipeg and was the site of an infamous railway accident in 1947.

Betty was taken to Winnipeg by air, trussed up on a gurney just like a mummy. Since the flight was not fully booked, she was perched on top of three seats without any extra charge. I was able to sit next to her. In Winnipeg, we were met by an ambulance and she was taken to the hospital.

I returned to Thompson by plane, feeling lonely and depressed, only to discover that I had to go back to Winnipeg immediately to confirm that I had a job and a place to live. The appointment for my teaching position had been arranged and I was soon on my way to it, despite my unfamiliarity with the streets and roads in either city. Soon, I was hopelessly lost and in a state of panic. Time was running out and I was at a dead end. Men are not supposed to cry, but the dam broke, which was most unusual for me. With my head on the steering wheel, I simply cried and cried with heartbreaking sobs, calling upon God for His help. How could one person bear so many ups and downs and crushing disappointments in life? My wife was extremely ill; I had no job, no place to live, and my children were with virtual strangers.

It took some time until I felt calm again and I soon found my way to the school as if being led by an unseen hand. Even though a little late, the principal understood, saying, "It is a bit tricky to find your way here the first time." I was most relieved. He took me to the classroom, explaining that the previous teacher was not available to update me on anything to do with the class. Little was said about my experience. He just seemed pleased that I could come and said I could begin right after Easter. We agreed accordingly. Imagine my relief to have one problem out of the way! Also, the investigation of our hoped-for place to live went well. In next to no time, with all finally arranged, I was reunited with my children and preparing to move south to Winnipeg. God marvellously took over and all three of my concerns were answered almost immediately.

On my last day in Thompson just before the Easter holiday, the loudspeaker announced directly after lunch, "Mr. Davis, please report to the office immediately." My heart plummeted—what now? Upon arrival, two teachers, who were good friends and fellow grade nine instructors, took me arm in one arm, and one said to me without explanation, "Come with us." When they pushed the double doors to the gym open, all was dark inside. Suddenly, the lights came on and students from all the grade nine classes sang heartily, "He's a jolly good fellow." I was completely flabbergasted. Evidently, the grade nine students had obtained permission from the administration to have a farewell party for Mr. Davis, with only grade nine students and teachers attending.

After some introductory remarks and some accolades, the party began in earnest. All the goodies had been provided by the students. The lad who had been a sparkplug in obtaining artefacts for our hut was the MC. Soon it was time to say goodbye. Guenther Neff's daughter was first in a long line of boys and girls. As I reached for her hand, she embraced me tightly and very emotionally began to cry. She clung to me for several minutes—such a long time that I was embarrassed. That started a new protocol. The girls all hugged me and the boys shook my hand. A shy First Nations girl timidly took my hand and confessed, "Mr. Davis, had it not been for my geese cross-stitch project, I would have gone crazy." The line was still long when the bell sounded ending the farewell party. The students from my class on *Mutiny On The Bounty* began the tidy-up and a few more good-byes and well-wishes were shared. The party boosted my sagging morale.

Soon after leaving my children again with strangers, the move to Winnipeg was completed. My sojourn in Thompson was now a sad part of my history—both as a preacher and a teacher. Betty was able to come home, but with the prognosis that there was little hope for any improvement. Though Betty was still able to be a mother and housewife, her limitations were significant even then. Our children again joined us, and we will always be grateful to Mr. and Mrs. Peters for the kind care they showed Bob and Beth during this time.

We were thrilled to be living on an acreage, which seemed to be everyone's dream goal, but in the course of time that we resided there we learned that acreage living is not all sunshine and roses. Our neighbour across the road was affectionately called "Shorty" Long. Shorty certainly was a big help to us in many ways. If I wanted to know anything about living on an acreage or just about anything else, he knew the answer. When I introduced our daughter, Beth, to Shorty, she immediately asked, "Well, is he short or is he long?" We both had a good laugh.

My introduction to teaching Special Needs children in St. Boniface presented a new challenge as they all had failed elementary grades at least twice. My main objectives were for them to become socialized, to learn how to get along with each other, and to follow simple directions. The students' short attention spans, along with many interruptions, were only a part of their problems. One game with many variations became my most successful activity, consisting of a list which involved many large coloured pictures of birds and animals. As the chalkboard was very low, I put a long line of the creatures along the rail and asked each child in turn to bring me whatever I asked. I used the class list to learn their names and study how they responded. I then made the task more challenging by changing the sequences, asking a child to choose the picture I called and give it to another student whom I designated by name. The variations were endless and we had fun. In this way, I learned much about their abilities, their personalities, and their friends.

Almost immediately after moving, we were confronted with elements of nature on our acreage which quickly acquainted me with some of spring's side effects. Some quite distressing problems were revealed. Arriving in the kitchen one morning, I discovered the inverted glass shade on the light full of water and dripping onto the table. This really surprised me as light fixtures don't normally collect water and leak. We learned that during construction the attic had not been properly vented. During the cold Manitoba winter, a thick layer of frost had accumulated on the underside of the roof. Since the plastic sheet on top of the insulation had holes in it to accommodate light fixtures, the only escape for the water was to drain down into the light fixture. Putting a pail on the table under the drip, I attempted to unscrew the fastener and pour the water into the pail with my single arm. Catastrophe! While I tried to balance the bowl on my shoulder, water began to squirt out of the hole in the bottom of the fixture and I instinctively ducked. The glass covering, the water and the repairman all landed on the floor in a big puddle.

The episode of the light fixture was only the first of several unexpected occurrences during the year that we lived there. One day when I turned on the water tap, it merely hissed at me as it sucked in air. The foot valve at the bottom of the well had failed. In this instance and many others, it was Shorty to the rescue. The recommended local repairman came and pulled up the flexible pipe and replaced the valve. Thankfully, the problem was easily solved.

The next surprise was rather nasty. Due to an extremely wet spring, the septic field had become water-logged. The aroma in the house suddenly became unbearable. We discovered about four inches of sewer in the basement. What to do? You guessed it—call Shorty. The sewer tank had overflowed and the unwelcome contents had backed up into the basement, which, thankfully, had not been developed. The man for the job came and pumped out the tank, but it remained for me to clean up the disgusting aftermath. Being so flat, many of the farmers' faced the same dilemmas with many of their fields flooded. Yes, spring had arrived!

It was 1970 when Lucy Kerfoot sent a puppy from her Sheltie kennel out to Manitoba by air. We named her Flurry and our small family very much enjoyed her company. Unfortunately, the dog was deaf and because she was unable to hear, she was shortly hit by a car and killed, another sad devastation for us to endure.

Three months passed quickly and my first contract ended. Even though I rarely saw the principal, he must have been pleased with my effort as he hired me for the fall at a different school which was strictly for special needs children. Summer seemed to depart relatively soon and it was time for school to begin once again for me in St. Boniface.

Classes were in the same building as some very needy students who were referred to as "Trainable." A number of these children actually needed a level of care which our school was unable to provide. One misfortune resulted in dire panic. On a beautiful spring afternoon, the teachers decided to take all the children on a walk beside the river, which was still running high. A fork in the trail by the river led up the high way and the low way. Failing to notice that one autistic lad had taken the lower trail, a head count upon returning to the school revealed him to be missing. Fortunately, just before his parents were called, the janitor found him clinging by his fingertips to the bank where the trail entered the rushing river. As he was in my class, I realized I had utterly failed to watch over him, though all the teachers were reprimanded. I was most fortunate that another year ended without tragedy.

I was busy at school and very busy on the home front as Betty's health continued to decline. Though Betty was still able to care for herself during the day, her hours must have been unbearably long. From her wheelchair, she was usually able to prepare supper and do some light domestic chores, but otherwise, little else. Weekends and holidays were more than welcome and she was always very glad when the children and I arrived home.

ON THE MOVE AGAIN

We really did not feel welcome in Manitoba, as it appeared to be divided into ethnic islands where newcomers did not fit in well. Here, if some new venture were suggested, it was met with a negative response such as "That has never been done here so why try?," whereas in Alberta, the same venture would be met with an enthusiastic, "Let's do it and see what happens." In 1971, we decided to return to Alberta immediately following the end of the school year. This time when I contacted a moving company and explained my previous dissatisfaction with movers, they assured me, "When you move with us, all will go well," and so it did.

Just before leaving, another surprise awaited me. My children had insisted that I retrieve cattails from a muddy ditch while returning from an errand early in the fall. Since then, the plants had hung suspended in a five gallon pail in the garage. One day, upon opening the garage door, I found the floor buried in about two feet of creamy cattail fluff. It instantly reminded me of the time Betty and I returned to our home following our wedding night to find our house christened with confetti. As I studied the situation, I was none too happy, as I had filled my rubber boots with water while collecting the cattails in the first place. The kids stated that it had been great fun as each blow erupted into a ball of soft fluff. How do you remove the result of the fight my kids had with their imagined war clubs? Enter our Electrolux vacuum cleaner. I do not now have any memory of how many bags of fluff were successfully sucked up or how long it took us to finish the job, but the humorous side of the battle surfaced and my displeasure vanished. Our family enjoyed many a chuckle over the incident.

Betty supervised the preparation for the move back to Calgary. We were relieved to see all our earthly belongings neatly loaded into a semi-trailer. Having been assured that they would be waiting for us upon our return to Calgary, we confidently watched the moving people pack up and leave.

On the way back to Calgary, we almost met with an accident. We had stopped at a motel in Regina and there was a very strong wind. It was downhill and downwind to our motel from the restaurant where we had enjoyed supper. I was wheeling Betty along the apron of the road with Bob and Beth running along beside us through the trees. The race was on but the elements were too much in my favour. Betty and the wheelchair nearly got away from me. I knew that if I tried to slow it down by pulling back on the handgrip with just one hand, the chair would swerve and Betty would be thrown to the pavement. I yelled at the kids, my voice indicating both humour and concern, "Help, Mom's getting away from me!" The little pneumatic wheels on the front of the chair were dancing a merry jig as they skipped over the small stones along the roadside. I eased back on the handgrip and immediately the chair began to swerve.

Betty showed no anxiety whatever but she joined in my alarm by shouting to Bob and Beth, "Hurry!" I suppose that they were about seven and ten years old. Bob was older but not any faster. They both scurried down the ditch, their legs going like little pistons. They really had to run to catch us. Fun and concern were having a tug-o-war as they came alongside, wobbling as they grabbed the arms of the wheelchair. We three were puffing like winded horses as they slowed the chair to a brisk walk. "Poof," I puffed, "that was sure a close call!" Betty gave us a good scolding for being so foolish, but when we began to laugh, she just gave us a reproachful look and commanded, "Would you get out of this wind?" It was a different story the next morning when we were pushing her uphill against the wind. We all had a good chuckle as we chided and teased her about the race. We didn't declare a winner. Of course, Bob and Beth insisted that they were in the lead when the contest was called off.

Betty and I had arranged to purchase the house next to the one in which Betty had grown up, as her mother's house was now rented by her cousin. We were so sure that all would go well that we even put down a hefty deposit toward the purchase. However, when the proposed sale of the property came to the attention of the city, the sale was refused, since two adjacent properties could not be owned by the same person as they might decide to join them. The area did not allow apartments, though this was far from our intentions. Our appeal was refused and our deposit was forfeited, but such is life. We had rented our lovely bungalow in Calgary to an older Christian couple when we went to Thompson in 1967 and we were reluctant to give them such short notice. As we needed a place to live in, we threw out the net looking for an alternative.

Before long, we discovered that 1665 Larkspur Way was empty, following the eviction of the occupant who had not paid the mortgage for months. This was similar to the situation that enabled us to rent the house in Dugald, Manitoba. We contacted the movers to arrange the time and place for delivery of our possessions. Soon, we were settled into the new lodgings which met all our needs, though I still carried Betty from the house to the car and vice-versa. Our children could walk to the local school, which was an added bonus.

The next hurdle was to find a teaching position. As there was an abundance of teachers looking for work at that time, the Calgary School Board did not require another Special Education teacher, nor were any other teaching positions available in the city. There was, however, an opening in Airdrie, which was a long drive from where we lived. Hence began a year-long trek all the way from the south side of Calgary to my new assignment north of the city. Our almost-new 1970 Dodge Monaco station wagon proved up to the task, but the morning and evening traffic at that time of day proved demanding.

My first year of teaching in Airdrie was very difficult as my classroom was adjacent to the open-area library. The librarian demanded that my class remain silent. Since my boys were much too old to be in elementary school and hated being there in any case, what to do with no suitable teaching material available? For the lads who were the most undisciplined, I chose a book which I thought would be of interest to them, recorded it on tape, gave them a headset, and let them sit in front or under a study center near my classroom. Since there was a craft room and a gym as well as some opportunity for outdoor activity, I managed to maintain both my sanity and order in the class until the year ended. My interaction with the principal, however, was distressing. When the school year ended, he gave a party for all the staff. As he gave each teacher an award, I thought, "He will be hard pressed to give me one!" He did, "Scrounger of the Year," which I still have. I was also given all the leftover Chinese food at the end of the party, which fed us for several days. Summer was more than welcome, but Betty's condition continued to worsen. Still, we managed with little outside help except for some arthritic treatments by a home care nurse.

As my teaching contract was renewed for another year in 1971, we gave notice to the occupants of our house in the city, sold it, and planned to build a new home in Airdrie which would end the nightmare drive and provide better accommodation for Betty. We contacted a builder and friend, Gordon Hewitt. The boys that I taught in the elementary school graduated—I use the term loosely—to the junior high school on the same property, and I moved along with them. My new principal was a gem and my classroom situation was much more suitable. As my wife and I believed in being part of a church in the community where we lived, we found a local congregation, which, although not Baptist, was evangelical. We enjoyed our time there.

Even though living on the acreage at Dugald had had its challenges, we took the opportunity to purchase land near Airdrie where I had hopes of starting a woodworking business plus breeding and selling our much-loved Sheltie dogs. I had been introduced to Shetland Sheepdogs when I lived with the Kerfoot family near Okotoks in 1953/54. After we had moved to our acreage, we intended to go into the dog-breeding business since we would have a lot of room. We hoped that raising Sheltie puppies from our Shelda Kennel would augment our income. As our children were growing and loved horses, it seemed like a good venture and would mean that I no longer needed to keep on teaching slow learners, which would be a welcome change and free up more time to spend with Betty and the family.

We agreed to purchase twenty acres of a forty acre parcel of land, with the assurance from the realtor that immediate subdivision would be no problem. However, upon applying in June, we were told that we would have to wait for a permit until September as the municipal authorities were on holiday. Construction could not start until then. My worst fears came true—building in the winter. We had given notice of possession of our new house in Airdrie at the end of the year. An added problem was the cost of the many test holes for water that were drilled before success. By Christmas, after many set-backs and with the house far from completion, we had to put our belongings in storage and find a place to live. Fortunately, we found a double wide mobile home in a farmer's field. I asked myself, *"Are all these distressing situations my fault or just the result of coincidence?"*

At this time, we decided to sell our much-loved Dodge station wagon for $2,250 and invest in a modified camper van—a Dodge Para Cruiser—which was air-conditioned and had a hoist for loading the wheelchair. It was expensive—$7,200—but ingenious: by inserting the key behind the passenger door, the doors to the hoist opened automatically and descended. Once the wheelchair and occupant were pushed into position and the key turned, the chair lifted and then stopped when level with the floor of the van. The chair was then secured with a turn lock. When the key was turned again, the door closed. It was much easier both on Betty and me than using our station wagon. Betty was situated almost between the front seats. The bed provided seat and belts for both children. This vehicle became our much-enjoyed home on wheels.

Because it snowed often that winter, getting to our new home in the farmer's field might have become a challenge, with only a trail across the field showing the way. However, our van managed to plow in and out like a tractor and we never once became stuck. We wondered when our lovely new acreage home would be ready, and finally, none too soon for our liking, the day arrived. By now, Betty's condition reached a new low. Since she preferred my nursing care in place of any other arrangement, we decided that I could become her full-time caretaker if I were to quit teaching, which I did. We rented an empty Quonset in Airdrie and began a woodworking business. I hired Glen Sherwin, one of my supposedly "retarded" students, who became my very faithful foreman, allowing me to come and go as needed.

Following the completion of our beautiful new home, we confidently applied for permission to form two small businesses. Both applications—one to do woodwork and the other to operate a small kennel—were denied by the municipal authorities. I was in shock. When I arrived five minutes late for the meeting, having been delayed at work, I found out that the council had declared both submissions, "Irrevocably denied." I had not even been able to explain their nature. When I had spoken to the neighbours about our plans for the property before building a house with special adaptations to make Betty's life easier, no one had given any hint of objections. They had simply said, "Do what you like. We do the same." Evidently at a council meeting, the neighbour across Highway 2 objected to the possibility of noisy dogs. What a double disappointment! Later, I learned that they were all members of the same club. Was this defeat an indication of what would follow? We were able to stay afloat financially for about two years by raising show-quality Sheltie dogs plus a couple of teaching opportunities—one in Beiseker and the other on a nearby Hutterite colony since I still was authorized to substitute teach.

Despite the rejection concerning a kennel, we still planned to breed and sell some puppies. Our first Sheltie was "Nugget," which we got from Lucy. We were expecting a good litter from her but she only produced one pup, which we kept and called Shelda's Golden "Bell," nicknamed "Ding-a-ling." She was pretty special to me as she was born into my hand and was my dog from that day on. Nugget didn't know how to look after her and I had to show her how to be a mother. When we called Bell, she would come running with one ear straight up and the other down. Bell, over time, gave us seven litters of seven pups each. We kept one of the pups which we called "Cristy." She grew up and was bred and we kept one more puppy from one of her litters. This one we called "Misty." We now had four generations of dogs living in our home. They all got along amazingly well together, but would not accept any other dog from outside.

During the day, time must have once again hung heavily on Betty. Fortunately, we had our dogs so Betty had some company and they provided her with an outside focus. A dog had always been part of our household and we did not view it a hardship to look after them. Keeping the records on the dogs and selling the puppies gave Betty something to do. We operated the kennel for almost seven years. Betty also kept busy with her needlework when she was able, and tried to take an active take part in church and community events.

BOOKS

During a visit to the Canadian Wax Gallery in Banff, Alberta, one day back in the '70s, I saw a wax statue of Pete Knight, the famous bronco rider and four-time World Rodeo Champion. Many articles and stories had been written about him and a book about his horse, Midnight, but no book had been written about this legendary transplanted Albertan. Charles Peter Knight had actually been born in Pennsylvania, on May 5th, 1903.

In 1976, I decided to write such a book, and *We Remember Pete Knight* became a reality. I wanted to straighten out the many rumours and conflicting stories that were circulating about his accidental death on May 23, 1937, from a fatal injury sustained beneath the hooves of a rank bucking horse named Duster at the Hayward, California, rodeo. As he stumbled from the arena, he knew he was badly injured and died on the way to the hospital a short time later from a broken rib puncturing his liver. One such story claimed that he had been in rough shape after celebrating his daughter's birth the previous night. In 1932, Pete met and married Ida Lee "Babe" Avant, of Hot Springs, Arkansas, taking his new bride on the rodeo trail with him. The couple had a daughter in April 1937 named Deanna. When the book was published, Pete's wife was angry because I had mentioned the rumour about Pete celebrating the night before his death. The actual record of the ride revealed that Pete was instantly thrown off his horse and its front feet landed on his chest.

Taking my tape recorder to record stories from his friends who were still living, I launched out on my project to tell the real story. I met so many interesting people who had wonderful tales to tell about Pete, speaking of him most highly. Knight was known for being a great human: humble, down to earth, and a friend to all. He had adoring fans and friends across North America.

While Pete was a young boy, his family moved to Oklahoma where they successfully worked Pete's granddad's homestead, eventually becoming stockmen. They relocated to Crossfield, Alberta, after Pete's dad saw an advertisement for cheap farmland. The Canadian government was looking for Americans willing to try to make a living in Canada. Canada is where Pete learned to ride bucking horses and eventually became known as "The King of the Cowboys," a legend in his own time. Canadians took him as one of their own and he became a rodeo hero to many.

I paid for the publishing of the book and was amazed when I later heard that his wife claimed all rights if the book were made into a movie. Thankfully, that never happened. The book sold well, both first and second editions, and I have one remaining copy in my possession. Betty and I spent many an enjoyable day at the rodeos and stampedes throughout Alberta selling the books to interested parties. This was our last great adventure together and I cherish the memories.

While visiting Bill and "Con" (Connie) Loree at their Midway Ranch near Nanton, Alberta, in the late 1970s, I asked why their house was such a long way from the main road, and the reason for what appeared to be an unused strip of land by the driveway. They explained that this place was here long before there were any fences or surveyed roads in the area. It had been Trollingers' Stopping Place at the crossing on Mosquito Creek on the original Macleod Trail, and Con's father had requested that portion of the trail between the house and the road be preserved as a reminder of those lost Pioneer days.

Stories of Fred Ings, Con's father, had appeared as a serial in the Western Producer Magazine and various other publications. These were taken from an original manuscript of Fred Ings' life, written in 1936, as he was dying from cancer. His wife had written all his memories down as he recalled them. It was Fred's wish to honour his contemporaries in this way. Fred recognized that he lived in a by-gone era significant to history. Born in Prince Edward Island in 1863, he came to Calgary in 1882, one year before the railroad. He worked on the Bar U and other ranches with such interesting and historical figures as John Ware, the freed slave and expert cowboy and rancher, and Harry Longdebough, known to history as the "Sundance Kid." When other places became too hot for them, saddle tramps and other fugitives drifted into Alberta to escape justice south of the border. Longdebough hired on with the OH Ranch in the early 1890s, and Ings describes him as a "splendid rider and a top notch cowhand" as well as a thoroughly likeable fellow. Longdebough's real troubles began when he joined up with Butch Cassidy and robbed trains.

Con wanted to have the manuscript put into book form. As I had just finished *We Remember Pete Knight,* I volunteered to do the editing for her. Thus *Before the Fences* came to be published in 1980. After the first edition sold, the family decided to have a second printing done in 2002, and they still have several boxes of the book left. Betty had passed away by the time this book was written and published and I had no wish to travel about alone selling it as I had with the book on Pete Knight. Instead it was sold through outlets and by word of mouth.

Bill and Con are both gone now and the ranch is being run by Con's daughter, Mavis, and her husband. I still get to visit them occasionally.

ON THE COLONY

Our woodworking business was not proving to be financially productive, so I needed a way to supplement our income. First, I was hired to assist the Industrial Arts teacher in the Beiseker school to help him design and build new tool storage racks for the recently expanded shop. It was a short-lived assignment due to some encounter he had with the new principal, and my much hoped-for employment ended abruptly. This was especially distressing because Betty and I had just hired May Bannerman to stay with Betty while I was away working. Trying to keep up with everything on the home front had become a losing battle. Coupled with this, Bob was becoming a handful. Though Beth and Bob were ardent defenders of each other in every other situation, at home they squabbled and scrapped, which was very nerve-wracking to both Betty and myself, and required much time and effort on my part. Having May around was fantastic as she did many domestic chores freeing me to tend to other matters and we did not want to lose her. Fortunately in the nick of time, I was hired to teach on the local Hutterite colony.

Just what do you know about Hutterites on colonies? During the Reformation, Dr. Martin Luther translated the Bible from Latin into German, allowing more people to read it. From the Sermon on the Mount, they learned the teachings of Jesus—that God loves us and wants us to love our neighbour and particularly, that we strive to do good, even when others treat us maliciously or violently. Also, in 1525, according to their understanding of the teaching of Jesus and His baptism, they began practising adult or believers' baptism, and were called Anabaptists. This baptism was declared a crime punishable by death in 1526 and thousands of Anabaptists fled from the German-speaking countries, of Switzerland, Austria and Germany, to Moravia. Anabaptists hailing from Austria's Tyrol Valley were identified with an early leader, Jakob Hutter; he was a hatmaker by trade and later became the Elder of the community in Moravia. Hutterites still carry his name today. Jakob Hutter is the reason the men often wear a broad brimmed black felt hat. During his time, the Hutterites, uniquely among Anabaptists, began to practice "community of goods," holding all their possessions in common as a church body and living in self-contained farming villages rather than working for individual wages and supplying their individual needs.

The Hutterites came to the United States seeking freedom from religious persecution in the 1870s. Later, following World War I, they came to Canada to avoid penalty for refusing to join the war effort, as they are confirmed pacifists. The arriving Hutterites bought large tracts of land. This alarmed the Alberta government and the Communal Properties Act was passed in 1942 to limit their expansion. The act was repealed in 1973. Each colony may consist of about 10 to 20 families, with a population of around 60 to 250. When the colony's population grows near the upper allowable limit, in order to preserve sustainable social relationships, its leadership determines that branching off is economically and spiritually necessary. They relocate by purchasing land and building a "daughter" colony.

There are three main branches—the Schmiedeleut, the Dariusleut and the Lehrerleut—each following the pattern set by their founding father. The book *I Am A Hutterite* by Mary-Ann Kirkby is an example of a family who saw no choice but to leave the colony because the wife had come from a group that wasn't technically Hutterite. The Hutterites do not intermingle with other peoples, and to my surprise, I discovered that any non-Hutterite is simply called "English," a term of derision pronounced with a very long "E" sound.

How we became attached to our first contact with a colony is now forgotten, though I do know it was most amiable. We bought produce from them and they gave us chicken innards which we used to feed our dogs, except for the livers which Betty loved fried with bacon. Betty sold them her beloved Singer sewing machine when her hands grew so gnarled she could no longer sew.

Shortly after school began in the fall, the teacher at their daughter colony became ill and was unable to continue teaching. She spoke German and very much enjoyed teaching the Hutterite children. I knew the teacher in the former colony, and, as it came to pass, Rockyview School Division asked me to take the place of the teacher.

The Hutterite school where I taught included grades one to nine. Those in grade nine were supposed to take correspondence courses by mail. Here I was in an entirely new situation. The colony supplied the school building and required materials and the division supplied and paid the teacher. This was not an ideal arrangement and I learned later that teachers in the division had the same opinion. It was by no means considered a promotion; rather, just the opposite, like a trip to Siberia in Russia.

The colony "boss" soon asked me to teach the grade nines. All were girls and he disapproved of the course material. He said, "Mr. Jeem, would you teach the girls?" So I did. Even then, they objected to the nature of my question-and-answer approach to the subject matter. When I launched a study on the origin of Hutterites, the boss told me, "Mr. Jeem, you teach them school and we will teach them what they should know." He also asked if I would mind if the little kids sat at the back so they could learn English. As I thought saying "no" to these adjustments would be worse than saying "yes," I went along with the changes. Learning was the purpose of education but it appeared now that reflective thinking was not to be a part of the practice. Simple rote memory was encouraged by those in control. The times tables would be an example if understanding how to use them were not necessarily a priority.

The children told me that they might start a new colony on the northern island of Japan, so I began a geography lesson on the country, including the island of Honshu. My friend, John Budd, with whom I worked in the Carpenter Shop at Prairie Bible Institute, was now a missionary in that country. He sent me a bundle of pictures of the island, which were all quickly "stolen." Pictures are a Hutterite no-no, at least on more conservative colonies. Since the Bible says, *"Thou shalt not make unto thee any graven image"* (Exodus 20:4, KJV) they considered pictures, especially of people, taboo. Alberta Hutterites had originally won the right to avoid having photos taken for their drivers' licenses, and in May 2007, the Alberta Court of Appeal ruled that it did violate their religious rights and that driving was essential to their way of life. At the time, approximately 80 photo-less licenses were in use. However, the Supreme Court of Canada ruled that the communities must abide by provincial rules that make a photo mandatory in order to prevent misuse as well as identity theft.

My rule about rules goes like this: a really good rule may have an occasional exception. A slightly mentally challenged lad of about fifteen was turning onto the busy highway off which his colony was located, and, by police estimate, was struck from behind by a car travelling about 70 MPH in a speed zone. This had happened quite some time before I came to the Colony. His mother, almost in tears, slyly showed me his well-worn picture when describing her terror (she had actually seen the accident happen). Sadly, his picture was now all she had by which to physically remember him.

The Hutterites' literal interpretation of the text is what led to this situation. The graven image in the Old Testament was a representation of the heathen idols of the countries which they had captured when they entered the Promised Land. Had they destroyed these detestable nations as God had commanded, there would have been no temptation to worship their false gods. God is just, fair, and kind but His kindness does not obliterate His justice. Today, our graven images are not necessarily objects but the obsessions by which we live: fame, power, education, buildings, cars, money, diamonds, collecting, travel, accumulating, or whatever captures you—for where your treasure is, there will your heart be also (Matthew 6:21). The Bible teaches, *"It is more blessed to give than to receive"* (Acts 20:35, NASB). I wonder how we measure up to this teaching, especially at Christmas, which is now primarily commercial.

Since learning did not seem to be the primary purpose of the school, I relaxed my objective of trying to teach the students the curriculum. Accordingly, I considered that perhaps a little diversion would be in order. Since I had been told of remnants of a corral on the west side of the colony, I suggested that we try to find the old enclosure. Of course, they agreed immediately. They all crammed into the camper van, which I used to go back and forth. (Much later, I purchased a little wagon.) As it was just one of my spur-of-the-moment decisions, I did not ask anyone for permission or tell anyone of our plans,

Off we went. I asked the girls to sing as they were allowed to sing a cappella—accompaniment with instruments was considered taboo, however. What fun we had, though the remains of the corral eluded us. It had obviously been torn down and ploughed under long before. There was a huge hill close by where one could see far and wide from the top so I asked, "Do you think we can climb it?" I did not even wait for a reply and up we went. We arrived back just in time for school to end that day. I imagine the kids had quite a tale to tell of what we had done. Long after, I learned that they had great fear that we all would come to harm as we were not driving a tractor.

I had gotten into the habit of not arriving before 9:00 each morning as the German teacher had an hour with the class before I appeared and often carried on until 9:30 or later while I sat at the back waiting patiently. Because of this delay, I began coming at 9:30 sharp. One day, a representative of the school division visited and asked to see me outside, which was very unusual. He said, "It has been reported that you do not arrive at school on time as you once did." I explained why and he smiled. Ever after, I was there at 9:00 with a big smile for the German teacher though he did not reduce his teaching time.

Just the same, the children enjoyed a long recess morning and afternoon while I took a break in the kitchen. From the start, I was asked to eat with the men at noon—the women ate on the other side of the room and the children ate elsewhere. I soon learned conversation was kept to the minimum. The rule seemed to be: grab, gobble, and go. I was soon back in the class for my preparation and recovery time.

As I stated previously, before I came to the colony, I had occasionally substituted farther west in Beiseker in the Industrial Arts class. Upon passing the colony, I had often noticed a man sitting in a shabby old upholstered armchair in front of an old barn. The chair was a curiosity as I had understood that such supposed comfort did not normally adorn any Hutterite colony. I always tooted and waved as I went by at the speed limit. Upon first arriving on the colony, I discovered his name was Peter and he became very friendly toward me. He soon quietly asked if I could bring him a bottle of wine if he gave me some money. I responded, "Peter, you know I can't do that!" He apologized profusely and it did not affect our friendship during all the time I was there. I soon discovered, however, that anything of value was kept under lock and key—especially the communion wine! The children told me that they once found a part bottle of wine hidden in a stack of bails. When I asked, "Did you have some?" the group just silently looked at each other, with guilt written all over them.

As I entered the classroom after lunch one day, the son of the "Big Boss" was kicking my coat up and down the aisle. As it was noon and I was not late, he should not have been in the school uninvited as stealing was not uncommon. As he ran by me on the way to the door, he said, "Mr. Davis, you are old and you stink." That told me their opinion of us lowly "EEEnglish"—obedience to those who they consider to be foreigners to them is not considered mandatory, not even to their teacher. Had I asked for him to be disciplined, he probably would have been spanked soundly. As his dad was one of the two main colony bosses (the Big Boss/financial manager and the church minister) I did not bother reporting him. There were also the Field Boss, the Pig Boss (Peter), the Garden Boss who had charge of the women who did all the work in the gardens, and so the hierarchy continued. Peter, my good friend and cohort, must have been the low man on the totem pole.

A WILD RIDE

School was interrupted one afternoon by some ladies bursting into the classroom crying, "Come quick, the old man fell down and is unconscious. Our men are all gone away! Can you take him to the hospital?" How glad I was for our camper van. The women heaved him into the vehicle and I was on my way instantly, surprised that no one came with me. I wondered, "Did he have a stroke, heart attack, or what?" We flew west all the way to the main highway and then south to Calgary. The old General Hospital was still standing then and I often had to take Betty there. Just inside the city limits, the speedometer fluttered near 100 miles per hour. With the pedal floor-boarded and warning lights flashing, I squeezed past a vehicle in the left lane which did not yield one inch. As I drove down the shoulder, I hit the end of a sawhorse parked under the overhead pedestrian walkway under construction. I checked the rear view mirror to see boards flying in all directions.

With my heart pounding, I arrived at the emergency entrance to be met by two attendants. Seeing the old Hutterite lying on the van's couch, they wheeled the gurney beside the wheelchair ramp and pulled him onto it like a sack of potatoes. Voicing their displeasure, they demanded to know, "What do you mean bringing him in here like that?" As the patient did not have any identification on him, I could only tell them that he was from the Beiseker Colony and reported that the women had called the hospital earlier.

Upon examining our van, I discovered that there did not appear to be any damage, except that the front left wheel cover had gone the way of the city's sawhorse. It is likely that I did not go back to the colony until the next day. The old fellow recovered and was soon back home, having suffered a diabetic seizure. My thanks were a tank of gas and a grateful word of appreciation.

The older students who were mostly girls in grade nine rushed to the window every time a strange vehicle entered the colony. On one occasion, Clara, an outspoken young lady, turned to the class and announced affirmatively. "No foot, no arm, no eye, and no ear—any old teacher is good enough for a Hutterite. Now they are sending us a black one." The principal of the school in Beiseker—a dark-skinned individual of recent immigrant arrival whose origin shall not be revealed—was getting out of his car and approaching the school. The town had raised such a fuss about his performance in Beiseker to the Rockyview School Board that the gentleman in question had been asked to leave. As he had a three-year contract, the man refused to resign and agreed to look over the "opportunity" at this colony. Further observation revealed that the man accepted the assignment at full principal's salary for the remainder of his contract, in accordance with the terms of the ATA's agreement. Clara's critical observation was, of course, accurate—I was Mr. No-Arm and each of the supposed defects was a description of teachers on nearby colonies.

In 1977, having been previously warned that my alleged replacement would be visiting, I was not surprised by the impending termination of my employment. Our woodworking business in Airdrie proved to be unprofitable. We could not compete with offshore products imported mainly from Asia. Making occasional articles from solid hardwood, such as end tables, toys, and benches, along with some repairs to furniture, just did not produce much. Even though we sporadically had a small market making shipping crates for oil companies, this spin-off from Alberta's major industry was not enough. I closed the rented Quonset and sold all the tools. Glen Sherwin, who had been especially capable at building the crates, was hired by Atco Trailer Company and served them well. One crisis after another had beset me during my entire lifetime and sometimes I felt that I could no longer cope. However, hope appeared in the form of an opportunity for a special needs teacher in High River, along with the news that Beth could attend Senator Riley School, with a class available for Bob at Spitzee School.

At this time due to the combination of the work, the extra expenses involved, and the state of Betty's health, we also felt it was necessary to terminate the dog-breeding business, which had become unproductive anyway. It turned out that purebred puppies at $200 each had no ready market; it was usually hard to find buyers, and the price out of necessity was often lowered to $75. Before moving to High River, we closed the kennels down and tried to find homes for the dogs with the exception of Bell. It was a very traumatic time for all of us. The whole family had enjoyed the venture and it was very difficult to part with our four-legged members.

> But godliness with contentment is great gain. For we brought nothing into the world and we can take nothing out of it. But if we have food and clothing, we will be content with that. (1 Timothy 6:6-8, NIV)

HIGH RIVER AND LOSS

We sold our beautiful acreage along with the twenty acres of land that we had rented out for pasture and moved to High River during the summer vacation. After purchasing an acreage in Alder Heights near High River, we moved in before school began that fall. All seemed promising. However, three further frustrations hit us like a Mac truck: cuts to funding cancelled my hope for a teaching position, there was no class for Bob, and Beth was unable to attend Senator Riley since we lived east of Highway 2. Bob, being dyslexic, was required to meet a Greyhound bus at 7:00 each morning for the hour ride to Claresholm where there was a class available for him. Beth, too, had a long school bus ride to Blackie.

Since Beth had already formed friendships at Senator Riley, the very first day she came home crying bitterly, which was very unusual for her as she generally brushed aside little troubles like chaff in the wind. This day, however, she was very distressed. The principal had informed her upon her arrival what the consequences would be if she did anything wrong in his school. Later she was ostracized by the girls in her class, evidently because of jealously over her athletic ability. She had been instructed by her teacher to hand an important assignment in by that Friday, but when she did she was told, "You cannot play basketball today as I don't have time to correct it." It was an intramural basketball game, and as Beth loved sports much more than school, she had had more letdowns than a person could handle. She expressed her frustration by trying to kick in her locker, which was not well received by the "powers that be."

After moving to High River, Betty's heath rapidly deteriorated. One day on the way to the hospital, I heard her moaning "*Grive!*" The sound seemed more like the groan of an animal than comprehensible human communication. What was Betty trying to say? Oh, "Dear Lord, she is saying "*Drive!*""

The moment that I had long dreaded was upon me. Betty was dying. Her very life depended upon my getting her to the hospital as fast and safely as I could. She had not seemed to be in any great distress when we had left the house a few minutes earlier. She had simply said, "I don't like this tickle in my throat. You had better take me to the hospital." As an afterthought, she had added, "Perhaps you had better let them know that we are coming." This appeared to be just another of many such trips to emergency, but the thought of taking her there almost unconscious, choking, and gasping for breath often haunted me. As I turned to her now, realizing the meaning of this strange moan, her face was already turning blue, her eyes had begun to roll in sightless gaze, and her breath came in choking, feeble gasps. Though barely able to speak, she had gasped out the desperate plea. I could do nothing to help her as my one remaining arm was needed to guide Skylark II. I felt helpless in that I could not even reach over and lift her lolling head. Every effort and bit of concentration was needed to get her safely to the hospital as fast as I could. Had I called for an ambulance, she would have been unconscious before it arrived. My inner being groaned, "*Go, go man, go!*"

The nose of our beautiful air-conditioned Dodge Maxi-van, which had been purchased with some of the proceeds of Betty's inheritance, lifted like a great whale rising from the deep as the accelerator hit the floor. The skilfully-tuned 360 motor rose to a roar as I felt myself being pushed back into the seat. The sudden thrust straightened Betty in her wheelchair momentarily as the vehicle surged ahead. Her head lifted from her chest only to loll sideways once again. Her hands groped feebly as she tried to grasp the arms of her wheelchair. "Oh, Dear Lord," I pleaded, "Help me."

> Do not be anxious about anything, but in everything, by prayer and petition, with thanksgiving, present your requests to God. And the peace of God, which transcends all understanding, will guard your hearts and your minds in Christ Jesus. (Philippians 4:6-7, NIV)

The lump in my throat dissolved. The hot rush of blood stopped hammering in my ears. My breathing eased. A great calmness came over me like being lowered into a pool of warm water. It was as though a trusted friend had laid His hand gently on my shoulder and whispered, "Be calm— everything will be alright." My world shifted into slow motion. Each detail came into sharp focus. I had mentally rehearsed this trip many times. We were going south from Alder Heights on Highway 2, approaching the gentle turn to the left where the municipal road goes straight south. "I must take the shortest route although it is the roughest," I decided as we plunged across the gravel-strewn shoulder and down the rutted rural road. I noted the cloud of dust in the rear view mirror as the vehicle bounded over the gentle rise and rumbled over the thinly gravelled furrows. A mental image of the ruts and potholes along this route filled my mind instantly.

Thoughts tumbled through my head like popping popcorn: *"Avoid the ruts on this short section. Be careful to slow down enough to make the corner on Glen River Road. Take care when you come out of the turn. Don't look at her; concentrate on the road. You can do nothing for her now. Be ready for the potholes after you turn. Be sure there is no one coming from the east. Don't stop at that corner."* Peripheral vision told me that Betty's head had fallen to her right. *"Good,"* I mused, *"Turn hard enough to straighten her up, but not hard enough to throw her head to the left. At least, she won't fall out of the wheelchair this time. We learned the seatbelt lesson the hard way, didn't we, Sweetie?"* I regretfully recalled.

"Go, Skylark, go like you've never gone before," I silently urged as we turned right onto the Glen River Road. Once again I felt the van's forward surge. "Potholes, potholes, potholes! Can I miss them?" I questioned. Betty straightened momentarily as we gained momentum, only to slump forward helplessly again. The roadside grass became a tawny blur. The fence posts flitted past in double time, and the interval between telephone posts seemed all too brief. I dared not look at the speedometer. My inner photograph of the potholes served me well; we scarcely swerved as they slid between the wheels. Thoughts continued to tumble through my mind: *"How fast can I turn the cemetery corner? It's banked a little. Check for oncoming traffic and use the inside of the turn if the road is clear. Good, it's clear. No cars from there to the bridge. Brake heavily going into the turn and downshift coming out. Turn the flashers on after crossing the canal bridge and pray that traffic is light. Yes,*

go right through town—it's shorter than going all the way to River Road. How glad I am that we have made this trip once already on an emergency basis." Now, as I raced to the hospital, I recalled an earlier trip that had prepared us for this ordeal. Then, the anxiety was nothing compared to the flash of fire that flooded my being as I recognized the reality of her condition. Thinking she was on the verge of dying, every second was of the utmost importance. I wondered who would be waiting at the hospital for us this time.

Two months previously, we had made a very distressing emergency trip to the hospital. One beautiful morning in June, we were getting ready to renew our oxygen supply. We brought enough each trip to last us about a week, storing the bottles on the deck. Each cylinder was about five feet high and weighed about eighty pounds. I could handle them quite easily with a little two-wheeled dolly made for that purpose. After putting about five empty tanks in the rear of the van, wedged between the bed and the cupboards at the back, I would wheel Betty into place between the front seats before securing the turn-buckle that held the chair firmly in place for her safety. On this occasion, I parked the van a little too far from the deck—a platform which we had built over the front steps to facilitate entry from the van to the house with the wheelchair. I dropped a piece of plywood between the deck and the lift to enable me to run the dolly into the van more easily before going inside for Betty, thinking it would be easier to put her on board with the plywood there. We had many things to accomplish so I suppose I was in a bit of a hurry.

Getting both of us ready to go was always time-consuming, and fighting frustration was a continuing battle. The plywood rested on the sides of the lift in such a way that there was about a six-inch drop-off from the plywood to the lift. "Not a hard problem to negotiate," I mistakenly thought. When the front wheels of the chair rolled off the plywood, I lost my one-handed grip and the chair flipped forward and hurled into the van. Betty's head barely missed the top of the door. Her face hit the linoleum-covered floor with a sickening thud. I kneeled beside my wife and sobbed, "Oh, Betty, I'm so sorry." Her face was lying in a spreading pool of blood. She calmly replied, "I'm okay, just get me up." The chair was jammed in the door and I could not lift both Betty and the chair. Thank God, Bob was home. I yelled frantically, "Bob, come quick." I think I roused him from a sound sleep. He came running out into the brisk morning air in his shorts. Together, we lifted the chair gently back onto its wheels.

Because Betty's seat belt was fastened, she and the chair was one unit. The force with which her face hit the floor must have been dreadful. Blood was still gushing from her nose. I mopped her face with paper towels the best I could. While she held a pad of towels to her face, I hurriedly secured the chair. "Surely," I thought, "there must be a quicker way to tie down a wheelchair." After making the chair safe, I turned the key beside the lift which activated the door-closing mechanism automatically. While waiting for the lift to rise and the doors to close, I asked Bob if he would call the hospital and tell them that we were coming.

Betty assured me that she was alright and that I need not hurry as she wiped the blood from her face. By now, her nose had stopped bleeding. When we arrived at the hospital, I did not see anyone at the emergency entrance. I took Betty out of the van as quickly as possible. *"I'm so glad for that lift but it seems to take an eternity for the doors to open or close,"* I fretted silently. Two attendants met us as we approached the door and they shepherded us right into the examining room. After checking elbows, knees, and wrists carefully, Dr. Jeeva said in his quiet and unflustered way, "She will be okay. There are no broken bones but she will have two beautiful, black eyes." He looked at me with a twinkle in his eye and chided, "And you will have some explaining to do in the next little while." A nurse carefully washed Betty's face and hands and we were soon on our way home again, complete with the oxygen on board. Betty hadn't even had to get out of her chair, and I was very relieved and thankful as I thought her injuries were much worse. The only aftermath was that for quite some time, Betty very much resembled a raccoon. Fortunately, during the seven years that Betty presided from her chair (and preside she did), this was the only serious fall that she endured.

That first trip Betty wasn't in any danger, as it turned out, but a dire situation truly existed now and everything was vastly different. There was no doubt of the seriousness of Betty's present condition. Competent hands transferred my dear wife to a gurney and she was taken to the emergency ward. Dr. Mercer was waiting for us and examined her at once. Earlier, we had transferred all Betty's medical records to this doctor and I had already discussed worst-case scenarios with him at an earlier time. Betty was soon transferred to a hospital bed, and by mid-afternoon, she had regained consciousness and seemed to be much improved. Dr. Mercer increased the rate of flow on her oxygen, but this was about all that could be done for her. My terror and the wild ride had not upset her in the least. She had cheated death so often that another trip to the hospital no longer bothered her. Now, she retreated into a state of partial oblivion where the inner powers of healing waged their silent war against death and disease. She lay quietly on her back with her gnarled hands folded on her chest.

Though Betty had often returned from the hospital when her condition seemed as bad or worse, I could not help thinking as I turned from her bedside that day knowing she was in good hands, *"Will she do it again or is this Betty's last trip to the hospital?"* All traces of her raccoon eyes had disappeared, but she still had furry, puffy cheeks, probably the result of the prednisone which had already added a year-and-a-half to her life. As Bob and Beth would soon be home from school, I hurried back to the van to bring them the news lest they arrive to an empty home. The children knew nothing of their mother's present condition. Perhaps this was just another one of many trips to the hospital and Betty would soon be home again, giving orders like a sergeant major. A sense of despair and weariness overcame me as I drove home in Skylark II.

My fears about Betty were soon to be realized. About a week after our harrowing ride to the hospital, Betty died. Her death occurred just as the sun was setting on October 17, 1977, at 5:05 PM. Even during this last stay in the hospital, Betty continued to tat with fingers that were gnarled and twisted like bird claws. By now, she only weighed sixty pounds. I often told her that she was my precious sack of sugar. Finally, she departed this physical world, having defied death on numerous occasions. A small, unfinished burgundy rosette adorned her bedside table. I stood and gazed out her hospital window to try to gain my composure. I seemed to sense her spirit leave the room as I looked at a burgundy cloud, just like a skein of yarn, floating in the sky below overhanging angel-shaped faces in clouds of the same colour. *"...We live by faith and not by sight. We are confident, I say, and would prefer to be away from the body and at home with the Lord"* (II Corinthians 5:8, NIV). So Betty was, and the clouds seemed to be affirmation. I rang the call bell and the nurse came and confirmed that she had died. Hers was a quiet, gentle departure, marked by a glorious sunset, the like of which I have never seen before or since. I phoned Beth and told her that her mother had just died in order to give her a chance to gain her composure before I came home. Betty's body was wheeled out of the room.

Beth met me as I parked by the special deck we had built shortly after arriving at our new acreage. I left the empty wheelchair in the van and ascended the deck. The lift would never be needed again. Beth and I continued to look at the spectacular sunset. Even the barbs on the wire fence shone like miniature stars and angel faces continued to smile down on us. Beth took an impressive picture of the western sky which we had enlarged and framed. She still has it. Beth said, "Well, Dad, isn't it good that we had her as long as we did?" Two years or more previously, Beth had been told by a good family friend that her mother might die anytime. Beth had said, "No, she won't. I am not old enough yet." What maturity for a young girl!

Bob really dissolved when he came home much later and knew immediately that his mother had died. When Betty was buried, I put the unfinished rosette beside her on the pillow along with the book *We Remember Pete Knight* in recognition of all the many Alberta stampedes she had attended with me and the many fun days we spent together. In response to Beth's question "What will you do to my mom's body?" Bob Snodgrass, the undertaker, told her, "With the casket you have chosen, your mother will look the same as she does at this moment fifty years from now." It was another sad day for me as I touched Betty's casket before it was lowered into the grave. A comforting verse popped into my mind, *"And I heard a voice from heaven saying…that they may rest from their labours; and their works do follow them"* (Revelation 14:13, KJV).

Betty's mother often said that Betty could organize the Roman army. It was certainly so in our family. Her death left a huge hole. Although our ideas and wills often clashed over the years, we were faithfully devoted to each other and I tended to her needs with loving care. Often, caring for Betty and meeting our needs were difficult, time consuming, and absolutely exhausting. Bob and Beth did not have a great deal of attention lavished on them as children, and they had to carry responsibilities far beyond their years. Though Beth adapted well to the situation, Bob apparently did not. I had explained to them that their mother required a great deal of care and I could not always be there for them and they seemed to totally understand.

However, in hindsight, I do regret that we could not spend more time just being a family, and I do recognize the contribution that they made during those very trying years.

> Naked I came from my mother's womb, and naked shall I return there. The Lord gave, and the Lord has taken away; Blessed be the name of the Lord. (Job 1:21, NKJV)

SEVEN LONELY, FRUSTRATING YEARS

During Betty's long illness and ultimate death, Bob would often lament, "When Mom is not here, we just have a house, not a home!" How very true and now this was our reality—perhaps more for Bob than Beth—at least outwardly. Though Betty had been able to make very little contribution in the house-keeping department in the last few years, her presence was essential. She had been the one who knew about our affairs, our schedules, what bills had to be paid and when, details about our children as well as an encyclopaedia of other details. Birthdays and anniversaries were her specialties. One particular faculty I relied upon and had become very convenient for me—I seldom needed to refer to the telephone directory when Betty was around. Once, when it came time to renew our auto insurance—a fact of which she had reminded me—I jokingly asked, "What's the number, Betty?" She immediately told me. I was surprised because we did not use the number more than once a year. No, our house was not a home without Betty!

Whenever Betty was hospitalized, which happened ever more regularly, it had been a gruelling round of work, eat, and rush in to visit her. However, even from there, she tended the home patch, always asking about meals, our Sheltie dogs, her devoted friends, and housekeeping chores. Fortunately, during the latter years of her life, we had had a lady do the washing and the weekly cleaning. There had been a time when I had tried to do it all—

the cooking, laundry, cleaning, and caring for Betty—plus making a living. Over time, it had become impossible to accomplish all those tasks in a timely fashion with one arm, especially with a growing family. Now, without a permanent job, I was not able to pay the mortgage on our property so I sold our comfortable home and moved to a rented farm on Tongue Creek Road, west of High River.

Brother Bill had invited us to spend Christmas in British Columbia with him and his most recent live-in. Since Bill had told my son Bob, "Just come and see your old Uncle Bill if you need anything," Bob and his friend decided to take the bus and left before I did. Beth had chosen not to go with us and was staying in High River with a girlfriend who attended Senator Riley High School. When I arrived, Bob was very upset and his friend had already left. Bob said, "Take me to the bus, Dad. I am not staying here." Bill's bad temper (which I had experienced as a child) had erupted and he had slapped Bob around, telling him, "Don't come crying to me if you can't get along with your dad!" Bill was living where he worked as a heavy-duty mechanic during the week. He had not winterized their mobile home and the sewer was frozen. His live-in asked, "What will our guests do?," and I will not repeat his vulgar reply. I stayed for Christmas because of his insistent previous request to meet his most recent affair, but left soon after.

On the way home while still north of High River, but in range of our local AM 1140 radio signal, I heard of a recent accident on Tongue Creek Road. I feared it was Bob. Sure enough! He had used our farm pickup to go tobogganing, lost control, hit the ditch, and drove through a barbed wire fence, spilling kids along the way. Some were hospitalized, one with a ruptured spleen. No, Bob did not have a driver's license. Later, Bob said, "My friend had a motorcycle license and he thought I was covered." Not so! Fears of having to pay fines and being sued simply boggled my mind—fortunately, neither happened. Bob only broke his little finger and was soon out of the hospital. The truck, however, was a total loss. How could a person absorb all the unexpected trials of life and still maintain their composure, their supposed sanity, and a hope for better things in the future? *"Cast your cares on the Lord and He will sustain you. He will never let the righteous fall"* (Psalm 55:22, NIV).

Unknown to me then, the owner of the farm where we had so recently moved caught our son and his friend playing chicken with his pickup and ours in the snow-filled pasture west of the farmhouse. Soon after arriving home, I was ordered to vacate the property immediately. My agreement to share the property with him equally had already created problems even before Christmas. My plans to raise my much-loved Pinzgauer cattle and have horses for my children evaporated. Rather than take my two pregnant cows to market, I sold them to the farm's owner at far less than they were worth. Our two horses and saddles I gave to Circle Square Ranch. Bob kept his yearling colt, Thunder, and later lost him playing cards with his boss. Now in hindsight, I realize that Bob was going through the same deep grief at the loss of his mother that I had felt when I lost mine, and coupled with rejection by his uncle, it was just too much for him. Striking out was the only way he could deal with the unbearable pain. Indeed, a mother is the rock and cement that makes a house a home!

We moved hastily into the Brewster apartment on the west side of High River. While moving, I had set a box of beautiful cups on the table to take with me. They were the cups that each graduating class gave Betty during her years of teaching dress-making at SAIT. I was distracted momentarily by some helper asking a question about the move. When I returned, the cups were gone. A young lad had put them in his pickup and was just leaving the yard. I raced to my car and tried to catch-up to him. Just as I did, the box of cups rose gracefully into the air and smashed onto the asphalt road. . The total destruction of that reminder of my wife was more than I could bear. Scattered before me lay a mangled stretch of colourful cornflake-sized pieces, no bigger than my thumbnail. Standing alone on the side of the road, I broke into uncontrollable tears. It took some time for me to recover my composure.

The summer of 1978, cousin David Trask's wife wrote that they had planned for some time to drive across Canada, dip their wheels into both the Atlantic and the Pacific and then return to Nova Scotia. One day while I was working in front of our apartment, Dave poked his head around the corner, saying, "Hello from Nova Scotia." Since their visit coincided with the Calgary Stampede, I asked them whether or not they would like to attend the parade which kicked off the events. While standing on the sidewalk, a complete stranger approached and enquired, "Would you like to buy some tickets to the Stampede?" I thought, "Oh, boy, a scalper! We must look like easy prey." He said, "I have three tickets which I cannot use. You can have them for the same price that I paid." Dave bought the tickets and we were able to attend the grandstand show and the chuck wagon races. These were very good seats, and I could have shot spit balls at Pierre Trudeau who was sitting three rows in front of us.

I had met Pierre Trudeau ten years earlier in Thompson, Manitoba, and had been repelled by his "charismatic" performance with the ladies and their babies. As a local pastor, I had been invited to attend the meeting. Just imagine! Bob Stanfield was also there. He was sitting at the back of the room and many people visited with him while Mr. Trudeau put on quite a "performance." I silently prayed, "Dear Lord, spare us from this man." How sad I was that Mr. Trudeau won by a small margin. Mr. Stanfield said later, "If I walked across Halifax Harbour before breakfast, the CBC would report in the evening news, 'Stanfield can't swim!'" We lost the best prime minister Canada never had. Even though Mr. Trudeau is held in high esteem in much of Canada, he is regarded with suspicion and not well liked in southern Alberta. His mandate of a Just Society by virtue of the Privacy Act provides a safe haven for criminals.

Mr. Trudeau also repatriated our Constitution and Canadians lost the British North America Act in exchange for forcing Canada's government offices to become bilingual, though Quebec was later allowed to ban English signage. The cost of packaging increased for companies who were mandated to have both French and English on their products, a cost passed on to Canadian customers. Metric measurements replaced ounces, pounds, inches, feet, and miles. No more inch our way or miss by a country mile! In the lumber industry, the new method of measuring became cumbersome to those used to the old way. In my humble opinion, Quebec has held the country hostage for one hundred and fifty years.

Trudeau's policy of multiculturalism hasn't helped our country either. The immigrants wanted to keep their language, way of dress, culture, and feuds. Not only that, they want to impose these things on us and to change our institutions to do so. All these thoughts rumbled through my mind at the sight of the man in question. I was determined to put him out of my thoughts and enjoy the day with my cousin.

How wonderful it was to make connection with some of my eastern relatives in the midst of my trials and grief. We had a great visit and much too soon Dave and Jennie were off. Sometimes God brightens the path along life's way. Before leaving, they invited me to come and see them, even if they did not have an impressive stampede in Nova Scotia! Their earnest invitation lit my fuse. Miriam Ross had not married since returning from Africa and she definitely became an added incentive to visit Dave and Jennie to see if I could light the fire of romance again—perhaps Miriam would take a second look at marriage! So it was in August of 1978 that I bought a return ticket to Halifax and phoned David that I planned to visit them. The money may have come from the sale of our acreage—nonetheless the flight was booked.

My holiday began with a free flight from the airfield in Cayley to the airport in Calgary with someone who had made that trip on several occasions. Did you know that a cow looks like a pear lying on its side when you are up in the air a thousand feet? The flight plan called for a direct connection to Halifax from Calgary by way of Montreal. At the airport in Montreal, the voice from above announced there would be a short delay in the flight, due to engine problems. I had expected to be in Halifax by supper time but instead I spent four hours watching sea gulls competing for scraps from flights that were being readied for take-off. Kindly, David waited at the airport in Halifax until I arrived. We got back to his house in Aylesford about two in the morning.

During the first few days, I kept busy washing and polishing the car he had promised to loan me, waiting for the date that Miriam had planned to arrive in Springhill following a thirteen-year stint in Africa as a missionary. On the morning of the third day before her expected arrival, I said to David, "I think I'll go to Springhill today and see if I can be any help to Mrs. Ross before Miriam arrives." He chuckled and replied, "Well, you are a big boy now. You don't need my permission." I was soon on my way, hoping that Christina would be home—not so! Shortly after parking in the drive, the neighbour came and told me, "Miriam and her mother should be home soon. They have gone shopping in Moncton today. Come on over to our house until they get back." I accepted their kind invitation and they even asked me to stay for supper, saying, "You can help us shuck some oysters which were just given to us for our meal."

After dark, the Ross' little Austin car finally chugged into their driveway. I curbed the urge to rush across the road and greet Miriam with a big hug and a welcome kiss as I would have done twenty years earlier. Stifling the desire to test her feelings, I walked slowly to the Ross' car where Miriam was busy examining her purchases of the day. She turned slowly and declared, "Well, I suppose you have had your radar out all the way all day?" A very astute evaluation of my anticipation! Arriving three days ahead of her announced arrival seemed to me to be a very good omen for my aspirations. Thus began a twenty day, unexpected respite from all the recent disasters in Alberta following Betty's death. My plans were to stay only ten days, but fortunately, Air Canada had a 13-day strike during this time and delayed my return accordingly. We enjoyed one day for each of the years since we had parted on the pier in New York harbour twenty years earlier—a sad parting indeed and now a hopeful reunion.

Miriam requested her Aunt Queen, a very austere lady, to be our chaperone on an anticipated tour around Cape Breton. In the middle of the night on the first day of the trip, I awoke and noticed that Miriam's blanket had fallen off her cot—she had insisted sleeping on it as she said, "You take the bed. I slept on a cot all the time I was in Angola." As I tiptoed toward her resting place, a stern voice commanded, "Let her sleep!" I returned to my bed feeling like a boy caught with his hand in the cookie jar. Our excursion was fantastic—the sea was always in full view and we saw many sites along the way, especially the Alexander Graham Bell Museum.

Lochlan MacDonald, a commissionaire and a survivor of World War I, escorted us from the parking lot to the museum, all the while entertaining us with hilarious stories. He had witnessed the flight of the Silver Dart on Baddeck Bay in Cape Breton, Nova Scotia, on February 23rd, 1909. This inaugural Canadian aviation feat was the result of the innovative thinking, entrepreneurial spirit, unrelenting determination, and the talented team of Alexander Graham Bell, Douglas McCurdy, Casey Baldwin, Thomas Selfridge and Glen Curtiss. These men had a common vision and formed the Aerial Experiment Association with the financial backing of Mabel Bell, Alexander's wife, and began building aircrafts and conducting experimental flights. A year and four months later, the Silver Dart, piloted by Douglas McCurdy, rose 9 metres and flew almost one and a half kilometres at 65 kilometres per hour. This first flight of a flying machine in the entire British Empire was a huge success. When I returned home, I corresponded with Lochlan MacDonald until he no longer had any involvement with the museum. An article in the High River Times reported the anniversary of that flight. The illustration depicted a tall lad following the plane on skates. He was wearing a tam o'shanter and I guessed that this had been Lochlan MacDonald. Volunteers on skates had pushed the plane into position for takeoff.

Upon returning to Springhill, Queen went her own way, most likely relieved that her duty to chaperone had been successfully completed. Miriam and I began several day trips. During this time, I helped her purchase her own car, which we industriously spruced up. We enjoyed each other immensely. One night, having just gone to bed, Miriam visited me on the far end of our upstairs bedroom and snuggled down beside me on top of the covers. The next night, I suggested, "It's chilly, crawl under," and she did. She assured her mother with the words, "I know the floor squeaks, but I want you to know, there is no hanky-panky going on upstairs." I think even then that we were closer in heart and mind than many married couples. To my surprise and dismay, she told me that even though she had experienced the most wonderful time of her life, marriage was not for her—"Thanks, but no thanks." I was horribly devastated once again.

The family who had first introduced me to Hazel Miriam Ross in 1952 during my first disastrous year at Gordon College has since informed me that Miriam died on February 14th, 2007, just two weeks after celebrating her 78th birthday. Evidently she died from an unexpected adverse reaction to the anaesthetic used for a rather routine operation. Truly, a once-dear friend was gone. Nineteen years earlier, she had said to me, "I let the drawbridge down once, but never again." Evidently, she had just changed her mind and regretted her decision to see me. While I continued to hear on an annual basis from the family that had introduced us, I continually hoped to hear from Miriam. Such was not the case, though the family usually informed me of events in her life. The only communication I ever received from her following my visit in 1978 were two letters that arrived soon after my arrival back home: a short letter saying, "No more letters or phone calls," and a very fat letter recounting, "Our wonderful twenty day time together." These memories I will always cherish—they have stayed in my mind, and it is with regret that I have not been able to extinguish them even now.

Miriam's memorial service records a remarkable history of service to others and a total of no less than seven earned degrees beginning with an RN in 1951 and a DD before her death. She was truly a remarkable woman who was loved and admired by all who knew her. My friends assured me it was probably better for both of us that we did not marry. In the nitty-gritty of married life, we would have been poles apart.

Back in 1978, however, by the end of the second week, I grew very concerned about my children. When the airline strike was over, I returned to Aylesford, gave back the borrowed car, and David took me to the airport in Halifax. After expressing my deep gratitude to him for his hospitality and his generosity in lending his vehicle, I boarded the plane for Calgary. Upon arriving home, two facts were to confront me: I went to Nova Scotia on an invitation and a pretext too soon after Betty's death and I had been away too long. Beth had stayed with a girlfriend, while Bob lived in our newly rented apartment.

Upon driving me to the little airport in Cayley, Bob had agreed to take our old Dodge station wagon to the body shop for minor repairs. This vehicle had served us well while Betty was alive. We had sold it to friends who also appreciated a good wagon. Much later, I bought it back with plans for a complete restoration. When I called the shop to ask if it was ready, a cautious voice replied, "Mr. Davis, you should have a look at your car before we work on it." The front of the vehicle was badly damaged. Bob had taken friends for a fast joy ride, hit the ditch, and then smashed into a farmer's field. I said, "Repair it anyway as it means a lot to me."

When I arrived back at the apartment after viewing the damage to the vehicle, Bob was still in a sleeping bag on the living room floor. There was a gaping hole in the bathroom door and the living room was in a shambles. To say that I lost my composure is an understatement. With my fresh disappointment and the stresses of my many challenges along with the lack of time, money, and energy, I was ill-equipped to understand or to deal with Bob's continuing rebellion and the difficulties they brought. I reacted poorly and got his immediate attention by giving him a swift kick in the backside with the side of my foot. A fight erupted with a lot of pushing and shoving. When it ended, Bob did not say much about my much-admired station wagon, which had been a gift from Betty—it had been purchased with some of the proceeds from her inheritance.

After cooling down, Bob told me that he had rescued a stray dog which he had locked in the bathroom. The dog ate a hole in the door big enough to escape and terrorized the room. Of course, we faced another eviction and a move to another apartment across the road from the hospital. We had already reduced our furniture and other belongings to the essentials. Most of the rest of our possessions were consigned to a secondhand store in the basement of the big building across the street from the Royal Bank in High River. Much later, fire destroyed the building completely, along with all record of consigned goods.

As it turned out, it was a mistake to repair the old station wagon. The long-awaited rebuilt motor and transmission were faulty and I traded the car in on a new Plymouth Volaré wagon at the same garage. It, too, proved to be defective and could have cost me my life while on my way to a substitute teacher assignment. On a chilly, misty morning, the car stalled in the middle of the southbound lane at Aldersyde as I turned west. It simply would not restart. The new electronic starting system was defective. Huge trucks blasted their horns as they tried to avoid a collision. My heart pounded. It was imperative that I not be late as I was usually the last teacher to be called. Finally, the car roared to life. With a much relieved, "Thank you Lord," I managed to arrive on time.

Early in the fall, a new teaching position for an English teacher became available in Cayley, which I accepted immediately. My assignment was to beef up the English program. I sensed immediate opposition from the grade nine students. They complained, "We are now supposed to take more English than we can get credit for." I enquired, "What have you been doing instead?" The reply was that they had just finished an arm-wrestling competition. After much discussion, we all agreed to do research and report on "survival in the bush." Once the reports were satisfactorily completed, we would plan an overnight adventure at a campsite at the end of the year with willing parent chaperones.

Before the next spring, our final move in High River came about in a similar manner. Bob must have had another noisy party while I was away. Evidently, there had been a lot of carousing, but no property damage. This time we relocated to an old two-storey house across the street from where

Joe Clark had grown up. The rent was more than reasonable, but the place was not very promising. The old coal furnace had been converted to natural gas and the foundation had settled so that the kitchen wall on the west side of the house did not quite reach the floor in the middle of the room. The upstairs rooms were quite warm simply because heat rises. We stored some things in the old garage at the back of the property by the alley. During a heavy rain, it flooded. Unwisely, I had not elevated much of the stuff and it was damaged, including many books—a set of cook books entitled *Cooking Around the World* among them.

Before the end of the school year, the district's superintendent visited my class. I was most anxious as that usually was the job of one's own principal, not the superintendent. His studious and serious attitude annoyed me. My principal, with whom I thought I had a good rapport, informed me that my contract could not be renewed the next year. When I reviewed all the things for which a teacher would normally be "let go," the principal had given me top marks. Upon enquiring as to why my contract would be terminated, he said, "Evidently, you did not support administration." Disagreeing, I phoned the superintendent and asked to see him in his office as a convenience to him.

The day and time were arranged. I sat in the waiting room of the superintendent's office for a long time, thinking, "I am expected to be punctual, why isn't he?" Finally, the door to the inner sanctum opened and he walked quickly past me, opened the door to the hall, looked cautiously both ways and motioned me to follow. We entered the storeroom and I sat on a pile of books, beneath a bare light bulb. He informed me that I was too much for the students and not supportive enough of administration. I do not remember our entire conversation, but his final remarks were, "Perhaps you might like to find a job pumping gas." You can imagine my dismay! The words that Robbie Burns in his poem "To a Louse" flashed through my mind: "O wad some Powr the giftie gie us to see oursels as ithers see us! It wad frae mony a blunder free us, an' foolish notion." Translated into more modern English, it would read: "Oh, that the giver of gifts would give us the gift to see ourselves as others see us."

My grandfather was a much respected educator as was my mother. I had done well as a Special Needs teacher, but as such, I was not at all suited to teach regular classes. The education structure was patterned after the military system to turn out cookie-cutter kids—the object being mass production and control. Having become a teacher because of the way I had been treated in school—with few exceptions—for twelve years, I was determined that no child in any of my classes would suffer the same fate. As stated earlier, the most I gleaned from school came from the large dictionary I spent so much time studying while enduring discipline in the hall. No teacher, with the exception of Miss Daley in grade eight and George Ryberg, who taught English in grade ten, showed the least concern or kindness toward me. A weekly class in Industrial Arts, called Shop, did, however, help make regular classes tolerable and dispelled some of my hatred and distaste for school.

With all of these calamities in my life, I visited a non-Christian counsellor who had been recommended to me and used a humanistic approach. Having unburdened myself to him, he exclaimed that my stress levels would register right off the chart. At times, I did not know how I was going to cope with all the problems with which I was beset.

The question arose as to what I would do now. From that day forward until the present, I have not had a very productive or full time job. According to government statistics, all the rest of my years proved to be below the poverty level—even now with the combined incomes of myself and my present wife. Other financial problems plagued me due to a misunderstanding with our Sears account. When I applied for a loan to buy my first pre-owned Volvo, they responded with, "Mr. Davis, you have a very poor credit rating as you did not pay the minimum on your Sears account for three months." Another bank near the Volvo dealership agreed to loan me five thousand dollars—the price of the vehicle—secured by my life insurance policy.

1981 ushered in changes of a different sort. A new employer, Walter Sapinsky, entered my life in a saving way and I enjoyed a much more stable income as an indoor/outdoor painter. At this time, I began working for him as a painter's helper. Painting clothes closets was my introduction to the business. I became known as the "Picasso of the closets," but I soon graduated to more enjoyable, rewarding jobs. Even Houdini would have found it a challenge navigating around those cramped spaces with a roller, paint brush and paint tray, all the while climbing up and down ladders which required real ingenuity and skill—especially considering I still found myself to be one-armed! Though I did have a somewhat steady income, I worked with and for Walter only as needed, which was not on a full time basis, so I sought other options.

On the way home from Calgary one day, Walter and I stopped at the Electrolux branch in Acadia to drop off a machine for repair. Walter had already decided to work by himself and not have the cost and hassle of extra bookkeeping and compensation, though I did work for him occasionally in other years. The manager told me out of the blue, "You should be an Electrolux salesman. You would make plenty of money," though I would have been content to earn only enough to provide for me and my children. Reality never matched these aspirations. I provided a much appreciated repair service and became Joe-Boy for returned warranty repairs, since that was company policy. No one wanted to do it as it provided no revenue. Income came only from the commission on the sale of new machines. I was wonderful at "show-and-tell" but a failure at "show-and-sell." One day, the new manager had filled the room with graduates from the remand center. All wore black jackets—not inspiring-looking representatives for Electrolux. They each signed up for a machine and left with the usual sales pitch. Neither they nor the machines they took were ever seen again.

While trying to sell Electrolux I found it necessary to place our small dog, Bell, or "Ding-a-ling," in a new home. Bob was working and no longer lived with me. Since I was away much of the time trying to earn a living, and Beth usually staying with her girlfriends, my poor dog was cooped up in the house for many hours at a stretch. Once when I returned home, Ding-a-ling ran out of the house to relieve herself while giving me a look that said, "Well, finally". Another time, she carried the nice fur hat I had purchased for winter out to the yard without me noticing. After I found it when the snow melted in the spring, the hat had shrunken so much it would not have fit a doll! The family we gave her to had several children who were crazy about the dog. Unfortunately, their parents separated and the dad took the dog to use as a bribe to have the children live with him. He sadly neglected her and one day when Ding-a-ling was running loose, she was struck and killed by a motorist. I was simply heartbroken.

Trying to sell new Electrolux vacuums was a real challenge. The manager's carrot-and-stick approach and his daily diet of "go, go, go, reach your goal" constantly pressured me to sell, sell, sell. However, although woman loved the machine, their husbands often refused the contract, preferring to buy a gun, fishing rod or some other more attractive investment. I became very experienced at repacking machines. I put one machine back into its carton thirteen times before it finally sold. Occasionally to add to my difficulties, the purchaser requested one that had never been out of the box. Having sold enough machines to meet the criteria for a bonus of a new suit, I was assured I would qualify. However, upon returning from a trip to Vancouver, I was informed that I had not qualified for the additional benefit as one of my contracts had bounced. Soon, the company required either cash or credit card but no personal cheques which added to my difficulties and became a real hindrance to selling. I never did receive the promised suit.

An Electrolux customer introduced me to Amway, saying I could really do well. After obtaining the request for a "Hope and Soap" order, you bought the product, found the person, collected the money and repeated the same. Along with all the phone calls, no one home, and no money, the business soon lost its appeal. I never even tried to sign up anyone with the company. Their regular sales meetings were also very much "Sell, sell, sell," with lots of enthusiasm. "Get others to join" was also one of their commands. My pyramid of success here was very flat-topped and soon another opportunity flashed across the sky.

The selling feature of Matol was inspiring. The inventor of the potent brown liquid declared it was the result of a long-ago miracle product which had been revealed to its discoverer in a dream—another pyramid get-rich-quick scheme. Another supposedly surefire way to get rich quick selling Herbal Life rapidly fizzled. Optimistic promotion at regular sales meetings produced few results.

My next undertaking was Purple Shield, the final layaway insurance to cover funeral costs. Again, one man who had done very well with the corporation enticed me to join. You were instructed to contact prospects who had requested information from the company, thinking it would be sent to them by mail. They did not expect to see a salesman at their door and my presence as a representative was often met with a cool or sometimes hostile attitude. Their expression often seemed to imply, "Are you here to remind me that I am only going to die?" That indeed is a fact of life, but usually not a very welcome one. I, myself, was the first to sign up. The policy has long since been paid in full and increases a small amount until required.

Since I demanded that my son make my plywood coffin, I expect that the policy will cover the cost. I gave Purple Shield my best effort, only to realize that I may have been a good teacher, but a very unproductive salesman.

Despite my failure at my other selling attempts, my next shot was with Dominion Windows. Mr. Trudeau had introduced the supposedly wonderful and convenient metric system. Preparing quotes was a nightmare as math had never been my forte. The company's home was in Toronto and they were expecting to expand out west into the booming economy. When the economy declined after this same prime minister enacted Canada's "share the wealth policy" called the National Energy Program, the company folded and returned to Toronto.

Late one night, the local RCMP detachment called for me to come for my daughter. Evidently she had been picked up for drunk driving. During questioning, the policeman treated her very roughly. I wanted to slap this officious young man around, but simply said, "Aren't you a bit rough?" He replied, "I will let you know when I want you to tell me how to handle a drunk." The reason Beth was apprehended and not her friend, Sandra, who had also been drinking was because Beth had traded places with her before the policeman reached the car; therefore, Beth was behind the wheel when they were caught. The policeman had obviously not seen them change seats. In court, she said nothing about this to the judge so that Sandra would not be implicated. Of course, Beth related this to me later. Her sentence was six weeks of house arrest and she was ordered not to drink. When I was on my way home at the end of the day, I occasionally saw her sitting in the upstairs window of her bedroom with her feet dangling out as she watched the cars go by. To my knowledge she obeyed the terms of her sentence. The police did not once check up on her.

By this time, we had arrived at 1982. I was my own supervisor for the R & N government-subsidized housing program under the CHAP umbrella to build our own house in Black Diamond. Under this program, the payments were extremely reasonable and our shelter was assured. I undertook to be my own contractor and asked my boss from Dominion Windows to give me a quote for windows from a copy of the plan—the Bell Shell—designed by the government. The company had ordered that all our stock be returned to Toronto as soon as possible. My boss could have provided me with quality windows, but, instead, he specified a mishmash of sliding windows with very poor insulating ability. Upon arrival, some of the windows simply did not fit the opening. After returning some and adjusting a few openings, they were finally installed. The construction of our house became a nightmare. Among other things that could go wrong, the location of the chimney was different in the basement floor plan than it was on the main floor.

Beth and I finally moved into our new home in January, 1983. Our housewarming was a memorable occasion. Beth lived with me until she left for university, whenever she was not staying with her girlfriends in High River.

Having my own property allowed me the luxury of building a one-car garage where I was able to practice my woodworking skills and hopefully augment my meager income. Over the years, it proved to be a welcome haven from my day-to-day difficulties and a place for some private time alone. Even with one arm, I managed to build many creative pieces, eking out a small profit.

During those seven frustrating years and the many that were to follow, there were no less than ten different occupations where I tried with all my ability to earn a good return for my efforts. None came close. However, as the Bible says, *"And having food and raiment let us be therewith content"* (1 Timothy 6:8, KJV). Since the Bible also promises in Romans 12:19 in part, *"I will repay"*(KJV), I had expected that one of these promising opportunities would provide a bundle of cash. Not so; like Tevye, the gentleman in Fiddler on the Roof, I kept asking, "What are You doing up there today?"

Throughout all this turmoil, I continued my efforts to track down a good wife. Does not God's word promise, *"He who finds a wife finds a good thing"* (Proverbs 18:22, NASB)? I thought that a man without a wife was like a fish out of water. I had probably "beaten the bushes flat" in my local areas.

During one such foray, an embarrassing event happened with a lady named Myrna. She was very attractive and could sing like a bird. I thought she knew me fairly well, but there was no real background in our relationship. I purchased a bouquet of roses and expected to find her alone in her office at a church in Calgary where she worked. *"Perhaps wedding bells will soon be ringing,"* I thought. To my utter dismay, I entered a room with several people in the middle of a committee meeting; Myrna was among them, taking notes. The pastor invited me to join them. I apologized and hastily departed, leaving the roses by a chair. Myrna never responded and that ended my efforts of trying to find a wife in southern Alberta.

This is by no means the full story of those seven sad years, but they recount more than enough to explain why they have stayed in my memory so vividly. I continued to search for a mate until I thought of another region. Totally unexpected results would finally come over the horizon like the rising of the morning sun.

Sow a thought, reap a word.
Sow a word, reap a deed.
Sow a deed, reap a habit.
Sow a habit, reap a character.
Sow a character, REAP A DESINTY.

Watch over your heart with all diligence, for from it flow the springs of life. (Proverbs 4:23, NASB)

III
PAT-TRISHA

Courtship and Marriage

The Lord God said, "It is not good for the man to be alone. I will make a helper suitable for him." (Genesis 2:18, NIV)

Since my attempts to find a new wife in Southern Alberta had not been productive, my thoughts turned west. Pat Ovans was a very good friend of Betty's. They had met at the Banff Springs Hotel in 1957, where they both worked as billing clerks and also roomed together. An agreement was struck that whoever married first would ask the other to be their maid of honour. Pat attended our wedding in 1959, but declined to be maid of honour because her engagement had just been broken. She occasionally came to Calgary from Vancouver with the Sweet Adelines, a four-part harmony barbershop group, whenever they had a competition in the city. As well, she spent several vacations with us over the years. Pat often stayed with Betty's mother in order to visit us. We always included her in our annual Christmas letter mailing. In 1982 on a stopover on my way to visit a relative in Ucluelet, British Columbia, I had attempted to meet her at the airport in Vancouver, but Pat declined because her mother was then very ill.

Two years later, I was on my way by car to visit Pat. She had replied by mail in February, 1984, that she would accept my request to visit her at Easter. Pat had given me directions to her house very explicitly and I found myself near on Wednesday, May 16, feeling quite confident now that all my utility bills were finally up-to-date. Fortunately, I had Pat's phone number since I was soon hopelessly lost. We kept her phone busy as she tried to direct me. I knew that the Lion's Gate Bridge was near her home and I crossed that bridge twice before going west on the north side and driving halfway to the Nanaimo ferry, before she finally told me to meet her in the White Spot parking lot on the main drag, not far from the Capilano Mobile Home Park where she lived.

Finally, I recognized a lady in a green coat looking like she was expecting the occupant of the car presently entering the parking lot. At long last, following many detours, the object of my search was in sight. What a thrill and relief! Since I was supposedly on my way to my relative on Vancouver Island, my first visit with her was short. Since it was her day off, she suggested we visit Stanley Park, and off we went. Among many interesting displays, we were impressed by a family of baby otters which were hitching a ride on their mother's stomach as she paddled around the enclosure. Among other things, Stanley Park is now famous for being the home of the largest urban great blue heron colonies in North America. The birds arrive in March and remain in the park until August. At lunch time, I asked for a suggestion regarding where we could eat, and Pat replied, "We could get a hot dog in the park."

I replied, "Isn't there something better?"

"Yes, but we would need a reservation, and it is probably closed by this time. Parking will likely be a problem, too," was her answer.

Fortunately, just as we approached the Ferguson Point Tea House, a very nice car was leaving. We parked there hopefully, though we could tell it was just closing. When we enquired as to whether they had a place for two, the waitress responded, "Just a minute," and returned shortly. Just then, a jaunty-looking individual arrived and asked, "What have you got?" The girl replied somewhat curtly, "Nothing!" then turned and said to us, "Please follow me." We were shown a table overlooking the rest of the restaurant. Since I had anticipated this, as I had told Pat earlier, I was very pleased. By now, I was beginning to wonder, "*Could this be the end of a seven-year fruitless search?*"

The next morning I was on my way to Nanaimo via ferry, and from there all the way across Vancouver Island to Ucluelet. Having travelled this way previously, I looked forward to a stop at Coombs Market, where good ice cream was sold at a popular restaurant. When I flew down the cliff-sided road by Kennedy Lake, I thought, "What a dangerous road on which to have car trouble." My destination was not far away; as I turned off, the exit sign said, "*Welcome to Ucluelet*" and below, "*Please Do Not Enter.*"

During my visit with Aunt Nina, my father's youngest sister, there were many long phone calls to Vancouver, which proved to be thoughtless of me. This rightly prompted Aunt Nina's somewhat annoyed remark, "I thought you came to visit me!" I was already anticipating a longer visit with Pat on my way home, which I duly arranged by phone.

I planned to arrive on a Friday so that we could at least share the weekend. Finding my way from the ferry to her house came easily this time. What all we did on that weekend, I do not now remember, but it soon passed all too quickly. When Trish indicated that she did not "anticipate growing old alone," I immediately responded with, "There is a cure!" Her comment may have been related to her mother's death, which still weighed on her mind. Needing funds for a prospective wedding spurred my desire to get back to work with renewed effort. Thus began my best-ever season selling Electrolux products.

Our long distance courtship mainly consisted of months of nightly phone calls and letters back and forth. I learned later that the mailman would play tricks on Trish, passing by her home saying he had nothing that day, and then back-tracking to fill her box with two or three letters (I wrote many!). In order to share the cost of the phone calls, we set up a signal— two rings and hang up; two rings on her end, and she would phone back; two rings on my end and I would return her call. We didn't have the special low rate plans that are available today. Our mail and telephone courtship was interspersed with a few occasional visits.

Though it may seem superstitious, picking up pennies had long been my habit. My dad's saying, "A penny saved is a penny earned," was changed to a prayer during my seven lonely years, "Please find me a good wife". The Bible states in Proverbs 18:22 (NASB), "*He who finds a wife finds a good thing,*" (though calling your wife a "good thing" does not seem to be wise!). John 15 declares, "*I am the vine, you are the branches*" (NASB), indicating a close relationship. The back of the now-defunct Canadian penny had two leaves on one branch.

Following further communication, it was arranged that Patricia would come to Black Diamond for a visit. By this time, "Trish" was my preferred name for her. I had arranged for her to stay with a friend when she arrived on Friday, June 15. On Saturday morning, I planned to have Trish join me in my almost-new house for breakfast. Since the possibility of a wedding had been discussed earlier, halfway between the orange juice and the toast I blurted out "Would you marry me?"—not a very romantic proposal! Since Trish obviously responded, "Yes," I suggested that we visit the jeweller in High River to see about a ring, which every engaged girl should have. I had kept the ring from my first marriage, "just in case." Now the time had arrived! Trish said that she had a diamond ring which she had inherited from her grandmother more than thirty years previously, and she had it with her.

Upon arriving at the jeweller's, I proudly placed my diamond—which had been a real answer to prayer when I bought it long ago—on the counter. Since it had a slight imperfection invisible to the naked eye, I had been able to purchase it quite reasonably. When Trish put hers on the counter, mine was dwarfed in comparison as her grandfather had been a bank manager in Halifax. We suggested that it be mounted in company with two maple leaves. The jeweller was anxious to demonstrate her ability and the design exceeded my expectations. Trish, sharing my enthusiasm, returned on June 30th to reclaim the results. Later, the jeweller requested permission to use the same design for others, which we readily granted.

The next day, the ring was on display on Trish's finger when we attended the Baptist church in High River, where it aroused considerable attention—both at the ring's design and my final removal from a seemingly endless single condition. Many prayers from that church had just been answered. Even though Trish was from good Anglican stock and had long since been confirmed, she declared her faith in my church on that Sunday. We thought that the wedding might take place sooner rather than later, although too soon, Trish was on her way home temporarily once again.

Plans for our wedding now shifted into overdrive, mostly by phone. Elmer Olson, my favourite pastor in Nanton when I was a boy, agreed to conduct our wedding ceremony, which was set for August 4th, 1984. Fortunately, Elmer was now living in Vancouver, and Laverne Ducomen, who once lived in High River and was willing to be my best man, was also now living in Vancouver. A friend of Trish agreed to emcee, another would take pictures, and her neighbour printed the invitations. Additionally, the community hall located at the Capilano Mobile Home Park near Trish's home was available. A caterer with reasonable prices was booked and all was set. My niece, Lynn, was able to attend, and cousin Carmen, her hubby Fran, and Aunt Nina arrived from Ucluelet in their motorhome, bringing with them the homemade wedding cake packed in the bathtub for safe travel! I spent a restless night before the big day with them in their home on wheels.

All was in readiness at the community hall when I arrived: guests, Pastor Olson, and my best man were already there. The arrival of the bride and maid of honour was arranged so that they would enter the side door just as the familiar strains of "Here Comes the Bride" began. However, the signal to the organist was given too soon. The organist had learned only the first few stanzas and she was well underway before they arrived at the door. They had to make a run for it, which they did while maintaining their composure. Trying to keep mine was a real problem. When the words of the promise, "In sickness and in health," were solemnly quoted by the pastor, I was briefly overcome by a moment of weakness as memories of my first marriage tumbled through my mind, and I nearly collapsed as Trish struggled to keep me standing.

The reception followed the ceremony and called for remarks from the newlyweds. When I tried to tell the story of my habit of picking up pennies for many years and how it had become a symbol of our wedding, I flubbed up and my niece came to my rescue. If Trish said anything, I do not remember now; however, when Trish saw her many guests, she bounced around like a ping-pong ball while introducing me. I finally gave up trailing her. The emcee gave a humorous rendition of the bride's history, as well as memories of their good times together. Food was shared by all. Finally the time for us to depart arrived; we were to catch the last ferry to Nanaimo then travel on to Qualicum Beach Inn where we had reservations. The inn had previously been a private boys' school. Although it was very late, we enjoyed a lovely dinner and our waiter treated us like royalty. Finally, we were on our way to bed. However, a surprise awaited me. When ready to turn in, Trish said, "Since this was a boys' school and you were a teacher, I will give you a history lesson before you get into bed." She read a large portion of the book retrieved from the bedside table which gave the history of the school and the inn while I stood impatiently at the foot of the bed. Believe me, it was a long lesson.

Irene Ingam, Trish's maid of honour, owned a summer cottage in Parksville and had invited us to attend church with her the next morning, which we did. This gave Trish the opportunity to visit with her as they had both worked together at B.C. Forest Products in Vancouver for many years. We stayed another night at the inn, though we were anxious to spend the remainder of our honeymoon with Aunt Nina in Ucluelet. After a refreshing dip in the inn's pool instead of a shower, we left Qualicum on Monday morning.

Aunt Nina's mobile home had a delightful attached little room, complete with a double bed, skylight, and a little wood-burning stove—just the perfect spot for a honeymoon and a place to stay free of charge while visiting her and her family. After a lovely meal at Carmen and Fran's place nearby, we retired there for the night. Just as we got into bed, remarking that no tricks had been played on us after the wedding, the sound of a clanging bell emerged from under the bed. I groaned, "Oh, no, the oldest trick in the book!" Carmen's hubby had excused himself from the table during supper and tied a trolling bell to the bed springs. I unwillingly got out of bed, used the little bedside rug as a creeper, slid under and began trying to untie the bell—by the way, with one hand! It was fastened with more knots than I could count. When I finally got back into bed, I proudly announced, "End of round one." This began a series of hilarious comments and much laughter. Nina said at breakfast next morning, "That's the first time I heard so much laughter when two newlyweds had just gone to bed."

Since Long Beach, which was near the mobile home park, had been an open-air hippie commune during the sixties and my cousin and her hubby were beachcombers, their yard was a museum displaying their discoveries, among which were many sizes of round blue iridescent Japanese glass fish floats. They attested to their successes with many other finds as well. We were fascinated by their collection.

What else for us to do—why not go for a walk on Long Beach? We parked our car at one of the many lots with trails leading to the beach. As we entered, we decided to leave our shoes by the path. Our first observation near the surf was a long pile of huge logs stretching as far as we could see. The wood had broken free from log booms, a system which evolved over the century to enable the forestry industry to move harvested trees from logging camps to saw and pulp mills located on the south coast. The logs are formed into slow moving rafts and held together by cables, then towed southbound, often through very rough waters. Occasionally, the booms break apart and thousands of logs float out into Georgia Strait and then wash up onto the beaches. We saw that someone had decided that they could section the abandoned logs into cedar boards, and some less–than–perfect boards were still lying around. We were surprised to learn later that Fran was the one who had done it. I could hardly believe that they had been split into boards, one by six inches, almost like sawn lumber, using a method similar to that used by the early settlers. The boards were used to repair their fence.

Trish and I walked and talked about our future plans in the bright sunshine and even played "keep away" with the surf. Leaving time arrived much too quickly. Finding the path where we had left our shoes proved challenging, since the trails all looked the same from the beach. At last we were successful, and able to recover our footwear and return to Aunt Nina's. The next day, we decided to repeat the expedition in spite of my sunburned feet and scalp. Carmen loaned me a big red bandana to tie on my head, turning my appearance into that of a pirate.

Following a very enjoyable visit with Aunt Nina and her family, we toured around Vancouver Island sightseeing. Trish phoned her cousin David in Esquimalt, just west of Victoria. Even though it was past midnight when we arrived, he prepared a lovely steak supper for us. That night, we slept in our sleeping bags on the living room floor. We visited other old acquaintances, including a special friend of my first mother-in-law. Emma and Bill Andison had worked together at CFCN for many years.

Esquimalt is the home to the Royal Canadian Navy, and four sites at CFB Esquimalt have been designated the Esquimalt Naval Sites National Historic Site of Canada. The base occupies approximately 10,000 acres at the southern tip of Vancouver Island. The facility dates back to the fur trade era, before the founding of the Colony of Vancouver Island in 1849. When Cousin David took us on a tour of Esquimalt, he pointed out several buildings in the Bay which were once used to store ammunition.

We boarded the ferry to Salt Spring Island in order for Trish to visit friends. They lived in a beautiful new home which partially hung over a cliff above St. Mary's Lake. Deciding to drive our Volvo up Maxwell Mountain proved a real challenge: it looked as steep as one of our Rocky

Mountains in Kananaskis Park, west of Black Diamond. However, our car rose to the occasion! The view from above was spectacular. Huge log booms appeared below looking smaller than a box of wooden matches. Speed boats resembled water beetles on a pond. We reluctantly departed as we needed to return to Vancouver, pack our many lovely gifts into our car, and return to Alberta. We had opened many of them before the wedding, but there were still some to be unwrapped on our return from our honeymoon. While packing our gifts, the glass top on a decanter popped off, landing on the spout of a teapot sitting close by breaking it off. Since this really disappointed Trish, we braved downtown Vancouver traffic to go to the store where it had been purchased. Although they all looked the same to me, after examining various similar looking teapots, Trish chose one.

Memory recalls two incidents from this time. Every time a pontoon plane flew overhead, I called Trish to have a look. She would appear instantly. Once, expecting to see an aircraft, she discovered she had to come to my rescue as I had shut my fingers in the car door and, being one handed, was quite trapped. This happened a second time after moving back to Alberta when I shut my hand in the rear door while trying to hold the rubber seal of the door in place. Trish was learning that there were definitely some disadvantages of me having only one arm!

Home to Alberta and a New Beginning

August 29th was moving day. It was a bright, sunny morning when the moving van arrived at 10:30, two hours later than expected. The park manager informed us that the van could not park by the mobile home as it would block traffic on the road. Instead, it had to park two blocks away in an open space. So began a day of shuttle service between the van and the trailer, using the help of our neighbour and their pick-up truck for the large objects and our station wagon for boxes and smaller items. After calling a third mover to help load, they were on their way by 5 PM. It was a long, strenuous day for all.

After a restless night on a cot borrowed from a neighbour, the next day was spent packing and repacking all our boxes of wedding presents and our suitcases into the station wagon. After much effort everything went in like sardines. Space had been left inside the cargo door for the cage to transport Whiskers, the black cat, so that we would have easy access. Our vehicle was ready for the trip back to Alberta. Since we still had the task of cleaning the mobile home before we left, we got to work with much-appreciated help from our relatives and friends.

On Friday morning, we were finally on our way—or so we thought! The cat had been sedated, his cage loaded into the car, and the cargo door firmly shut. We made one last check of the premises. Then as we were pulling out of the driveway, we became aware of a very bad smell coming from the rear of the vehicle. Oh, no! The cat had pooped in his cage! Trish tried to open the cargo door, only to discover that it was jammed. We had to unload many of our carefully-packed boxes from the side door to enable Trish to crawl over the top to unlatch the rear door so the cat cage could be removed. While she was cleaning up the mess and the cat, a neighbour came over to help me wrestle our stuff back into the car. With Kitty safely back in his spot and the door fixed, we were on our way with all our neighbours waving goodbye.

It was late in the day when we reached Canmore. Stopping for gas and a meal at the Esso station, I felt really weary and so parked behind the station and slept for about two hours. Unknown to us, the highway from Bragg Creek to Black Diamond, about an hour's drive, was under construction. As it had been raining heavily for some time, the road was in a terrible condition and the drive an absolute nightmare. Finally, at 4:30 AM, we arrived home to another unwelcome surprise. Though the electrical utility company receptionist had assured me that my bill was up-to-date, her new boss found out that I still owed a small amount which had been overlooked. The boss had a policy that any unpaid bill would cause the power to be cut off immediately. Mr. Erdman, a company employee and my neighbour, tried to tell him that I was away getting married and would settle the bill when I got home, but authorization to leave the power on was denied. That early morning as we entered a dark house, we noticed a smell that was not too nice, but being exhausted, we both just fell into bed, relieved that we had a flashlight in the car.

When we awoke, it was to discover that both fridges had long since defrosted, and in the warmth of summer, the food had decayed, leaving a sickening smell. Thankfully, my neighbour had kindly removed the rotting mess while checking the house. The contents of the freezer were lost. This was a most distressing event to welcome us home! On Sunday, we turned on our trusty Electolux vacuum, which we loaded with a product, called T-3, designed to clear the air. We opened all the windows, then escaped to my old church in High River. It was an opportunity to introduce Trish to all my friends and to give our house time to air out. Friends at church were glad to see Trish and to share my joy: my search for a new mate had finally ended. After the church service, coffee and goodies were served in their large fellowship hall, where we enjoyed a long visit with everyone. No one was anxious to leave and we all shared in the exchange of lots of good humour. We returned to Black Diamond to attend church in the evening. What a surprise awaited us!

Just as church ended, the pastor announced, "We will now depart to the Davis's to welcome them home." Horrors of horrors! My jaw dropped and Trish gasped, nearly fainting. Recovering slightly, I stuttered, "Give us twenty minutes." The party had been announced in church that morning when we were not there. The Black Diamond congregation is known for its spontaneous activities. When the people arrived, the door burst open and an avalanche of tables, chairs, people, and goodies poured in as if by magic. The invaders simply took over as if with orders from above, and presently everything was ready amid much chatter. We had a wonderful time! With hilarity and congratulations, the party ended, and again, somewhat magically, the tables, chairs, and people disappeared.

On Labour Day Monday, reality suddenly dawned. Though our guests had left no mess, we faced the task of clean-up as a result of the power having been turned off. The notice tag still hung as a grim reminder on the front door knob. A Labour Day slogan caught our attention: "God put work in our life. He expects us to put life in our work!" We thus began attacking the mess. For three days, Trish worked on the stinky fridge with all manner of cleaners, all to no avail. Our friend, a fridge repairman, even changed all replaceable insulation, again without positive results. Finally, we just put it out on our back deck. A fellow came by and offered us $50 for it, even though we told him, "It stinks." He took it anyway—but we never saw him again, nor the money.

One day, while on an Electrolux house call, I spotted a fridge and stove on sale for $600.00. We purchased the pair and gave our stove away. We sought no recourse from the power company. Since the boss had refused to be lenient, I was not about to give him the sadistic pleasure of knowing how much distress his decision had caused us. Scripture says, *"For ye had compassion of me in my bonds, and took joyfully the spoiling of your goods, knowing in yourselves that ye have in heaven a better and an enduring substance"* (Hebrews 10:34, KJV). In our case, the spoiling was all too true. Reverend Hale from High River gave us a fridge for the basement which he no longer needed. God provides at all times, including these: *"...seek ye first the kingdom of God, and his righteousness; and all these things shall be added unto you."* (Matthew 6:33, KJV)

On September 9th, another surprise awaited us. The moving van arrived while we were in church on a Sunday morning. Half of Trish's belongings were already in the basement by the time we arrived home. "In them there days," as my daddy would say, "We never locked our doors." We didn't either, especially if only gone for a short time. The movers reluctantly (with no apology for not telling us of their unexpected arrival) put Trish's belongings where we actually wanted them—especially the chesterfield. I had told her while in Vancouver, "I really like your chesterfield!" She had replied, "Remember, when it goes, I go with it," which really gave me ideas about the possibility of a future together.

In order for Trish to meet all my friends in High River and Black Diamond, we decided to have another wedding reception at my old church in High River. We worked on a fairly extensive invitation list, and because we had set the date for two weeks' time on September 21st, Trish did most of the inviting via phone. We planned a sit-down dinner and program to follow and prayed for good weather. Part of the dinner menu included Jello fruit salad, a favourite of mine. The day finally arrived. My half-sister, Ann, and her family and dog arrived the night before from Edson to stay with us, so we had a full house.

People started arriving at the reception around 6:00 PM and soon all the tables were full. We were at a head table and it was wonderful to look out at all "my" friends, which were now "our" friends and family, including Bob and Beth, who had come out on a snowy night to help us celebrate. Spontaneously the room broke into laughter as bowls of Jello salad, some half eaten, others untouched, started appearing in front of us, and the emcee said, "Eat to your heart's content, Jim!" What a hoot! We were just getting over this joke when in came a scraggly old tree on a stand, obviously dug out of someone's back yard, loaded with money. Tied to every branch with red ribbon were boxes of red Jello—a year's supply, I am sure! By this time, we were weak with laughter. People told jokes and sang songs—a real "roast Jim" night. It was just a tremendous time of fun and laughter, and a joyful memory.

Soon after Trish's arrival, we encountered an experience entirely new to her. The Williams family asked us to care for their children as the mother, who was Inuit, was in Inuvik, and the dad was working. Supposedly, we would care for the children in their own home, but it didn't end up that way. There were two older girls, two younger boys, and a baby who cried continually. The girls fought so much in bed that we let one sleep with us. The boys who were in the basement bedroom awakened screaming in the middle of the night just when the baby had finally fallen asleep on the chesterfield in the living room. I ran downstairs to see what had happened. As I knelt by the bedside, one of the youngsters reached out his hands and jammed his fingers into my eyes. Instant pain! My eyes ran with tears. Finally, the boy, who was having a nightmare, relaxed and drifted back to sleep. Fortunately, their mother returned and we only had them with us for a day and a night. As they grew older, the girls came to Sunday school with us for quite some time, but none came to know the Lord as far as I know.

Trish's mobile home in Vancouver sold relatively soon after our return to Alberta. In response to my love for Volvos (plus the fact that it was too expensive to repair the old one), Trish purchased a demo from Halford and Valentine Co. in Calgary. I named the car "Honey Bun." When the new one was no longer under warranty, we bought a second-hand Sprint, a little three cylinder, in order to reduce expenses.

Another exciting event took place in 1984. In 1982, when Beth was eighteen, I had asked her if she would be interested in locating her birth mother. "Sure, why not!" was her reply. I knew that her birth mother had been born in Coledale, Alberta, a small friendly town where everybody knows everybody. Through a friend from that area, I was able to get the name of the local doctor, who it turned out was the family doctor who had looked after Beth's mother. He suggested that I talk to Beth's birth grandmother first, which I did, explaining the situation to her. She seemed very pleased with the thought of meeting her granddaughter after all these years, but was not so sure her daughter would agree to the idea. She promised to follow through and get back to me. We thought it was a lost cause because we did not hear back.

Then, one evening in 1984, I picked up the phone and the voice on the other end said, "This is Beth's mother." What a surprise! We had a long, pleasant conversation. She called Beth as well and then Beth called me and I called the grandmother. The phones were really buzzing that night. It was a few weeks later that Beth and I met her mother and grandparents for dinner. What a good visit we had and what a thrill to be part of that scenario in my daughter's life. I could see many similarities between mother and daughter. Beth spent three weeks with her new found family that summer. Trish and I were invited to the grandparents' home in Coledale for Thanksgiving weekend that year, as part of a family reunion in the truest sense of the word and with much sincere thanksgiving.

On New Year's Day, Trish and I chose, "We shall thrive in '85," as our motto for the coming year. That August, to celebrate our first anniversary, Trish and I decided to head out to British Columbia to visit our friends, Wayne and Tannis Morris in White Rock, and use their home as our base to visit many of our friends in Vancouver, back at the mobile home park, and on Vancouver Island. It took us two days to drive out there and we spent the first night in a campground near Field. It was dark when we pulled in. We planned to sleep in the back of the station wagon, which meant covering the windows with garbage bags and a blanket over the windshield to give us some semblance of privacy. We crawled into our sleeping bag and the next thing we knew we sat bolt upright, striking our heads on the roof of the car, as the 6 AM train rolled through, blowing its whistle and shaking the car on the way by. What a rude awakening! We hadn't been able to see just how close we had parked to the railway tracks. All we could do was laugh. This was our introduction to camping. Thus began our long-time custom of an annual holiday, camping trips around the time of our anniversary: a practice that fulfilled both the objective of celebration and summer vacation. As my daddy would say: "A change is as good as a rest," although Trish didn't usually get much of the latter.

Our camping trips were usually a Monday to Friday stint, which necessitated much preparation on the part of Trish as it entailed having enough food for five days. Since I was hooked on outdoor fires, the wood was my responsibility. Boxes originally used for bananas were filled with the scraps from my wood-working hobby as well as with other stray pieces that might come my way. Garbage bins at construction sites were the main source of my pyrotechnic efforts. It was always good to get away as there was nothing tying us to home. Our cat, who had been old in the first place, had died of kidney failure. We had taken him to a vet but that proved to be disastrous, as the man had not much kindness for us or the cat. Earlier, though, whenever we had needed to be away, the cat like all cats had fended quite ably for himself. A dog is a companion; a cat is just an observer.

In February, I was hired to teach English at a school in Calgary called Foothills Christian Academy. Driving in and out was very challenging. Teaching went well and I really enjoyed the class. Unfortunately, the opportunity was short-lived and only lasted five months, as I had been hired on a temporary contract to fill in for a teacher. It was to prove to be a fact that during our years together, our combined income—as Trish also worked at odd jobs—would be considered to be below the poverty line by government standards. Since Trish became my wife, however, we have never had an overdue or unpaid bill: we have always had food, clothing, and shelter. As the Bible proclaims, *"But if we have food and clothing, we will be content with that"* (1 Timothy 6:8).

LIFE ENRICHED

On February 18, 1986, while doing an Electrolux service call at a house in Longview—a village about 8 kilometres from Black Diamond—I spotted a little grey poodle-cross dog in the porch area as I was making my departure. The customers explained that he had arrived on their doorstep a few days earlier, and that advertising and posters had yielded no results. As they already had a dog of their own, they felt they couldn't keep him. I directly phoned Trish to ask if I could bring the dog home with me. She agreed and the little dog hopped into the car quite happily. As we drove home, I ruminated we would probably give him to a good home or take him to the SPCA the next day as we had not been considering getting a dog to replace our cat. *Wrong!* Trish and the dog bonded immediately and he was here to stay.

We called him "Willie the Wanderer," which was an accurate characterization until we had him neutered soon after his arrival. Willie would disappear for hours whenever he was let outside or if he got out on his own, rain or shine. Once he came home soaked to the skin, so Trish and a friend decided to follow him the next day. He took off running, ears flying, with the girls in hot pursuit, heading straight for a trailer park about five blocks away. The pursuers lost him when he arrived in the park. After going up and down each street, they found him at a trailer madly wagging his tail, nose to nose at the patio door with a little Chihuahua. The mystery was solved! The Chihuahua's owner said the courtship had been going on for a while and she was planning to have her dog spayed. Trish told her that

Willie was to be neutered as well. They each felt a little guilty putting an end to the budding romance!

Willie loved people and made friends with everyone. He went everywhere with us in the car, either sitting on Trish's knee or sleeping in the front seat when we left the car. As a result, one evening, he gave us an awful scare. We had parked the car on the third floor of a parkade in downtown Calgary to attend an evening meeting in a hotel next door. Willie was with us as usual. The meeting dragged on longer than we expected and consequently, when we returned to the vehicle, our little dog was more than anxious to relieve himself. Because of the late hour, most of the cars had long since left, so there were not any tires available and there was nothing but cement around. Willie ran over to the wall overlooking the very busy street below where there was a big tree and some grass as part of the sidewalk. He spotted that and leapt off the wall. Trish screamed, "He just jumped," and took off running in high heels down to the ground level with me close behind her, both expecting to find a dead or very injured dog. We rounded the corner, and there he was, standing on the sidewalk, shaking like a leaf, and totally confused by all the lights, traffic, and noise. Miraculously, Willie did not appear to be hurt, only terribly shaken. Trish kept an eye on him all night, and when the vet checked him the next day, she was amazed that he had no broken bones, not even his toes! He definitely was a survivor.

One winter when I was working in Calgary, Trish also had a job at the time and so we couldn't leave Willie at home. I decided to take him with me with the understanding that he would be quite happy in the car with me checking in on him from time to time. Soon, I realized it was much too cold to leave him in the parking lot so I had no other choice but to bring him into the office with me. He spent the day peacefully curled up under my desk on an old down-filled jacket, seeming to enjoy all the attention he got. Willie was a big hit with everyone and they really missed him when those weeks came to an end.

In 1986, we got a so-called "tourist tent." Putting it up was always a challenge, and without exception almost caused a divorce! Since then, we have steadily climbed the ladder of camping luxury: from tent to a borrowed tent trailer which friends used for a week and left at a special site at Interlakes Campsite in the Kananaskis. Subsequently, I saw a small Trilium Trailer for sale in Black Diamond which we bought. This served us well for twelve years. Next, we upgraded to an aged motorhome equipped with a bathroom, which to us was a real luxury. However, when the holding tank exploded on a steep hill on the way to a friend's campsite, we quickly changed our mind. Fortunately, we sold it for more than we paid for it, but the convenience of a camper van enticed us to buy another on the recommendation of our very dependable mechanic. The van was in for repair and, as the owner was moving back to Nova Scotia, it was for sale. This turned out to be our last and most enjoyable improvement, which we dearly appreciated for seven years.

One of our most memorable summer holidays, apart from camping, was a visit to cousin Carmen and Fran's summer hide-away at Barclay Sound, a body of water not far from Ucluelet on Vancouver Island. This trip was in conjunction with Expo '86 in Vancouver, a spectacular event, and a chance to spend the day with our daughter, who happened to be in Vancouver at the same time in a ball tournament. I think we took in one of her games as well.

Barkley Sound and the Broken Group Islands comprise one of the three main recreational components in Pacific Rim National Park. The Broken Group Islands consist of over 100 islands, islets and rocky outcrops scattered in the centre of Barkley Sound. The popularity of these islands is due to the fact that they provide a true west coast experience in sheltered water as Port Alberni is not normally subject to the extreme ocean conditions seen farther west in the open waters around Ucluelet. We followed Carmen and Fran to Torquart Bay east of Ucluelet, the first ten miles on pavement and then another fifteen miles on an old logging road barely wide enough for two cars to pass. At the end of it was a beautiful bay with many boats on the water and tents and RVs along the shoreline. Torquart Bay is considered one of the safer launching points for accessing the Broken Islands. We unloaded all our equipment onto a dock where Fran had his Zodiac tied up, loaded it up, and off we went. We seemed to be out in the middle of nowhere, surrounded by water and islands that were scattered here and there.

After about half an hour, we rounded a bend and what appeared to be a small white building with a blue roof came into view. This was home away from home—a float house—anchored to a large rock face and floating on logs. As we got closer, we could see a large deck on the front and shutters and colourful floral window boxes on the little house. What a paradise!

Inside was a large kitchen, complete with wood stove and fridge, a living/dining area, and a bedroom. There was a larger bedroom in the loft above, accessible by ladder. No motion could be detected when other boats went by.

We sure got our fill of seafood while we were there. Each morning, we went out and checked the crab traps Fran had scattered around the area, marked by buoys, and they usually brought in a good supply. We would have crab sandwiches, crab chowder, and crab casseroles. Other days, we went fishing for cod and salmon. Though we never caught a salmon, there was always next time. Other days were spent sitting on the deck, watching boats go by, reading, and playing scrabble.

The sunsets in the evenings were spectacular, reflected in the water around us. It was like living in another world those ten days and very difficult to leave. We were, however, able to make two more visits to that wonderful spot—one the following year and another four years later. Fortunately, I recorded both major and minor reflections in my daily diary—a big wire-bound notebook—each year, for which I am now very grateful. It is nothing compared to a computer, but much better than my hit-and-miss short-term memory.

Still always short on money but somehow always able to pay our bills, it was necessary that I find some means of filling the coffers. Though I still painted on occasion with Walter Sapinsky, it was very sporadic. I was given the opportunity to teach special needs children at the nearby First Nations reservation school in Eden Valley. It was an absolutely hair-raising fiasco. Any white man who enters either a Hutterite colony or a reservation is usually considered a foreigner or a trespasser. They are often viewed as someone who is trying to change their culture. Fortunately, a new policy is presently in operation to change that attitude at Eden Valley.

In 1988, I turned in my Electrolux demonstration sample and also my franchise. I had had my fill of trying to sell under their "Rah, rah, rah, go, go, go" pressure coupled with managers changing like dirty socks and breaking their promises. I gave up my contract with the company and joined A to Z Vacuums, working alongside the Electrolux repairman who left the company to start his own business. Once again, I became Joe-Boy, but this time, I managed to earn a meagre stipend. I paid the reasonable wholesale cost of the repair and charged the customer for pick-up and delivery. Following the retirement of the fellow who started the business, his relative, Hanif, took over. My supplier, a Muslim, and I have done business together over many years. He remains my very good friend. During our entire relationship, we have never had a disagreement. At the request of a former patron, I recently had a machine repaired by him though it meant asking a friend to take me to Calgary as my driver's license had been rescinded. Through the years, I have made many good friends and acquaintances, who still refer to me as the "Electrolux man."

As well, a shock awaited me when Mount Royal College hired and fired me before I had even begun my employment, with no reason offered. However, a so-called bonanza soon emerged which required selling promotional pins, caps, and pens which were made in China for a fellow named Peter. It, too, quickly fizzled as did the imaginary business. Then a sure-fire way to wealth appeared in the form of Amway, which also failed to meet my expectations—getting orders, filling them, delivering them and then collecting the money proved costly, slow, and unproductive—the "Hope and Soap" business, as I christened it, soon petered out. That summer, a celebration of our church's 40th anniversary was a welcome reprieve from my depressing efforts to earn a living.

Though there were far too many challenges in my life to relate, I will recount one more. I was exploring every option that arose and none proved successful. "Just keep trying" appeared to be my only hope for success. I responded to an opportunity to sell ads at the North Hill News for a small military paper printed at their facility called *Roundup*—a rather strange name for an armed forces publication designed only to be read by military personnel, as it sounded more suited to a ranch-type operation. It was an experience which I really enjoyed, although it had little result financially. Being informed at the outset that it would only be a supplementary income, I was not surprised when it only provided enough for gas money. The job required lots of travel with little payoff, since advertising budgets were already committed and the base of interested clientele quite small. The venture was doomed before I even began—it was just another "Joe-Boy" job. However, it did lead me to at least one thrilling experience. The military representative from the base at Curry Barracks was a fine officer. On one occasion, he invited me to accompany him to lunch at Curry Barracks and then on a tour of the Museum. To say posh is not sufficient. I felt like royalty. The visit to the museum to see the replica of World War I trenches was very revealing. 1989 ended—busy, hopeful, and still short of money. Yes, there is a reason for this annual account of financial disappointments. I had expected that God would fulfill my expectations of Romans 12:19 (NIV), *"I will repay,"* by my own efforts, not His.

Early in 1990, financial assistance appeared from an unexpected source through the government which provided both our CMHC mortgage and now assisted us to make our monthly payments. Our income was considered to be below the poverty level so we were not required to pay income tax. Our mortgage payment now was determined by an amount which equalled 28% of our declared income, making our payments quite small. The monthly amount was only over $200 for one year, when Trish deposited the money from a GIC policy which had matured. At the time, I was distressed that in spite of my efforts, I was unable to earn more. How this ended up being a great benefit was to appear in the future. This new mortgage plan later proved to be the miracle that fulfilled God's promise to repay.

The year 1991 brought many changes. A friend told me about the Gideons—the people who place Bible in hotels, motels, hospitals, and other public places. Having been introduced to a ministry within my comfort zone and experience, we gladly joined the organization as a couple. The Gideons, an international association based in Nashville, Tennessee, have been placing New Testament Bibles that also contain the Psalms and Proverbs in Canadian public schools at the grade five level since 1936, when permitted by those in charge. The emphasis of separation between school and religion has adversely limited the numbers given out, especially in more recent times. Once, it was almost considered to be "a rite of passage," but now it is often not permitted or at best, reluctantly allowed. One objection from a volatile home and school member will shut down the opportunity for many students to receive the Holy Word in this fashion, though many parents still support the distribution. Apparently, we are to believe that the makeup of Canada and the social values have changed since the time of the first distributions of the Scriptures to students, even though it's printed in stone over our Parliament doors "He [God] shall have dominion from sea to sea." Even the politicians don't all believe that now. It's sad.

The local "camp" (or base of operations) is a very close-knit community for both men and women. We each have personally handed out hundreds of New Testaments to those with whom we have come into contact, in addition to visiting as many grade five classrooms as possible. Trish and her group of ladies have handed out New Testaments to graduating nurses in the local hospitals each year. The camp hosts a Harvest Banquet, held annually in High River, as a fund raiser for our local area. The proceeds from the banquet and donations have purchased many thousands of Bibles to be distributed throughout the world. Trish and I have been dedicated members of this most worthwhile organization for over twenty years, serving in various executive and camp positions and I as Zone Leader for seven camps in Southern Alberta. The leadership position also included speaking engagements at Gideons functions upon request. We really enjoyed this part of the ministry as we got to travel and meet so many fellow Gideons in the province. Sadly, the time for my replacement is at hand due to the limitations age has imposed upon my ability.

By 1991, our church, the Black Diamond Gospel Chapel, was growing and had purchased a derelict, half-constructed building which had been abandoned during the recession of the early 1980s. Pastor Henry Fehr envisioned that the building could be transformed into our new church, and under his leadership the congregation embarked on an adventure of building and raising funds. With many donations of money, labour, and even some materials, as well as some scrounging, the church building gradually came to fruition. The work served to fuse us all together as we had a common goal, and I recall a joy-filled time. The first service took place in the new building on July 19, 1992 and a grand opening was held on October 11, 1992, with Pastor Fehr dedicating the building to God.

That same year in January of 1992, the church established a Men's Fellowship Breakfast which met successively in various restaurants in Black Diamond and Turner Valley. "In those days" as my daddy would say, five to seven men was about the average. Each paid his own way. Twenty years later, twenty or more men meet in the Fellowship Hall in our church. The men take turns bringing breakfast with a vast array of delicious menus. Besides food, the men enjoy a special time of fellowship and Bible study. Recently, the study time has been spent discussing the pastor's previous Sunday's sermon with all men taking part. Many times the discussions are very involved and on topic, but occasionally we get going down insightful "rabbit trails." When it is my turn, my faithful wife supplies an interesting menu. Recently, a regular member brought his very tasty quiche, which is said to be "not real men's food," but we just drool and gobble it up.

By now, I was well aware that God had not yet decided to fulfill His promise in Romans 12:19, *"I will repay"* (NIV), to compensate me for the loss of my right arm. Our bank account was in the red. "No money now," is still my theme song. Our Volvo had sat in the yard for months with no buyer in sight. Finally, our neighbour offered $5,500—the list price was eight or nine thousand dollars. For me, it was a sad parting. However, with money in short supply, we could not afford to repair it. The new owner later loaned the car to someone who subsequently was involved in a bad accident but suffered only a broken leg. The police told him in any other car, he would have been killed. Before we sold the Volvo, we had already bought a second hand Sprint which was occasionally very hard to start, a problem that was never solved.

In August, 1994, we outran an impending snowstorm, hoping to find a camping spot before it hit. No such luck! Seeking shelter, we arrived at Kozy Nest Kabins which unknown to us was the location of Crowsnest Lake Bible Camp. While getting breakfast, children from the nearby camp arrived on our doorstep singing Christmas carols. To our surprise, about four inches of snow had fallen during the night.

This accidental discovery began a longstanding relationship with "Crow," as we now call the camp. We spent ten years on the planning committee for a seniors' retreat weekend there, with a group known as the "Keen-Agers.". The retreat has been held on Victoria Day weekend in May since 1956. We have attended every year since 1995, a total of 17 years. During this time, we made many good friends, enjoyed good food, heard excellent speakers and music, and always came away feeling uplifted and refreshed. Keen-Agers is still going strong today.

On one such weekend, we went on a day trip to nearby Sparwood, British Columbia, to go swimming. I was surprised to see Harold Butler in a restaurant there. He had been one of my daughter Beth's hockey coaches many years ago. He said, "Beth is the best female hockey player I've ever seen and she was a real joy to coach." His comment pleased us immensely and we shared it with Beth.

Beth was the athletic one in our family, excelling in every sport she tried. She had played baseball in the summer and hockey in the winter, and won many medals over the years. Her passion now is golf as she tries for that elusive "hole in one."

Bob, on the other hand, became our artist. At an early age, as I watched him draw the outline of a horse without lifting his pencil, we discovered that he was very artistic. Since art classes didn't work out for him, he was pretty well self-taught. In his adult life, his artistic skills have enlarged to include carving, both in wood and in elk horn. His elk horn carvings vary in size from wall-hanging scenes to a three inch ornament of an eagle landing on a stump. His woodworking projects include everything from furniture down to children's toys. Unfortunately, making a living doing this kind of thing is next to impossible so it is simply a hobby which he enjoys and is exceptionally good at.

My attempts to find gainful employment continued. Despite my failure at other sales attempts, I did try the NSA water purifier. Efforts to produce a living wage by selling this system also proved inadequate. My endeavour evaporated as quickly as steam from a tea kettle. Brita was the choice of most people. I faced the fact that my ability as a salesman was sadly lacking and this was neither my calling nor the answer to my financial difficulties. Fortunately, that fall, I began working for Ken Field, who was a great employer. He was manager of a company called Job Jar Maintenance. As it involved mostly painting, similar to the work with Walter Sapinsky, I found it most enjoyable. He was both generous and always cheerful. Unfortunately, he sold his business—a deal that did not include me. Worry over money once again became our constant companion.

At this point, a friend waxed eloquently about selling a chemical cleaning product that he had invented called a "surfactant." By then, my experience with grandiose promises of getting rich quick had been nothing but negative, and I decided to pass the opportunity by. By this time, I had come to realize it is better to trust in God fully rather than in people's promises, schemes, or one's own effort—*"It is better to take refuge in the Lord than to trust in humans"* (Psalm 118:8, NIV). To my knowledge, this product too came to nothing.

I intensified my efforts to supplement our income by spending more time in our combination shop and garage. You might wonder how a one-armed person could turn out such items as tables (large and small), rocking horses, ladder chairs, chests, benches, coat racks, and cutting boards, to name just a few. The cutting boards were made of strips of various types of wood (maple, walnut, and mahogany) laid edge to edge and glued together and then shaped like a large ping-pong paddle with a handle, otherwise known as a paddle board. I used clamps of all shapes and sizes to hold everything, a great substitute for my missing arm. Of course, I had to be very careful around saws, sanders and other wood working equipment, as I certainly didn't need to lose any part of my remaining extremity. There were a few close shaves though. These projects became my outlet, pleasure and passion, and the shop became a comfortable haven although very little financial benefit resulted.

On January 10th, 1993, our pastor marched up the aisle of the church and announced before the gathered congregation that he had been guilty of infidelity and was resigning from the church immediately. Trish and I were simply stunned. It was a devastating time for the church family and it took us some time to recover our equilibrium. In June, Pastor Art Siemens and his delightful wife, ElLee, answered the call to serve in Black Diamond. Art lovingly brought healing and proceeded to minister at our church for seven years, before retiring from the senior pastor position and becoming a pastor to seniors, as well as serving faithfully as the local hospital chaplain. ElLee and Art became friends to all who knew them, serving the congregation and community with devotion and commitment. It was a sad loss to the community when they pulled up stakes. Having moved away after thirteen years here, their occasional visits are most welcomed by everyone. Art and ElLee hold a special place in both my heart and that of my wife.

Our church celebrated its first mortgage burning on February 10th, 1994. The following spring the parking lot was paved thanks to a generous donation from a member. Also in 1994, our church joined the AGC—Associated Gospel Churches. About this time, I discovered that I had some trouble hearing. A hearing aid proved to be more of a problem than a solution for the selective hearing loss which my wife could doubtless verify. Meanwhile, in October, Trish began working locally at the Spice Cabinet, repackaging products into smaller amounts for retail sale, adding a little more money to our sparse income.

Another supposedly great opportunity to earn a normal living also ended in failure. A printing company located in Pincher Creek advertised a position to sell ads in their area for a regional brochure, competing with one that was successful and well-established. After trying my best for several days, covering the area from Pincher Creek to the British Columbia border, I had managed to sell just one small ad to a gentleman who I knew. The territory was too far from Black Diamond, the travel costs expensive, and the prospects disinterested. I began to think I must be a slow learner or just simply desperate.

A fellow I had met introduced me to a company named Modern Vac. This proved to be unproductive—just more "Go, go, go; sell, sell, sell." Their home office was in Edmonton, which produced more problems than solutions. Since I was somewhat known locally as the "Electrolux Man" anyway, I soon abandoned this occupation.

Another "sure-fire" way to make money appeared in February, 1995. Melaluca was presented with great enthusiasm. The product falsely claimed to cure all ills. That year we visited my brother, Bill, in British Columbia when returning from our wonderful stay with cousin Carmen on their float house. Offering a half-hearted apology, Bill said, "I am sorry for being so mean to you when you were a kid." As my daddy would say, "Better late than never." I accepted his apology.

Our church had cause for a big celebration when on May 5, 1996, the Black Diamond Gospel Chapel was able to burn the second and final mortgage on the property. What a grand day that was—free and clear of debt in just five years. A few unexpected (though no less welcome) jobs kept the wolf away from the door, especially with Trish still working at the Spice Cabinet. Then, in July, at a jobsite while up on a stepladder painting near the ceiling, my left arm refused to work. What a surprise! I was to learn that I had suffered a small stroke. Shortly thereafter, I was rushed to the Foothills Hospital in Calgary with severe angina. Two stents were inserted into my heart while I watched the process on a television that the doctor used to do his work. Seventeen years later, a few more "little strokes" called transient ischemic attack (TIA) have seriously taken their toll (although fortunately angina has not returned). The strokes cause a brief interruption of blood flow to part of the brain and cause temporary symptoms. The TIAs disappear on their own, but sometimes cause minor damage.

That year, friends treated us to a stay at Lake Louise. Generously, they insisted that we take the room overlooking the lake. Having broken her ankle and with her leg in a cast, Trish was treated like a queen in her wheelchair and always given first place in line for meals. Our friend tucked a $50 bill in my shirt pocket and simply said, "You might like a cup of coffee." Yes, life does have its bright spots.

Attempting to sell Mannatech "glyconutrients" products for health, weight, fitness, and skin care was another fiasco. About this time, I inadvertently backed over our dear little Willie the Wanderer, our little poodle-cross. This poor doggie, who had a special attachment to Trish, died instantly on our driveway. He ran behind the car while on his rope as Trish waited for the car, trying to get to her. Trish saw it happen and was hysterical! We buried his ashes beneath a tree in Sandy McNabb Campground, where we often let him run. What a shock for both of us and such a sad end for our loyal little mutt. In Willie's later years, he had become quite deaf and had some health issues which, among other things, required a special diet, consisting of a mixture of cooked hamburger, hard cooked eggs, ground egg shells, and rice, which he really enjoyed. As our dear Willie was twelve, we had started to realize the time was coming when he would need a lot of special care, which we would have been only too happy to provide for him, along with increasing medical costs. However, his tragic death relieved us of that concern. We missed him so much and vowed we would not get another dog.

My introduction to a computer came when our good friend, Alec Kerfoot, upgraded his and gave me the old one. I had high hopes of using it to write my book, so much so that I got rid of my left-hand Dvorak typewriter, a move I have since regretted. I soon found that using a computer was definitely a two-handed operation even having the keyboard programmed for left-handed typing. After many attempts to master it, I gave up and gave it to a young lad to play games on. Pen and paper was now the only way to go. The government continued to subsidize our mortgage, giving us some freedom from the pressing need for a greater income.

On our way to our annual visit with Cousin Carmen and her husband at their summer home on the float house, we narrowly escaped death. We were less than an hour from the fishing dock where we had arranged to meet Fran when the car's motor sputtered and died just as we topped a mountain road. Fearing disaster, I took what I thought might be my last glance at my wife and gave full attention to our wildly bucking station wagon which no longer had any power steering nor power brakes. Several turn-outs appeared along the way, though none was long enough to stop in. Our speed increased alarmingly as the car flew down the mountainside. "Help me Lord!" was my constant prayer. After what seemed forever, we ground to a stop on a gravel stretch where the road leveled out at the bottom. All I could do was open the hood in the common distress signal and offer another heartfelt prayer for help.

Just ahead of us, a motorhome was parked on the side of the road. Going up to it, I tapped on the driver's window. A very startled Chinese man yelled "No speak English" and sped away, showering me with gravel. It was raining by now and watching the many cars zip by, it never entered my mind to stand on the side of the busy highway and hold up my arm. Fortunately, an identical vehicle to ours came to a stop amid more flying gravel, and a lady got out. After explaining our dilemma, she had a chat with her companion and they generously agreed to take us to our rendezvous in Barkley Sound. They were on their way to Ucluelet, as bees had driven them from their campsite that morning.

Upon approaching a garage in Ucluelet, we were met by a mechanic who knew our cousin's wife very well. He said, "Leave it to me. I will pick up your car, fix it, and you can come back when your holiday is over." Time was going by quickly! The lady obligingly led the mechanic back to our car and we were soon on our way down an old logging road to the fishing dock deep in the woods.

When we arrived, we spotted Fran walking back to his Zodiac. He had just given up on us. The driver signaled our arrival by honking the horn. "*Thank you, Lord, that he is still here!*" I silently prayed. As my daddy would say, we were rescued "just in the nick of time."

Because of our close call with death, we enjoyed our annual vacation even more than usual, feasting on the daily diet of seafood. Trish and Carmen shelled crab, their preferred bounty from Barkley Sound, while freshly-caught rock cod, those ugly denizens of the deep, were favoured by the men. Fran's favourite fishing hole was not far from the float house and always met our need. We had expected to have salmon on occasion, but trolled most of one afternoon without success.

Fran and Carmen's objective was to enthral us with their everyday delights. They were fabulously successful, but again as my daddy would say, "All good things must come to an end sooner or later" and for us it was much too soon. Fran drove us back to Ucluelet. Much to our regret, this was the last year we were to spend at this idyllic location. Trish and I felt that the drive was just too long and Carmen was dealing with health issues. She died one year later and was followed by Fran the next year.

We arrived back in Ucluelet to discover the problem with our car had been the alternator, a relatively inexpensive repair. We had forgotten our food hamper in the station wagon so we quickly tossed the smelly contents into a dumpster and headed out on our long return trip home. What thoughts beset us as we began the long upward climb on the Kennedy Lake Mountain road! Had we gone over the cliff, we certainly would not have survived, and it is doubtful that our bodies would ever have been discovered. Arriving home safely was never so welcome.

As the twenty-first century approached, a world-wide atmosphere of dread settled around the globe like mist rising from a huge rotting swamp, fueled by media hype and get-rich quick artists. Threats of international food shortages, power failure, transportation problems and such brought about by the collapse of computer systems were daily fodder. Some soothsayers even predicted the end of the world. However, nothing happened and the world gave a mighty sigh of relief. Although we never added one can of beans to our larder, many people purchased power generators and extra fuel to stave off possible disaster. In many places, power generators sold out to the extent that manufacturers were forced to produce many more. January 1st, 2000, dawned as it had from the beginning of time, just as God promises in Genesis 8:22, *"While the earth remains....day and night shall not cease"* (NASB). So it has been and so it will be until the end of time (which is all in God's hands, not ours). The next summer, brand-new power generators were a dime a dozen at garage sales, selling for a pittance of the original cost. Just shows how easily people panic and jump on the bandwagon of popular belief or fears.

That year, four years after losing Willie, our poodle-cross, we decided another dog would make a nice birthday gift for Trish. Before long we heard an ad on the radio looking for a home for a little Shih Tzu/terrier cross. We couldn't get there fast enough. We fell in love with him immediately, and it was Trish's birthday the next day. He had just been with the owner for three months, but after nipping her two year old daughter, she felt he wasn't safe to have around children and very sadly decided to let him go. Because he was so full of energy, we named him Sparky.

The vet thought he was about two years old. We later learned that our home was his fourth, which explained why he seemed so traumatized at first. After months of TLC, he gradually settled in. We discovered he was not a good car traveller and was terrified of being shut in, as we discovered when we left him in a portable kennel one day. We had done this with our other dog and he was quite content, but not Sparky. Upon our arrival home that day, there was blood on the kitchen floor and all over his paws from trying to claw his way out, ripping his toenails in the process. What a shock! He was also scared of thunder, firecrackers, and anything that went bang. He never did get over that.

One of the highlights of his little life was to go camping with us. He would sit in the driver's seat of our camper van while Trish was packing it up for a trip. Sparky was a very happy little dog who loved his walks, especially when we went to the field near our home where he could run free. He was a great companion and we loved him dearly.

The next year, the world was again in a state of chaos when Islamist terrorists flew hijacked American passenger planes into the twin World Trade Towers, creating both instant disaster and long-term disruption to travel and to lives. Later, on a domestic flight, I was frisked so thoroughly that they asked me to remove my belt. Imagine an old man with one arm being able to disrupt a flight from Calgary to Saskatoon: absolute foolishness and caution taken to the excess. The next terrorist attack is sure to come, but I very much doubt it will be by aircraft!

Thankfully over the years, our mortgage assistance subsidy continued on an annual basis as our yearly income was never steady. The only income of which we could be assured were the Canadian pensions we received. Camping, now our only annual holiday, continued as usual with the majority of work falling on Trish. Most of our trips were to Sandy McNabb Campground, in Sheep River Wildlife Sanctuary near Turner Valley, or Canyon Campground in Peter Lougheed Provincial Park, which became our favourite as all the sites were paved. Providing firewood and driving were my main contributions to the outings. Though not very exotic, we enjoyed the times away from home just the same.

Our church had been without a pastor for eleven months but everything was working amazingly well. The congregation stepped up to the plate, filling in for the pastor in handling day to day business as well as some Sunday services and all the committee work. Fortunately, Pastor Art Siemens was still on the scene to provide a steadying hand. He arranged to have a visiting pastor come each Sunday and we were well ministered to. It was truly a spiritual growing experience which brought the congregation into a tight community of sharing, caring brothers and sisters. In September of 2003, Pastor Matt Martens and his wife Carla arrived on the scene to take on the leadership. However, when he was introduced as the senior pastor, people looked rather perplexed due to his being so young. Right away, he fit in and the church has thrived under his leadership. I was appointed by the board as an Honorary Elder.

My woodworking efforts were enhanced by the purchase of a huge pile of left-over hardwood from the Tsuu T'ina Reserve where my son worked. Some went for firewood but the majority was targeted for many projects. My paddle-shaped cutting boards became popular and many sold.

Canadians were undergoing considerable stress with events over which they had no control. Court decisions were coming out in favour of gay marriage although many people, myself included, believe it is morally wrong and a backwards step. The family is the basic building block in society; when the family fails, the nation will soon follow. Then, a mad cow scare decimated the beef industry as countries closed their borders to Canadian beef.

Meanwhile, Trish and I were undergoing our own very stressful time. We badly needed a car, but we did not know how we would manage until we were able to borrow ten thousand dollars from Manulife. I still held on to the promise that God would repay.

In 2004, a westerner named Stephen Harper became the Conservative Party leader in Canada and the Reform Party ceased to exist. Coincidentally, his wife Laureen was born and raised in this area.

During this time, I made four chairs that converted to a stepladder for kitchen use, two in oak and two in spruce, but they unfortunately proved too cumbersome for household use. Right then we needed the money badly so that we could replace both front windows of our house, which had begun leaking during heavy rain storms. A generous friend came to our rescue and gave us three boxes full of grass-fed Angus beef along with a $1000 cheque, which was the cost of the repairs. How very true: "...*my God will supply all your needs*" (Philippians 4:19).

Between Christmas and New Year's, we bought a package for a mid-week stay at Kilmorey Lodge in Waterton Lakes National Park. For once, we had a real holiday. The staff treated us royally. Sadly, this historic old building burned completely to the ground five years later. The owner has vowed to rebuild a new lodge, although not an exact replica, bearing a strong resemblance to the original. However, at the present time, has not been able to cut through all the red tape with Parks Canada. Sadly, 2004 was also the year of the tragic tsunami in Southeast Asia. While we were enjoying a wonderful holiday, people on the other side of the world faced devastation.

As 2005 rolled around, the scope of the disaster from the tsunami was incomprehensible, so many lost lives and lost dreams. The disaster was triggered by a 9.1 earthquake off the coast of Indonesia and killed over 230,000 people. It was the single worst tsunami and one of the deadliest natural disasters in recorded history.

Sometimes one tragedy after another occurs, testing the faith and endurance of everyone. In our own country, four Mounties were gunned down in a Quonset in rural Mayerthorpe, Alberta, on March 3 by James Roszko, while they were executing a property seizure on the farm. This was the worst one-day loss of life for the RCMP in 100 years. Roszko then killed himself.

Trish and I were both greatly honoured to attend a luncheon May 25th for Queen Elizabeth II, hosted by Premier Ralph Klein. The gathering was held in the Roundup Centre in Calgary. Our invitation came from our Conservative representative in the Alberta Legislature, Ted Morton, asking us to join him and his wife at the celebration. What a thrill! We were amazed to see many of the guests dressed in very casual clothing. Even though Her Royal Majesty had seen many ceremonies in her honor, she looked surprised to be met by a circle of First Nations people pounding loudly on drums and chanting, "Iya, iya, iya." Had my arm been long enough I could have touched her as she was being escorted to the head table. The luncheon plate was very artfully decorated, but not very filling.

Trish had managed Ted's campaign office in Black Diamond and this was his way of showing appreciation for all her efforts. I, myself, went door knocking with him. On First Street in Black Diamond, I chose the snowy side of the block. Ted chided me later, asking, "How come all the nice-looking ladies were on your side of the street?" Obviously, he had noticed!

A company endorsed a line of credit on the equity in our property so that we could pay out our mortgage at a much lower rate. My woodworking projects provided us with some income but we still had to be very frugal in order to survive. At the back of my mind was always the question, "Is this God's time?"—it was not!

Like I said, sometimes disaster piles on disaster. In August, Hurricane Katrina struck New Orleans and southeast Louisiana with a vengeance, causing massive damage and loss of life. Even today, the area is struggling to recover, both economically and environmentally.

Pastor Art and ElLee started an SOS luncheon in 2005 to be held on the second Tuesday of each month from October until May in the fellowship hall of our church. The initials stand for "Serving Our Seniors" and the event is a celebration of LIFE ("Living Investments for Eternity"). At first, there were only two or three tables, seating up to twenty-four people. As people became aware of the event, more and more began to attend and the luncheons grew larger every year. Trish still works on the planning committee and spends quite a bit of time shopping, helping to prepare and serve the meal, and cleaning up. Entertainment varies from month to month and gives us old people a chance to get out for a good meal, some fun and laughter, and to meet others our age from the community.

For Christmas 2005, we were blessed to have our daughter, Beth, with us from Saskatoon. The visit was absolutely enjoyable and it was a pleasure to have her. However, our icy trip to take her to the airport for her flight home was hair-raising and we ended up arriving late. Beth made it on board with just seconds to spare, and then, wouldn't you know it, she waited on the runway for two hours while they de-iced the plane.

Sometimes blessings pile on blessings. When a friend cleaned out his freezer, he only asked a token for a big bag of grass-fed beef. Yes, God more than meets our need for food, clothing, and shelter when we fully trust Him. We always seemed to have just enough to get by—but not enough to get me into trouble!—and we still managed to go on our beloved camping excursions.

Thankfully for Canada, Stephen Harper was elected Prime Minister in January 2006. Things seemed to be looking up. We were even able to buy a 1996 Volvo sedan from Ollie Hux at a price that was very reasonable and affordable. I very much like the Volvo make—I do not worship them, but they are comfortable, stable, endurable, and a pleasure to drive. When the vehicle was rear-ended five years later, the insurance company paid out one thousand dollars more than the purchase price. Not many cars appreciate over time! I felt like I had been paid to drive my beloved Volvo all those years. "God is good, all the time," as my good friend, Pastor Art, so often quotes.

That summer we attended a concert of Quartet Jamboree presentations at Harmattan near Red Deer, Alberta. A particularly lively quartet sang a song about "chickens" and asked all to join them by flapping their wings. When I flapped my single wing, Trish turned to me and said, "You must be a utility grade," sending the whole row into laughter. The quartet must have wondered, "What's so funny?"

In the fall, I volunteered to be a Sunday school teacher for grades four, five, and six. There were three teachers per class, with each of us teaching two weeks out of six. It was great to be back in the classroom with students once again, and I enjoyed preparing for each lesson. I felt that it was important for the children to memorize significant verses in the Bible and encouraged them to do so with a rewards program. The church at that time was in a vibrant growing phase, so we had perhaps eight to twelve students each week in each class. I even found time to make a table for my classroom as well as some of the props (including a very impressive-looking fireplace) for the Christmas program that the students presented each year.

A tragic event occurred on December 17, 2006. The daughter of our neighbour was involved in a terrible car accident near Vulcan. This lovely young lady, who was a leader in our youth group at church, was on her way to work the morning after graduating from the University of Lethbridge. She may have dozed off, having enjoyed a late night, and hit the ditch and rolled. She was instantly killed when she was thrown from the car. That Sunday morning in church, her parents were called to the foyer and informed by two police officers. When the announcement was made at the end of the service, the congregation vented a collective gasp. Trish and I were particularly affected, having watched this young lady grow up. She was a very special girl to both of us. As in the loss of my arm, *Ecclesiastics 9:11 correctly pronounces,...the race is not to the swift or the battle to the strong, nor does food come to the wise or wealth to the brilliant or favor to the learned; but time and chance happens to us all.* (NIV)

In 2007, I received the sad news that my first real love, Miriam Ross, an angel in human garb, had died from an adverse reaction to anesthetic. Memories came flooding back and I recalled her comment that "no one could ever take our memories from us." How true—and at times, how unfortunate to be tormented with thoughts of what could have been. At that time, I decided to put the story of my life on paper and began to write my memoirs.

The church evolved and grew to the point that it was decided to hire a youth pastor. We had been depending on the generosity of a few adults to lead the youth, and it was felt that the time was ripe to add another pastor to the payroll. Previously, the church had only had short-term intern youth pastors. The new youth pastor began in June of 2008.

On my 80th birthday, our good friend Bob Lochheed invited us to keep him company when meeting his friend at the Calgary airport. You can imagine my joyful surprise when I saw my daughter coming down the escalator. The family had organized a party in the fellowship hall at our church to celebrate my big day. It was complete with a special cake with my picture on it along with my favourite Bible verse, *"I can do all things through Him who strengthens me"* (Philippians 4:13, NASB). Many of my friends attended and it was truly a day to remember.

My hearing had really deteriorated by this time. A new hearing aid did not prove too helpful and I found it impossible to hear anything in a crowded room. So much for getting old—you can't hear, you can't see, and you can't do much else either.

Following a confrontation with the youth pastor at the church over the necessity of disciplining a student in my class, I decided that it would be my last year of teaching Sunday school. In June, I resigned from the last teaching position I would ever have. In my opinion, the young youth pastor overstepped his bounds and treated me without the respect due someone my age. The years I spent teaching were most rewarding and I was glad to have had one more opportunity to use my skills in this way. Parenting styles had changed and perhaps not necessarily for the better. As well, my health was not what it had been, and the church had decided to add a Saturday night service and there just would not have been enough students Sunday morning to warrant more than one or two classrooms. This second service was not successful, and was cancelled after one year. Nevertheless, no matter the reason, it was gut-wrenching to realize my days of teaching, a profession I so relished, were over; in the months to come, I mourned that fact. A friend had given me a frog ornament and, during this rather difficult time, seeing it reminded me daily to F.R.O.G.—fully rely on God.

In May, 2009, we noticed lumps appearing on both sides of our dear Sparky's neck: lymph nodes, as the vet revealed. Test results were not good and we were told he had lymphatic cancer. The vet gave him from two to four months to live. He was so active and full of energy it was hard to believe this was happening. By August, Trish realized that Sparky could not go as far on his walks without sitting down and he seemed to be short of breath as well. He fainted on two different occasions which really scared us. Back to the vet and x-rays showed fluid on his lungs. Medication to provide some relief helped a little, but we knew now it was just a matter of time.

Two joyous events occurred in August. One was our twenty-fifth wedding anniversary. Friends joined us for dinner at the Turner Valley Golf and Country Club. Where, oh where did the time go so quickly? Following the meal, we continued our celebration at the home of good friends for the husband's seventy-fifth birthday celebration.

The second was attending our son's wedding on August 22nd. Bob and Michelle had known each other for some time, so we were very pleased when they decided to tie the knot. As they are both horse lovers and Bob is somewhat of a cowboy, a western theme was the order of the day. It was held outdoors on a sunny (albeit windy) day. The bride and her attendants arrived in a horse-drawn buggy and the groom and the groomsmen arrived on horseback. Fortunately, everything went smoothly. Daughter Beth was with us as we welcomed our daughter-in-law into the family. It was a very special day indeed.

A sad day arrived on November 9th when Sparky didn't have the energy to walk from the bedroom to the living room, refused his breakfast, and seemed extremely disoriented. The vet talked with us for half an hour to help us with the final decision. She couldn't believe that Sparky had lasted as long as he did, three months beyond the predicted time. We had to let him go and as Trish picked him up, he licked her face as if to say, "Thanks for everything." We held his paws as he went to sleep, tears flowing, but we knew we had done the right thing for him. What a dear and faithful companion he had proved to be over the years. We buried him behind the garage with a sidewalk block for a marker. Little did we know that we would be moving from that house just six months later—God works in mysterious ways. Trish and I made the decision that Sparky would be our last dog and, with nothing to tie us to a house any longer, we began to discuss other options.

On January 12, an earthquake devastated Haiti, with approximately 316,000 people dying, 300,000 injured, and 1,000,000 homeless. Even when these things happen, we know that God is in control. Seeing the aftermath of this event, one realizes that our struggles and problems are sometimes minor compared to those of others. Most people hoard things, but in the end what are they but mere material possessions with only momentary value? One never knows when it is our last day, so each day should be richly lived to the glory of God.

> My brethren, count it all joy when you fall into various trials, knowing that the testing of your faith produces patience. But let patience have its perfect work, that you may be perfect and complete, lacking nothing. (James 1:2-4, NKJV)

"I Will Repay"

Now to him who is able to do immeasurably more than all we ask or imagine, according to his power that is at work within us, to him be glory in the church and in Christ Jesus throughout all generations, for ever and ever! Amen. (Ephesians 3:20-21)

Trish and I began thinking that sooner rather than later we would have to make a change and give up our lovely house, as it was getting beyond our capabilities to manage any of the maintenance required. A lovely condominium complex had been built just off Highway 7, east from Black Diamond. We decided to visit it and fell in love with the show suite. Not only was it the right size for us, but the building had a ground level, heated garage, which was a very important feature for me as my Volvo would be protected from the elements. A friend suggested, "Why not try to sell your house and find out if you will have enough money?" That very spring, at a time of real-estate decline and much to our surprise, the house sold for $260,000, thanks to our good friend and realtor, Howard McColister. This was more than the price of the new condo!

Our moving day was set for May 1st, 2010. Friends helped us set up and manage a huge garage sale as it was necessary to severely downsize. The leftovers were donated to Bibles for Missions and the Salvage center in Okotoks. Probably the hardest part of that time was getting rid of all my woodworking materials and tools. I had spent many long and happy hours in that shop (along with some frustrating ones, too!). But there comes a season for everything and it had become difficult for me to accomplish much in that area lately. *"There is a time for everything, and a season for every activity under the heavens"* (Ecclesiastes 3:1, NIV). When moving day arrived, again our good friends from the church and my son, Bob, moved us in double quick time. By that evening we were unpacked and living in our beautiful new digs.

My faith in God's promise in Romans 12:19, *"Do not take revenge my dear friends, but leave room for God's wrath, for it is written: 'It is mine to avenge; I will repay,' says the Lord"* (NIV), was miraculously answered, and with perfect timing, too. After sixty-one long and depressing years financially, there finally shone a silver lining. My days of deep despair, like Jonah in the belly of the big fish, came to an end.

Before I end my story, I must tell you about the "phantom pain" that has tormented me ever since my arm was so violently taken by that machine. It is said it is worse in people who have undergone a traumatic amputation. The pain can be absolutely excruciating and nothing provides relief. Now, in my senior years, it has actually gotten worse—sometimes it's as though I can feel my thumb being ripped off. Long ago when I was a pastor, doctors told me they could perform a lobotomy (an operation on the brain) to get rid of the pain, but the side effects could be severe such as speech and hearing problems. I responded, what good would a preacher be if he stuttered and couldn't hear?

God has kept all his promises. The scripture that came to me all those years before in the hospital, Isaiah 41:10 and 13, states,

> So do not fear, for I am with you; do not be dismayed, for I am your God. I will strengthen you and help you; I will uphold you with my righteous right hand...For I am the Lord your God who takes hold of your right hand and says to you, Do not fear; I will help you. (NIV)

Even in all my pain and trials, His presence is always with me and looking back and reminiscing about my life has shown me that God's hand was always upon me. To Him I give all glory and honour and praise. More than sixty years ago when I was lying in my hospital bed after losing my arm, I really did think that life would not be worth living. Here I am in my eighties and I marvel at the road I have travelled. Truly, truly, God has repaid in so very many ways. Though I lost my first love, He provided me with two beautiful, devoted wives who brought unimagined comfort. Along the way, I have had the joy of two children and many good friends, mentors and acquaintances, as well as support in various shapes and sizes from so many unexpected avenues, all of them gracing and blessing my life. I look at the things I accomplished, from the types of employment I have held, to the beautiful woodworking pieces I have produced, to the organizations I have been a part of and contributed to. Despite not having any money or family support, I managed to garner quite a bit of education and succeeded in graduating. In spite of my disability, my wives and children and I have always had a decent roof over our heads, food on our table and clothes on our backs. Even with sometimes severe financial restrictions, we enjoyed many vacations and the quiet of the wilderness in our very own camper. I was also able to indulge in my passions of woodworking and spreading God's Holy Word. Yes, indeed, all my needs over the years have been more than met in abundance—now we even have a wonderful new home in a condo project that is entirely paid for. Often we search for the windfall when we are already reaping it day by day. Praise our Lord that He loves us and cares for us in every way, ever more shaping us and leading us home. *"Even so, come, Lord Jesus"* (Revelation 22:20, KJV).

> His master replied, "Well done, good and faithful servant! You have been faithful with a few things; I will put you in charge of many things. Come and share your master's happiness!" (Matthew 25:21, NIV)

Biography

Jim Davis was born March 13, 1929, into a family of three boys, just before the "Great Depression." His family struggled to survive the hardships of that period. Jim lost his mother when he was eight. During his early years, he faced many difficulties and had to go out to work as a teenager. While in high school, he became a Christian and following graduation attended the Prairie Bible Institute in Three Hills, Alberta, during which time he lost his right arm in a tragic farm accident. Following graduation from PBI, he enrolled at Gordon College of Theology and Missions in Boston, Massachusetts, for another four years, obtaining his Bachelor of Science in Education. He worked on a farm, in store security, and as a car salesman prior to attending Bible school and becoming a pastor. Later, after obtaining his education degree, he became a teacher of special needs students at various schools. Since that time, he worked as a salesman of many things—from advertising to vacuum cleaners to so-called "miracle" products—and as a house painter. He served on his church board as secretary and also in the position of Deacon and Elder. Over the years, he was a Sunday school teacher and served as Sunday School Superintendent as well. His woodworking skills contributed many pieces of furniture to his church and various other places. After joining the Gideon ministry, he served as Zone Coordinator as well as in several other positions. He has two adult children, and at the age of 85, lives quietly with his second wife, Trish, in Black Diamond, Alberta, a town southwest of Calgary.

CPSIA information can be obtained at www.ICGtesting.com
Printed in the USA
LVOW13s0030020814

397137LV00007B/35/P